What people ar

The Silent I

Publication of *The Silent Messenger* would be an important addition to the scholarly literature on world religions, as well as a book in high demand by a growing audience for readable works on Meher Baba. The Hopkinsons' previous book, *Much Silence,* is regarded as the most accessible biography extant of Meher Baba's life. Tom Hopkinson was perhaps the best pure writer among the hundreds of authored books about Meher Baba, and this new text is guaranteed to be well received by a significant number of potential readers.

Allan Y. Cohen, PhD, Harvard University, Compiling Editor, *The Mastery of Consciousness* (Harper & Row, 1977; in UK, Eel Pie Publishing Ltd., 1977), author, "Meher Baba and the Quest of Consciousness" in *What is Enlightenment?* (Paragon House, New York, 1985), retired Professor of Psychology & Religion (John F. Kennedy University, University of California at Berkeley, Pacific School of Religion), Consulting Psychologist, Pacific Institute for Research & Evaluation (USA).

The Silent Messenger

The Life and Work of Meher Baba

The Silent Messenger

The Life and Work of Meher Baba

Tom & Dorothy Hopkinson

MANTRA BOOKS

Winchester, UK
Washington, USA

JOHN HUNT PUBLISHING

First published by Mantra Books, 2019
Mantra Books is an imprint of John Hunt Publishing Ltd., No. 3 East Street, Alresford
Hampshire SO24 9EE, UK
office@jhpbooks.com
www.johnhuntpublishing.com
www.mantra-books.net

For distributor details and how to order please visit the 'Ordering' section on our website.

ISBN: 978 1 78904 056 2
978 1 78904 057 9 (ebook)
Library of Congress Control Number: 2018947816

A CIP catalogue record for this book is available from the British Library.

Design: Stuart Davies

UK: Printed and bound by CPI Group (UK) Ltd, Croydon, CR0 4YY
US: Printed and bound by Thomson-Shore, 7300 West Joy Road, Dexter, MI 48130

Contents

The Messenger

... God speaketh once, yea twice, yet man perceiveth it not. In a dream, in a vision of the night, when deep sleep falleth upon men, in slumberings upon the bed. Then he openeth the ears of men and sealeth their instruction. That he may withdraw man from his purpose... He keepeth back his soul from the pit and his life from perishing... If there be a messenger with him, an interpreter, one among a thousand, to show unto man his uprightness... He will deliver his soul from going down into the pit, and his life shall see the light. Lo, all these things worketh God often times with man. To bring his soul from the pit, to be enlightened with the light of the living.

Holy Bible, Job, Chapter 33

Much silence makes a mighty noise.

African Proverb

Tom & Dorothy Hopkinson, taken outside the Meher Baba Centre, Hammersmith, London by Laurie Kaye / Date unknown / Private collection.

Preface

When our earlier book *Much Silence* appeared in 1974, there were already in print a great many books dealing with the life and work of Meher Baba, some of them of the highest importance. But among them was no reasonably short record of Baba's earthly life, conveying also some impression of his teaching, written in language everyone could understand and without assuming knowledge most readers would be unlikely to possess.

Such a plain man's introduction to Meher Baba, *Much Silence* sought to provide, and since its first appearance in Britain, it has been published also in the US; reprinted several times in India as a paperback; published as a paperback in Australia; translated into French and Spanish, as well as into German to be brought out at their own expense by Meher Baba devotees in Switzerland.

During recent years, however, there has been a fresh outpouring of books about Meher Baba, among them some by close companions, men and women who had spent their whole lives in Baba's service. These not only provide a wealth of new information, but also many delightful anecdotes and stories which bring his presence vividly before us.

Meanwhile in the external world, events are happening and changes taking place which appear to threaten not only the existing order but the future of the world itself, so emphasising the supreme importance of the message Meher Baba brought.

Faced with this fact and with the wealth of new material available, we have found it impossible simply to reprint our earlier book or to make only minor alterations. We decided therefore to write it afresh under a new title, retaining what was valid, but making use of the devoted work done by others, and of the further understanding we feel we have gained through study and discussion over the past fifteen years.

Rather than confront readers with a long list of book titles before meeting the subject of them – Meher Baba himself – we have transferred the bibliography to the back pages.

T. and D. H. 1989

Dorothy once explained that she and Tom wanted to bring the relevance of Baba's life and message into the present, for the future and everybody. *The Silent Messenger* was their answer to this, involving years of discussion and study, and seven years of writing. Some of Tom and Dorothy Hopkinson's research for the book was actually first hand, as over the years they travelled to India and spent much time listening, learning and talking to Baba's closest companions. This rich experience, along with their personal relationship with Baba and how he touched and changed their life, runs through the writing itself. In the narrative Tom and Dorothy also share the extraordinary story of how they came to meet and were drawn to follow Meher Baba.

The main body of the text had been finished by Tom in 1989, not long before he passed away in 1990. Dorothy received the manuscript in 1992 and she asked me to annotate her input directly onto it. This task took months of reading, discussion and working together several times a week – quite a feat at her age and with her visual impairment. It was touching to see her responding to the text as if Tom had freshly written it and they were composing it together. Dorothy passed peacefully away aged 90 in August 1993. The eventual compiling of the materials I received from Dorothy started from 2014.

In acting as editorial compiler I have done my utmost to respect the integrity and quality of Tom and Dorothy's original work. The compiling process involved checking for accuracy and consistency throughout, in both text and quotes, and verifying sources used. It was also necessary to assemble and to some extent create the front and back sections of the book including a bibliography of similar ilk to that in *Much Silence,* and source a suitable map that is also mentioned.

Tom's style of narrating draws together many resources not all of which are footnoted. The Bibliography and Acknowledgements, however, are comprehensive in showing his written source materials. Tom's skilful condensing of quoted extracts, including his use of English over American spelling in some places, has been left untouched to give flow and consistency as a whole.

The passage of time from the writing till now has been of notable significance. Many of Baba's close companions have passed away, and Tom's own footnotes on this have been supplemented to update the record.

Other changes over time, such as to Indian place names, have been left as in the original text, preserving Tom's writing and literary authority. Here too, extra references extend Tom's notes and are marked with the 'Ed.' abbreviation.

There are occasional instances where Tom uses words and expressions that might seem rather uncomfortable or dated, such as using masculine terms of reference. These place the book in its time. Only a few adjustments, for the sake of consistency, have therefore been made.

Happily many of the messages and writings drawn on and listed in the bibliography are today accessible online – a resource that Tom and Dorothy would have embraced wholeheartedly.

Since this book was written, many new Meher Baba works have been published and can be found listed on Baba-dedicated websites.

Shelagh Rowling, 2016

Foreword

The Silent Messenger is Tom and Dorothy Hopkinson's final book together, a searching and profound work for a world in turmoil. With biographies of these two extraordinary people, Sir Tom and Lady Dorothy, available online it remains to say that anyone privileged to have met or known them holds them in the highest and warmest regard.

Tom, knighted for services to journalism and a distinguished author, has been described as the most truthful editor and journalist in the twentieth century, encapsulating transparency and honesty. A pioneer of photo-journalism, he went on to expose the Sharpeville massacre in South Africa; and he once told me, cup of tea in hand, how he had interviewed Nelson Mandela in prison and how he had overwhelmingly felt that if anybody could lead South Africa out of the apartheid mess it was in, it would be Mandela.

Dorothy was a strong, practical (eldest of ten) yet deeply spiritual person with remarkable powers of insight. She gave many a profound talk on a whole range of psychological and spiritual matters. She lovingly encouraged so many people to find their way through life and its problems, and to open their hearts.

An incident that Dorothy used to relate during her final year was how Tom once returned from work upset, having had a disagreement and treated a colleague unfairly. He felt guilty and could not shake the incident off. That night he dreamt he was standing, holding a dirty handkerchief when he saw Meher Baba coming towards him. He could not find a pocket or anywhere to hide the handkerchief. Baba came right up to him and said, "I am not interested in your sins. Is your heart open?"

Tom and Dorothy never talk down to their readers, impose their beliefs or make assumptions. With this as a foundation, *The Silent Messenger* is a remarkable and thought-provoking book, but the reader may judge for themselves.

Shelagh Rowling 2016

Part I: The Life of Meher Baba

Introduction

In the life of each one of us come moments when we ask ourselves –

Who am I? Where did I come from? What is the purpose of my life? What will happen to me when I die?

Each of us assumes happiness to be the aim of life; we are all, in our own ways, pursuing happiness throughout our lives – why, then, do we never overtake it? Which of us, in our secret heart, considers him or herself happy? Which of us believes that those about us – partner, children, parents – are truly happy? How many of us, looking honestly around, can say we know *one* truly happy man or happy woman?

In every age men and women are haunted by these questions. No access to power or accumulation of possessions, neither absorption in work nor abandonment to pleasure, ever entirely drives them from mind. And when we are old, sick, poor, impotent or deserted, the unanswered questions rise up like ghosts – and we realise, when it seems too late to do anything about them, that they were of deeper concern to us than all the activities on which we are spending and have spent our lives.

At such moments the thoughts of most men and women turn

to religion. And in their essential message all the great religions speak as one. They tell us that the aim of life is to love and serve God, and that the way to achieve this is to love and serve our fellow beings, putting their happiness and well-being before our own.

People judge religions, however, more by what their followers do than by what they say, their actions rather than their words. And we see that religious bodies which praise poverty have amassed vast wealth, and while preaching humility exercise worldly power. We see too that, while all proclaim the 'brotherhood of man', their followers wage wars and kill each other for material and political advantage, or simply for belonging to a different creed. Sometimes indeed for belonging to a different branch of the *same* creed, so justifying Jonathan Swift's bitter words that "we have just enough religion to make us hate, but not enough to make us love one another".

Whether a person were born a Jew, a Muslim, a Buddhist, or a Christian would make no difference: if they *lived* their religion they would find it impossible to kill their fellow beings, or to enrich themselves through others' ignorance or weakness. Holding fast to the same truths, in whatever language or form of words expressed, they would pass their life without surrendering to hate or worldly values, but equally without retiring into monasteries or caves. They would not escape suffering, but would learn to understand it and to grow by means of it. Through understanding, and through serving their fellow beings – without expecting reward or gratitude for doing so – they would find, first, tranquillity of heart and mind and, later, the glow of inner happiness.

Lasting truths, however, if we are to recognise and accept them, must come to us in contemporary dress, restated in the light of our expanding knowledge of ourselves and of the universe – which itself, we now know, to be continually expanding.

The writers of this book believe that such a restatement of

the deepest truths in terms of the contemporary world has been made in our own day by Meher Baba, who was born in 1894 and whose earthly life came to an end in 1969. This conviction is the result, first, of having met Baba and the lasting – indeed the ever-deepening – effect of that experience; and secondly, of a study of his life and writings which has now extended over many years.

Baba said of himself: "I am not come to establish any cult, society or organisation – nor even to establish a new religion." "I have not come to establish anything new – I have come to put life into the old." "To affirm religious faiths, to establish societies or to hold conferences will never bring about the feeling of unity and oneness in the life of mankind... I have come to sow the seed of love in your hearts so that, in spite of all superficial diversity... the feeling of oneness, through love, is brought about amongst all the nations, creeds, sects and castes of the world."

What kind of being was Meher Baba? And what was his effect upon those who came into his presence?

Meher Baba, date: 22 February 1954. Location: Town Hall, Masulipatnam, Andhra, India. © Meher Nazar Publications.

Chapter 1

Meeting Meher Baba

Meher Baba was of medium height. As a young man he was of slender build, and films show him moving with a graceful, floating walk – with which he would often cover thirty miles a day for days on end, so that even the strongest of his companions found it hard to stand the pace. Later, following two severe car accidents, any form of movement became painful and his body grew thick. But when you put your arms around him – for Baba would often embrace his followers or allow them to embrace him – he appeared to be at the same time firm and insubstantial, as though having solidity but little weight.

As a rule Baba wore Indian dress, with sandals or else with his feet bare and, since they were never confined in shoes, his toes stood out separate and strong. His hands looked powerful enough to crack stones, but he moved his fingers with astonishing delicacy, as though playing some invisible musical instrument, to convey his unspoken message. While doing so he would often look up at his interpreter with a humorous, trustful glance. His expression changed continually, but it was through his eyes that the pattern of thought and feeling was conveyed. Intensely black, they would in a few seconds lovingly greet his audience, sparkle with laughter, or contemplate some situation with a sternness there was no escaping or resisting. At different periods Baba wore his black hair at varying lengths, down to his shoulders and below in early life; later, short and brushed back from his high square forehead, or else braided into a pigtail. He had a powerful hooked nose, giving him in one or two photographs the look of a 'Kurdish brigand'. His skin – which was neither dark nor fair but something in between, as might be expected from his Persian origins – was unusually sensitive.

Simply to come into Baba's presence was for most people a profound experience. Some, on first seeing him, burst into tears. Some flung or tried to fling themselves at his feet, an attempt which those about him were always ready to forestall. One or two laughed hysterically. Many found themselves smiling with a happiness they could not explain, but which to their own astonishment they did not try to hide. Almost all, whatever the anticipations with which they had approached him, found it difficult, even painful, to leave his presence.

What made the experience memorable, and any description of it difficult, is that Baba had not – like royalty or most political and religious leaders – a set reaction, even a gracious and dignified reaction. He responded to every individual afresh, giving himself in immediate contact. So it was as if, to each man or woman who approached him, he embodied something that person had been waiting for throughout a lifetime. What is it we have all, each one of us, been waiting for throughout our lives? An intense experience of love. Meher Baba radiated love, so that it appeared to even a casual visitor as though Baba loved him or her in some quite special way.

Once over the first reaction to his presence, it was noticeable that Baba seemed far more alive than anybody else. In a crowd, however large, he was invariably the centre, and everyone in it was governed by the same impulse, to draw close enough to make contact with him. A film, made in the 1950s in the USA, shows Baba in a crowded dining room of men and women seated at small tables. Moving from group to group, he has the effect of a lamp carried round a darkened room. As he approaches a table, the sitters raise their heads, gaze up, animate, smile – and then, as Baba moves on, they dwindle down, relapsing after he has passed, into the zombie-like condition normal to us human beings.

Mani (Manija S. Irani), Baba's younger sister, has described the reaction of Indian villagers to Baba's presence, though they had no idea who he was:

> When we were on the road walking, mile after weary mile, sometimes passing through villages and towns on the way, or walking on lonely stretches of country roads, passers-by would somehow not be unduly distracted by the rest of the party in robes and turbans, but when their eyes fell on Baba they would stop their chatting and stand quite still, just looking at Baba as he went by, then turn round and follow him with their eyes till he was out of sight.[1]
>
> (And of his effect on children Mani related:) Wherever Baba was and where there were any children they somehow always came to Him. I remember in 1952 on the plane to the US – of course, nobody knew who Baba was – the children would walk down the aisle and constantly stop where Baba was sitting and caress his coat or look up at Him. And their mothers would be after them, "Don't disturb that gentleman!" Then Baba would smile, the mothers would relax and forget to scold.

Baba was never frivolous or flippant, but he disliked needless solemnity and loved jokes and entertaining stories which those about him would save up for his enjoyment. At the 1958 gathering of his followers at Myrtle Beach in the US, following some profound discourses, Baba said: "*Now*, what do you want? One more discourse, or music and jokes? Personally, I want jokes, but let's keep your wish. I want you all to be happy..." And among those close to him, Baba kept a special place for one Kaka Baria[2] whose flow of inconsequential chatter, expressed in a confusion of languages created by himself, provided entertainment and distraction.

An aspect many found surprising was Baba's utter absence of self-importance and refusal of special treatment. He lived austerely, took only the plainest food, invariably travelled by the cheapest class. Except on the rarest occasions, he would never allow outward signs of reverence such as bowing or kissing his feet. In November 1962, when the whole *mandali*,[3] or group of close companions, bowed solemnly before him, they recalled with astonishment that this was the first time for twenty-two years they had been permitted to do this. Baba himself, however, frequently bowed down, and those he bowed to were the poor, the afflicted such as lepers, and the unappreciated. During a visit to the United States in 1952, it was noticed that Baba remained seated as he always did when people were brought to meet him. But each time a black family or person entered, he stood up.[4]

An immense dignity surrounded Baba, and an authority which could in a moment overawe aggression or hostility, but in general his manner was disarming, and even while remaining seated, he came out to welcome you. Unlike those spiritual leaders who cultivate aloofness and permit contact to be effected through a haze of condescension, Baba would often express a childlike candour and simplicity, against which the armour of the sophisticated offered no protection. "When I am with sadhus" (holy men), he said once, "no one is more serious than

I. When I am with children, I play marbles with them. I am in all, and one with all. That is why I can adapt myself to all kinds of people, and meet them where they are."

Baba's sister, Mani, in her *Family Letters*[5] tells of a man who came to see Baba with a long list of questions he was determined to have answered. Baba motioned the visitor to sit beside him, and he sat there quietly taking in Baba's presence – and only on leaving did he confess the reason for his visit which till now he had entirely forgotten.

Quentin Tod, an actor who was one of the first Westerners to attach himself to Baba, described his meeting with him in London in 1931.

> What impressed one most was his rather wild quality, as of something untamed, and his truly remarkable eyes. He smiled and motioned me to sit beside him. He took my hand and from time to time patted my shoulder. We sat for several minutes in silence and I was aware of a great feeling of love and peace emanating from him; also a curious feeling of recognition came to me, as if I had found a long-lost friend.[6]

Before going to meet Baba, Tod said he felt unprepared and shaken, "as though about to undergo a major operation."

A similar sense of awe was experienced by two young men, a dancer and an artist, living together. They were anxious to meet Baba, but in view of all they had heard about him and the reverence with which he was surrounded, they approached in a state of inner trepidation. As they came towards him, Baba held out his arms and with a twinkle in his eye addressed them through his interpreter with the one-word enquiry, "Chums?"

It was in 1952 that the writers of this book first met Meher Baba. The unlikely venue was the Charing Cross Hotel, just off Trafalgar Square in the middle of London. Baba was on his way back to India after a visit to the United States during which he had suffered severe injuries in a motor car accident he had foretold long before. Dorothy and I (Tom) had only recently settled down together, and though Dorothy had been in contact with Baba for ten years, I knew little more of him than his name and that Dorothy was devoted to him.

After waiting for a while in a corridor, we were called into a room of the kind used for small business meetings. On a settee at the far side of the room sat a figure in loose white clothes, with one leg raised and enclosed in a plaster cast. Behind him and to the sides I was aware of a number of Indian faces, but once we had entered I could look at no one but Baba and Dorothy, and for Dorothy I was soon in deep concern. She had been placed in a chair a few feet from Baba, facing him as he sat sideways on the settee, and I had been motioned into another chair by his feet. I thus found myself in the situation with which every journalist is familiar, that of spectator at someone else's drama. In the present case it was proving to be a silent drama. Baba, as I knew, never spoke, and Dorothy was so overcome at being finally in his presence, that she was finding it impossible to speak. Her lips opened, her eyes gazed pleadingly at Baba, but not a word came out. She was quite paralysed.

Baba's hands fluttered in gesture, and a soft voice behind him asked: "Why do you not speak?"

Struggling, Dorothy finally managed to stammer out, "Because I c-can't s-speak."

Baba smiled benignly. His hands moved again, and the voice replied, "Neither do I speak."

Encouraged, Dorothy was able to bring out: "But you, Baba, don't speak because you don't want to speak… I'm not speaking because I c-c-can't speak."

Baba's hands moved again, and the voice said reassuringly, "I will help you."

As I followed the drama, and the effect Baba's presence had on all about him, I was already trying to find words for the scene and for Baba himself. Sentences were piecing together in my mind, the mind of an observer, interested but not personally involved.

Suddenly Baba turned and looked into my eyes.

"And what have *you* come here for?" asked the voice in the background.

Caught off my guard, I uttered the first words that came into my head. "I only wanted to see you."

Baba flung up his arms with a delighted smile, and the voice enquired, "And do you *like* me?"

The words entered me like a bullet. I found myself struggling to bring out the reply, "I love you, Baba." For a moment I thought I might achieve it, but, inhibited by nationality, upbringing and journalistic detachment, the most I could manage was, "Yes, Baba, I like you."

L-r: Fred Marks looking at Baba, Meher Baba (seated). Behind Baba: Eruch Jessawala, (unknown), Adi Sr., Will Backett behind Adi, (unknown group). To the right of Adi Sr.: Delia de Leon & Homa Dadachanji. 18 July 1956, London Airport, UK. © Meher Nazar Publications.

"And I like you," came the voice, as Baba smilingly leaned forward.

In these contacts, as in thousands of others, Baba revealed his power to cut through the artificial personality we all create for self-protection in our everyday lives, and to touch that inner self which lives on somewhere in each one. The sense Baba conveyed was of loving acceptance without criticism or reproof. Soothed by such acceptance, the timid cease to feel exposed; the worldly, the resentful and the self-absorbed, instead of guilt, experience relief; the desperate sense a trickle of new hope, because for the first time someone is seeing us, as in our heart we long to be, and as – with the help of such love and understanding – we feel we may yet become.

Notes

1. *Tales from the New Life*, p. 180
2. Ardeshir S. Baria; *Kaka* is a term of respect meaning 'uncle'.
3. A Sanskrit word meaning a group or company. As with other words which he took over, Baba gave this one a special significance.
4. "Memories of '52" by Filis Frederick, *The Awakener Magazine*: vol. XIV, no. 2, p. 10
5. *Eighty-Two Family Letters*
6. *The Beloved*, p. 28

The young Merwan Sheriar Irani at 16 years old. Location: St Vincent's School in Pune, India. Date: circa 1910. © Meher Nazar Publications.

Chapter 2

Early Life

Meher Baba means 'Compassionate Father', Meher being an adaptation of the name Merwan which formed a part of Baba's full name – Merwan Sheriar Irani. He was born at Poona[1] in India of a Persian family on the 25th February 1894, at 5.15 a.m.

At that time Baba's father, Sheriar Mundegar Irani, was already in his middle forties. From the age of thirteen Sheriarji had been a seeker after spiritual truth, roaming the country as a monk or dervish, in Persia first, and then in India. Failing to achieve the enlightenment he sought, he visited the home of his sister in Bombay,[2] who urged him to marry and bring up a family. It is said that in a dream an inner voice assured him that one of his children would achieve what he had not, by becoming a great spiritual leader. "There was none like him," Baba said. "It was because of him that I was born as his child." Sheriarji followed his sister's advice and took a wife, a girl in her teens, Shireen[3] Dorab Irani (also known as Shirinbanoo and later Shirinmai), settled down and set himself to earn a living. As a child he had received no education but he now started to educate himself. Even while working as a gardener, later as an estate manager and teashop owner, he learned to read and write four languages and gained a reputation as a poet and singer.

Shirinmai, unlike her husband, was an educated woman; "as intelligent as she is fair," said one of her friends. Merwan was her second son, born when she was only sixteen years old.

> Before his birth, (it is recorded) Shireen had an unusual dream. She had dreamt being led into a wide open area where she was surrounded by a large number of alien faces, a multitude that extended on all sides to the horizon. The faces stared at her steadily and expectantly till she woke up... The dream was interpreted as symbolising the birth of one who would be loved and esteemed by large multitudes.[4]

Merwan was born in the Sassoon Hospital in Poona, where a slab in the wall commemorates the event. The house to which Shireen brought her baby was a small one with two main rooms, plus kitchen, bathroom and garret, which her husband had bought and repaired. It was known as the 'Pumpkin House' because of a large round stone beside the entrance. For a couple of years the family moved into a flat, but then came back to a larger house in the same street as their first home. This house, visited today by many Baba-lovers, is No. 765 in the section of Poona once known as Butler Mohalla but now renamed Meher Mohalla. Here Baba grew up with an older brother Jamshed; three younger ones – Jal, Behram and Adi; and his sister Manija (Mani), another sister having died at the age of six.

Shirinmai called Baba her "most beautiful child", and would later talk of her many worries over her precocious son.

> Merwan has been my problem even as a child... he was very active and mischievous from the time he was able to toddle, and would walk out of the house when my attention was distracted. This often compelled me, when I was especially busy with housework, or had to go for my bath and there was no one in the house to look after him, to tie one end of my sari to his waist and the other to the bedstead. Even then I could not always keep him out of mischief. Once (this was about January 1895, when Baba was not yet one year old), I had left him playing on the floor. Returning to the room some minutes later I was horrified to see him playing merrily with a big black snake (a cobra)... I rushed forward, but the snake slipped quickly out of the house and was never seen again.[5]

To English people the name 'Poona' suggests an India of garden parties and polo-playing officers, but in fact this city stands on the junction of two rivers and is an important cultural and educational centre. It had been chosen as the seat of the then Bombay government because, though not more than 120 miles distant, it offers a far pleasanter climate during the hot season, being 2,000 feet above sea level. Here from the point of view of schooling, the family was extremely well placed.

Merwan began attending school at the age of five and at fourteen entered what was considered to be the best school in Poona, St Vincent's High School (Roman Catholic), from which he graduated in 1911 at the age of seventeen.

His childhood was a happy one. Untroubled as yet by a sense of his own destiny, he was lively and mischievous, though naturally gentle and unselfish. He took great pleasure in games, particularly hockey and cricket (he was a batsman and wicket-keeper) and long after he ceased to play would enjoy watching cricket matches. His sister Mani recalls him saying on busy days that there was this and that to be done when he "would much rather be watching a game of good cricket."

Aptly nicknamed 'Electricity' by his friends, the boy was also a good runner and strong walker – as his companions would learn later in life during their immense journeys over the Indian countryside.

In his studies he is said to have been quick to learn, methodical and punctual. This is easy to believe since later in life he was punctual to the minute and insisted that every task had to be tackled in the most practical and economical way. His special interest lay in poetry. Besides reading widely, he wrote poems in English, as well as in Gujerati, Urdu, Persian and Hindustani. Some were printed in a Bombay newspaper, and at the age of fifteen he had a story published by his favourite boy's adventure magazine – the *Union Jack* of London. But just as avidly as poetry he would read detective magazines or Edgar Wallace stories, and one of his earliest followers, Ramjoo Abdulla, recalled many years later that what had first drawn him to Baba was a common enthusiasm for Sexton Blake. Merwan was also intensely fond of music, loved singing and had an exceptionally sweet voice. "He had a rich juicy voice" was the description given long afterwards by one of his closest companions, Adi K. Irani.

Once school was over, Merwan's enjoyments were like those of other boys. A couple of elderly Parsis kept a small shop near St Vincent's and the old lady often gave cold drinks or handfuls of sweets to Merwan and his friends. The old man, with his eye on the profits, would chase them away from the front of the shop, and the kindly old lady would beckon them round to the back. A photograph of this time (1907) shows a boy with brooding eyes and a full-lipped humorous mouth. He wears a trim dark jacket, with tucks in the sleeves to be let out as he grows taller and what appears to be a school badge pinned to the pocket. His hair, which would later become dark, was at this time reddish-gold.

Merwan had one habit, however, not common among boys of twelve or thirteen: he was fond of solitude and would slip away by himself to sit for hours at the 'Tower of Silence'. Both his father and grandfather had been keepers of the Zoroastrian Tower of Silence in the Persian village where they lived, and now young Merwan found the tower near Poona his natural retreat for silent contemplation. These towers, on which Zoroastrians expose their dead on gratings to be devoured by vultures, caused horror among early Western travellers brought up to regard burial in the earth as the only proper way to dispose of bodies, even though it meant setting aside large tracts of useful land in which the dead, after a more or less expensive funeral, decay slowly in the dampness of the soil.

The Zoroastrians, however, consider exposure of the dead as the method best suited to their arid climate, in which vultures are the natural scavengers; it is also the one least costly or harmful to the interests of the living. Towers of Silence are built away from towns and villages, but at no great distance, and often in situations whose wide outlook over the countryside, combined with the purpose for which they are constructed, might well induce profound reflection in a meditative mind.

At the age of seventeen a new period opened in the boy's life. Not far from Poona was Deccan College, at which Sir Edwin Arnold[6] and other distinguished men had been professors. The finest educational institution in the province, it was one of the few which already, in the days before the First World War, allowed considerable freedom to its students.

Merwan entered Deccan College in 1911. Here, as at school, it was literature above all which attracted him. He read Shakespeare, Wordsworth, Shelley and many other poets – English, Indian and Persian. But the poet with whom he was enraptured and continued throughout his life to quote – for Baba possessed the faculty of recalling almost everything he had ever read – was Hafiz, one of the greatest of Persian lyric poets, whose work expresses the deepest spiritual experience in the language of passionate love.

During his first year Merwan passed his examinations with credit and was active in social life. Here, as at school, he was accepted as a natural leader to whom others went for advice or called in to arbitrate in their disputes. Outside college, he founded the Cosmopolitan Club. Its rules, which forbade quarrelling, gambling and bad language, might be thought naive. But there was nothing naive about the insistence in its constitution that anyone could belong regardless of community and caste – an attitude rare indeed at that time and place.

In Merwan's education, therefore, East and West were blended, Western schooling against a background of the East, with studies and fluency in several languages, and this may have helped to evoke early in life the determination to draw people together without regard to race, creed, class or colour. During his second year at Deccan College, however, an event occurred, outwardly of small significance, but which put an end to Merwan's studies, disrupted what had been hitherto a conventional and happy life, and set on foot the transformation of his whole nature through a period of the most intense suffering. This was an encounter with an aged woman named Hazrat Babajan. At the time of the encounter she was said to have lived already for one hundred and twenty-two years, and in other ways she was no ordinary old woman.

Hazrat Babajan had been born in about the year 1790 in the mountainous country of Baluchistan to the west of India, daughter of one of the chief ministers to the Amir of Afghanistan. Exceptionally beautiful, she was due to be married as a girl of fifteen, but was already overwhelmingly drawn to the spiritual life. Rather than marry, she disappeared from home and had already spent half a century of wandering before she found a Master, through whom at the age of sixty-five she achieved the complete spiritual enlightenment she had always sought – a state to which the term 'God-realised' is applied, meaning that she had realised to the full the divine aspects of her nature and now lived continually in the enjoyment of God's presence. A Muslim by religion, she went in 1903 on a pilgrimage to Mecca, appearing around 1907 in Poona where she made her home under a neem tree in what was known as the Malcolm Tank Road.

It is not uncommon in India to see holy men dwelling underneath trees which they have adapted to form shelters. Babajan, however, built no shelter for herself but simply perched, exposed even to the drenching storms of the monsoon, with merely some sacking as protection. Only ten years before her death, in 1931, did her disciples with great difficulty obtain permission from the authorities to construct a small shelter for her, which since Babajan refused to move had to be built around the tree. Objection was based on the fact that her neem tree stood at a busy crossroads, so that the traffic at times was dislocated by the thousands of pilgrims who came to gaze at her, to kiss her hands, or to escort her on her daily walk to the public gardens in which she would sit for hours looking out over the river.

At the time of the encounter with Merwan, however, there was no such shelter, and Babajan was sitting under her tree on the morning in May 1913, when the boy came riding home from college on his bicycle. As he passed the tree he looked up and their eyes met. He knew quite well who she was, and when she beckoned to him he went over to her and she kissed him between the eyes. No word was spoken, and after sitting with her for a short time, Merwan remounted and rode home. From that day he would go every evening to sit with Babajan, usually without a word exchanged. "I was drawn to her," he later said, "as steel to a magnet." And whenever he spoke of her he would use the words "matchless", "incomparable". He often also referred to her as 'Emperor', and it is noteworthy that she herself took the name Baba (father) Jan, and would flare up if anyone addressed her as Amma (mother) Jan, since women are held to be the weaker sex and God-realisation is not for weaklings.

So their silent meetings continued, and then one night in

January 1914, Babajan was in a more talkative mood. As Merwan, having kissed her hands, stood humbly before her, she pointed her little finger at him and uttered the words: "This child of mine will after some years create a great sensation in the world and do immense good to humanity."

This powerful assertion, following the many hours of silent contact between them, had a shattering effect.

For some moments Merwan remained standing before her and then went home. It was late and he went straight to bed. Hardly had he lain down before he began to suffer alarmingly; through his body passed what seemed to be fierce electric shocks, causing him agony mixed with intense joy. Before long he lapsed into unconsciousness, and when his mother found him on his bed the next morning his eyes were vacant, he was unable to speak or move, and she supposed he had been taken seriously ill. Not until the fourth day did he show any recovery of consciousness and then remained for nine months in a state which amounted to continual trance, showing no interest in his surroundings and no inclination for food or drink. Whatever was put before him he gave away to beggars or dogs, or put into some drawer where it went bad and stank. He appeared never to sleep, and if he embarked on any action would be liable to continue it for hours in complete unawareness of the outside world. Once, leaving his home to go to the Bund Garden, he walked there and back three times without a pause, a distance of fifteen miles. On another occasion he remained for three days lying down near his old haunt, the Zoroastrian Tower of Silence. His parents became desperate. They supposed he had 'gone out of his mind' and he was placed under medical treatment, but the sleeping draught and morphia injections given to him had no effect.

Many years later Meher Baba spoke to some of his followers about his experiences at this time:

When I was a boy I did not know anything. I had nothing to

do with spirituality… I preferred games and I found myself the leader of others.

One day, when a friend gave me a small booklet on the Buddha, I opened the book to the place that told of the second coming of the Buddha, as Maitreya, the Lord of Mercy, and I realised all of a sudden, "I am that, actually", and I felt it deep within me. Then I forgot about it, and years passed by. Babajan called me one day as I was cycling past her tree, she kissed me on the forehead; and for nine months, God knows, I was in that state to which very, very few go. I had no consciousness of my body, or of anything else. I roamed about taking no food. My mother thought I was mad, and called the doctor. My father understood, but said nothing. The doctors could not do anything… I took no food but tea, which my elder brother Jamshed, who loved me very much, gave me. One day, all of a sudden, I felt nature's call. I wanted to move my bowels, but it was impossible because I had not had any food, I sat there and had no stool. Then I saw, with these gross[7] eyes of mine, circles and circles, whole universes. From that moment, instead of the Divine Bliss that I was in, for nine months, I was in such tortures that none in the world can understand. I used to bang my head to relieve my pain. I scarred my head on floors and walls.[8] I could not contain myself. It was as if the whole universe was on my head. I used to break windows open with my forehead… My sleepless, staring, vacant eyes worried my mother most… In her anguish she could not refrain from going once to Babajan and demanding to know what she had done to me… Babajan indicated to my mother that I was intended to shake the world into wakefulness, but that meant nothing to Shirinmai in her distress.[9]

This condition of acute suffering persisted until November 1914, when some degree of normal consciousness started to return. Baba later explained that the kiss given him by Babajan had carried him into the bliss of God-realisation, and that the intensity of his sufferings was due to unwillingness to come down into normal consciousness which was essential for the work he had to do. Babajan herself used to quote to Merwan certain Persian lines which mean: 'Having gained freedom, you have come back as prisoner (to free others)'. Merwan's eyes now gradually ceased to be vacant and he started to take small quantities of food; he had become, he said, "like an automaton possessing intuition." At this moment a friend brought along a poor young man, Behramji Irani, who would become one of Baba's most devoted followers and to whom he offered to teach Persian. Behramji made rapid progress and Merwan's parents, delighted, tried to get him to accept other pupils, which he refused though continuing to instruct Behramji.

As Merwan's mind began to focus more directly upon everyday life, his mother insisted that he should take up some employment and in 1916 he joined a theatrical company as manager. But before long when the owner died he was glad to come back to Poona. Here he was put in charge of his father's teashop, and later of a toddy or palm-wine shop. In neither capacity was Merwan a success, being always more concerned with meeting people's needs than with taking payment for what they had consumed. And in the toddy bar he would often urge the drinkers, usually among the city's poorest people, to drink only moderately or give it up altogether. However, he applied himself wholeheartedly to all menial labour, washing up bottles, cups and dishes, sweeping the floor, washing over the tables and benches.

The toddy shop was in a section of Poona known as Kasba Peth, which would become the base for Baba's work from 1917 to 1921, and it was here that he gathered his earliest disciples and formed the nucleus of his mandali. One of these, Dr Abdul Ghani, a friend of Baba's from his schooldays, has commented on his choice of Kasba Peth, the fishermen's locality of Poona, on the banks of the Mula River. It is, he says, "reminiscent of the early association of Jesus Christ with the fishermen of Galilee." Moreover "the Hindu local populace... though religiously orthodox to an extent, evinced a sort of camaraderie with the Muslim element there, over their common allegiance to the spiritual genius of the place – the shrine of the famous Muslim Saint Khwaja Salauddin."[10]

A revealing glimpse of Baba at this period has been given by his sister Mani, known to all Baba followers as Chairman of the Avatar Meher Baba Trust in Ahmednagar.[11]

> In the days when Merwan worked as helper in his father's toddy shop, there was an old man who used to come there regularly. He was an opium-taker as well as a toddy (palm-wine) drinker, but he was no idler. He worked and supported himself by his own efforts, and if he chose to spend his small resources on opium and toddy, he did no harm to anyone and owed no man anything. The old man made his living partly as a *chumpi-wallah* (a man who does Indian massage with the fingers), and partly as a 'waker-up' – that is he would call round at any time and rouse people for a small fee by rattling on their doors and windows. Among his regular customers were the mullahs who had to be up to summon their followers from the minarets at the hour of early morning prayer.
>
> The chumpi-wallah had one unusual habit. When he had taken a few drinks he would start to doze while still standing up. Once asleep, he would lean forward, and still further forward, till at last he folded up like a penknife and his head was almost resting on his feet.
>
> This old man had taken a great liking to young Merwan.
>
> "Merwanji," he used to say, "you are the only one I trust, so I want you to make the arrangements for my funeral. I want a good funeral, mind, one that people will talk about

and remember for a long time to come. So, Merwanji, you will see I get a good funeral, won't you?" Then he would hand over to Merwan a coin or two, to be added to the small hoard which was accumulating slowly.

"Don't worry," Merwan would reply. "You'll get your funeral."

At last a day came when the old man did not wake up from his sleep, and Merwan planned his funeral. Not only all the old man's friends and fellow drinkers, but everyone who knew Merwan and his family, were asked to come. There were musicians with their instruments, singers, dancers... and the procession winding its jubilant way through the streets attracted bystanders in such numbers that the tail soon lost sight of the head.

Then more and more people tagged on, saying: "What a procession! Anyone can see this is some rich man's daughter getting married. There's bound to be a feast. Join in and keep going – we'll be sure to get a share!"

In the end it seemed that all other activities had been abandoned in Poona for the day, and the whole town was taking part in the funeral which Merwan had organised for his friend the old chumpi-wallah.[12]

As Merwan's hold on life strengthened, he felt an impulse to travel and particularly to visit the homes of great saints or Sadgurus. It was in this way that he came in December 1915 to visit the temple of Khandoba where a renowned saint and master, Upasni Maharaj, had been living for three years on water, and had been reduced by his fasting almost to a skeleton. Upasni Maharaj was no less remarkable a being than Hazrat Babajan. By religion he was a Hindu, a tall heavy man, usually naked except for a gunny cloth and sandals when he went out. He had a lowering look and piercing eyes. His behaviour was often strange and he sometimes appeared mad. He once lived for over fourteen months in a bamboo cage, only three by three and a half feet, taking nothing but coffee once a day. Two years after Merwan's first visit to him he became a Perfect Master, the highest of spiritual states, and on his death in December 1941 the village where he lived became a place of pilgrimage. The part Upasni Maharaj played in Baba's life was a decisive one, and Baba has left his own account of their first meeting.

> When I came near enough to him, Maharaj greeted me, so to speak, with a stone which he threw at me with great force. It struck me on my forehead exactly where Babajan had kissed me, hitting with such force that it drew blood. The mark of that injury is still on my forehead… With that stroke, Maharaj had begun to help me return to ordinary consciousness.[13]

At all times, Baba has explained, there are in existence five Perfect Masters who carry the burden of responsibility for the world's spiritual guidance and direction. And in addition to the two, Hazrat Babajan and Upasni Maharaj, who had made Merwan aware of himself as Avatar, there were three others who played a part in his acceptance of the task. Their names were Sai Baba, Tajuddin Baba and Narayan Maharaj.

Sai Baba had arrived, no one knew whence, at the village of Shirdi in the Ahmednagar district sometime in the 1870s, and began to live as an itinerant monk, eventually making his home inside the mosque itself.

> When calm he was as gentle as a lamb, but when roused up he was liable to be exceedingly fierce. As the years rolled by the number of his devotees went on increasing. From his rich visitors he asked for money, and there and then gave it away to the poor standing near. Thousands of his devotees were Hindus, and, though he was a Mohammedan, they performed *Arti* (a ceremony of devotion) in his honour… A stone slab in

> the mosque used to serve him as a pillow. One day in that year (1918) it was accidentally broken to pieces. Sai Baba, seeing the pieces, said that the breaking of the slab meant that it was to be the last day of his life: and it proved to be so.[14]

Three years before this, in December 1915, when Merwan was emerging from his period of agonised suffering, he had felt impelled to visit Sai Baba at Shirdi. At that moment a crowd was escorting him in procession, and when Merwan made his way through the throng and prostrated himself before Sai Baba in the road, Sai Baba gazed at him and exclaimed "Parvardigar!" (God Almighty, the Sustainer). He then directed Merwan to visit Upasni Maharaj, who had formerly been his own disciple.

Previous to this Merwan had already visited Tajuddin Baba at Nagpur. For a great spiritual figure Tajuddin Baba had an astonishing background. He had once been a soldier in the service of the British, but on attaining the sublime state known as 'God-realisation' had given up the military calling and settled in Nagpur. Here he was so besieged by crowds asking him questions, wanting his blessing and demanding to have their various desires gratified, that he resolved to take refuge where he could be pestered no longer.

> One evening he went naked to a tennis court where Europeans were playing, and began to behave like a madman. As a consequence he was sent to a lunatic asylum, where he lived for seventeen years. Even there hundreds of people called upon him with a view to receiving his blessing. In the last year of his life in the lunatic asylum the titular Chief of Kampti, near Nagpur, paid him a visit. The Chief was well aware of the fact that Tajuddin Baba was a Sadguru[15] and as sane as himself. He persuaded the saint to leave the asylum and stay as his guest at the palace in Nagpur, where he would not be troubled by worldly people. Tajuddin Baba accepted the

> invitation, and passed the remainder of his life in the Chief's palace... He breathed his last in 1924. At his funeral no less than thirty thousand people were said to have been present.

The last of the five, whom Merwan also visited in the year 1915, was Narayan Maharaj. He too was utterly unlike the conventional picture of a great saint or holy man.

> Sadguru Narayan Maharaj lives in a large, well-furnished bungalow. He wears costly clothes and adorns his person with jewels. He is a strict vegetarian and eats very little. He plays the role of a great Bhakta, and offers prayer and performs ceremonies regularly. His pilgrims number thousands, and he has built a large inn to accommodate them. He has also built a beautiful temple in honour of the Hindu God Datta, into which he goes twice a day. Though his mode of living is that of a rich man, he is regarded as 'God-realised'. He is said to have become an itinerant monk as a child and to have become spiritually perfect at the age of twenty-five.[16]

Of the five Perfect Masters concerned with Baba's recognition of himself as Avatar, therefore, four were men and one a woman, three were Muslims and two Hindus, while Baba himself had been brought up in the Zoroastrian faith. Baba himself has explained the significance of this:

> From the viewpoint of Divine gnosis (knowledge), the Muslims progress from Oneness to Manyness and the Hindus from Manyness to Oneness i.e. the Hindus (who recognise God in many forms) and Muslims (who accept God in only one being, Allah) represent the extreme and opposite points of a diameter of a circle with God as the Centre. Zoroastrianism is mid-way between the two extremes and hence the choice at this juncture of a Zoroastrian Form in me as the vehicle of

spirituality derived from Hindu and Muslim sources.

Bal Natu, who quotes the above passage, goes on to remark that "in this Advent, the Avatar of the Age chose the English language to explain spiritual truths. This indicates that Meher Baba is also for the Westerners, among whom a good many are Christians."[17]

To this might be added that, coincidental with Baba's adoption of English as his vehicle for communication, the language has spread from being one among several languages in use over wide areas, to become the accepted means of communication between nations, and seems likely over the next half century to develop into the first 'world language' – one which most peoples will know and employ in addition to their own, and which will be understood wherever one goes.

From the day when he had been struck with the stone by Upasni Maharaj, Baba started to revisit Babajan with whom he would sit for about an hour each evening. He went almost daily also to the Parsi Tower of Silence or wandered on into the jungles beyond, where he would repeatedly knock his head against stones, wrapping his brow with a handkerchief to conceal the bruises from his family. Twice a month he visited Upasni Maharaj with whom he also exchanged letters, none of which unhappily have been preserved. Finally in July 1921, Merwan, now three-fourths normal in behaviour, went to live for six months with Upasni Maharaj at Sakori. They would spend a number of hours each day together, and sometimes whole nights behind closed doors which no one was permitted to approach. As a rule they sat in silence, but sometimes Merwan would sing. By the end of that year Merwan had recovered full consciousness and Upasni Maharaj solemnly handed over authority to him. He instructed his own disciples, much as John the Baptist did with Jesus, to leave him and stay with Merwan for the future: "I have given my charge to Merwan. He is the holder of my key." Later he stated publicly: "This boy will move the world. Humanity at

Meher Baba's family. Location: Baba House, Poona. *L-r:* Shireenmai (Baba's mother), Mani (his sister), Adi Jr. (his brother), Jal (brother), a servant, Sheriar (his father). Photographer not known. Date: 1922–23. © MSI Collection.

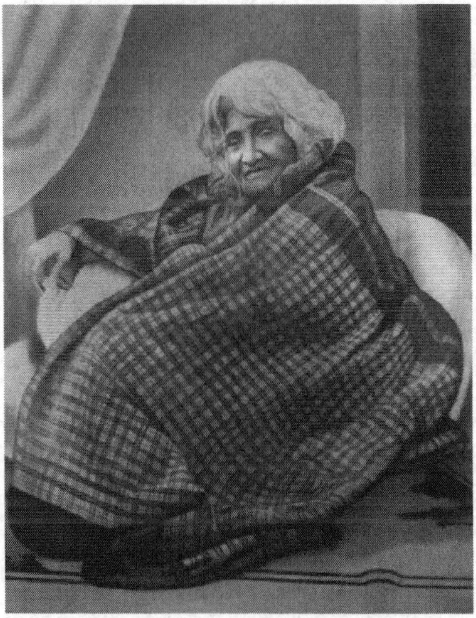

Hazrat Babajan (circa 1806–21 September 1931). © Meher Nazar Publications.

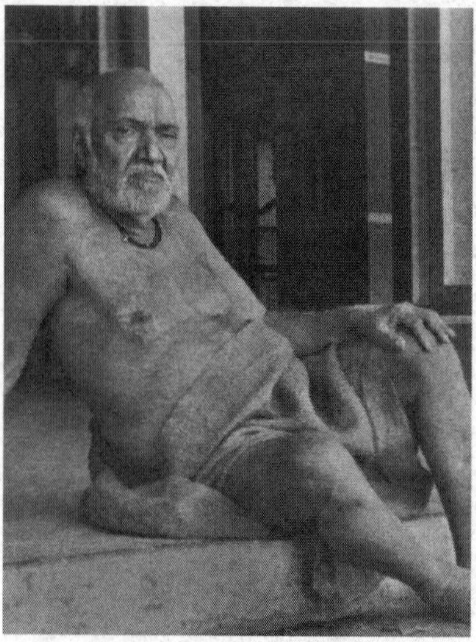

Left: *Upasni Maharaj* (15 May 1870–24 December 1941). © Meher Nazar Publications.

Right: *Tajuddin Baba* (27 January 1861–17 August 1925). © Meher Nazar Publications.

large will be benefited at his hands." He referred to Merwan as the 'Sadguru of this age', and told Behramji, "Your friend is God-realised; carry out every command and every desire of his." Finally he himself addressed Merwan by the title 'Avatar'.[18]

So now, at the age of twenty-seven, Merwan Irani had become Meher Baba and was ready to begin his life's work for mankind.

Notes

1. Now known under the Indian form of its name 'Pune'.
2. 'Mumbai' (Ed.)
3. Often spelt 'Shirin'. (Ed.)
4. *The Beloved*, p. 5
5. *Listen, Humanity*, pp. 244–5
6. Author of *The Light of Asia*, the life and teaching of the founder of Buddhism, told in verse. First published in 1879,

Left: *Narayan Maharaj* (20 May 1885–3 September 1945). © Meher Nazar Publications.

Right: *Sai Baba of Shirdi* (died: 15 October 1918). © Meher Nazar Publications.

it made Buddhist thought widely known among educated people in Victorian England.

7. 'Gross' i.e. physical, as distinct from inner perceptions.
8. 'Baba's room', in which he used to hammer his head against walls and floor, can still be seen at the house in Meher Mohalla already described.
9. *The God-Man*, p. 244
10. *Twenty Years with Meher Baba*, p. 45
11. Mani passed away on 19th August 1996. Of herself she said: "I was born with just one ambition – to be with Baba." (Ed.)
12. Told by Mani to a group of Baba-lovers at Meherazad, Christmas 1975, and noted down by the authors.
13. *Listen, Humanity*, p. 249
14. This and following extracts: *The Perfect Master*, pp. 24–6
15. A *Sadguru* is 'a man or woman who has become one with

God, but remains on earth for the help and guidance of others'.

16. For a fuller description of Narayan Maharaj see *Glimpses, Vol I*, pp. 114–7
17. *Glimpses, Vol II*, p. 273
18. The *Avatar* is not man become God, but God become man. The best-known and most accepted earlier manifestations have been Zoroaster, Rama, Krishna, Buddha, Jesus and Mohammed.

Standing: Babu Cyclewalla, Hormusji Vajifdar, Sarosh, Baidul, Slamson, Nervous. *Seated:* Behramji, Rustom, Baba, Ghani, Gustadji. *On the floor:* Burjor Dahiwalla, Adi Sr., Ramjoo, Raghunath Karmarkar. Location: Ghatkopar, 19 October 1923. © Meher Nazar Publications.

Chapter 3

Intense Activity

Having now fully recovered consciousness and accepted his role as Avatar from the Perfect Masters of the time, Baba withdrew for a period of concentration before launching out on a life of intense activity. For this purpose he left his parents' home and went to live in a hut only six feet by ten, inadequate even for a monastic or prison cell, which he asked a friend to build for him. He has described this period of his life himself:

> For about four months (January–May, 1922) I stayed in a small *jhopdi* (thatched hut). It was built for me temporarily on the edge of some fields in what is now the Shivajinagar

> area of Poona. In this manner I began to live independently, surrounded by men who formed the nucleus of the *mandali*. One of these was the first to start addressing me as 'Baba'. Some of the men were drawn intuitively to me long before they had any clear idea of my inner state. Others were attracted to me by hints from Babajan and Maharaj. And still others I drew directly to me.[1]

Asked why he chose to confine himself to such cramped quarters, Baba replied: "It does not inconvenience me, for walls do not bind me. For certain kinds of work which I have to do in non-physical realms, I prefer to shut myself up in a small place." And throughout life, when the nature of such work demanded it, he would instruct his followers to construct a hut, or sometimes to find and prepare a cave, in which he remained closeted for a period ranging from hours to weeks. Often the site chosen would have special associations with a Master or holy person from the past, and once in Italy he spent a night and a day fasting in a cave near Assisi which was associated with St Francis.

Meantime Baba was making contacts among young men in the neighbourhood who, beginning as friends, transformed themselves before long into disciples. It was with a group of forty-five of these that in May 1922 he set off on foot from Poona to Bombay. Twelve of them were Muslims, eleven Zoroastrians, like Baba's own family, and the rest Hindus. On reaching Bombay Baba rented a large bungalow which he named Manzil-e-Meem (The Master's House) where he established his first *ashram*.[2] There were fifteen rooms, but there was to be no furniture; only blankets were allowed for bedding, without bedsteads, mattresses or quilts. Each morning the men went out to work at various employments, but in the evening they had to come straight home, and their life was governed by strict rules to which – as to any instructions from the Master – absolute obedience was required.

All must retire to bed by 8 p.m. and be up each morning at 4 a.m., since the early hours are best for prayer and meditation. Before this they had all to take cold baths, including even a sufferer from asthma, who found to his surprise that after a while he had lost his asthma. Meals were vegetarian, but all were obliged to eat heartily of the simple food except during periods of fast. Drink and sexual intercourse were forbidden. Anyone going out off duty must leave purse and money behind, and while on duty not more than two annas (two pence) might be spent on refreshment, a sum which at that time would have paid for tea or a cold drink. All earnings went into a common fund for the benefit of all, and no one was allowed to own any personal possessions. Each man was instructed to keep the holy days and observances required by his own religion.

But though the regime was strict, life in the ashram was far from gloomy. Baba was fond of all kinds of games, for which regular times were allotted, and of music and singing. He often took his followers to the theatre and cinema. Free speech was encouraged and the group had its own governing body at which the members were expected to speak out freely. The same practice was encouraged by Baba's habit of suddenly asking a follower to say exactly what was in his mind – a technique familiar in the West to students of psychoanalysis – and at breakfast he would often ask one or another to recount his dreams.

To certain of his companions Baba gave nicknames, usually based on some peculiarity or mannerism. In time these gradually replaced their own names, until only their relations or old friends remembered what they had originally been called. Two such early companions would later become known to tens of thousands of Baba's followers from all over the world as 'Pendu' and 'Padri'. Pendu, whose real name was Aspandiar R. Irani, was a relation of Baba's who joined him when he set out from Poona to Bombay. He himself has often described how he came by his nickname.

> Every morning at 5 a.m., after we had washed and dressed, we gathered round Baba, sitting in a circle, and at this time I would often be sleepy. Baba would be very sharp with anyone who dozed off and so, to keep myself awake, I would rock a little from side to side. Because of this habit Baba said I was a pendulum, so I was known as 'Pendulum', later shortened to 'Pendu'.

Padri's name was given him because of his habit, when young, of always wearing black clothes so that he looked like a priest or 'padre'.[3]

Despite the regularity of ashram life, it was understood among Baba's followers that he never allowed life to settle into a fixed routine, the unexpected was always just around the corner. On one occasion Baba ordered followers who were then fasting to collect two hundred beggars at the ashram. In Bombay there is never any shortage of beggars but Baba did not want sturdy able-bodied rogues, only the truly suffering or disabled. When gathered together, bathed and clothed, Baba himself took part in serving them and even, to their astonishment, garlanded them before they left. Another time, when the whole party was subsisting on nothing but water, Baba ordered no fewer than eight hundred beggars to be assembled, fed and clothed, but this time the able-bodied might also be included. Once, possibly because of some murmuring over the simple fare, Baba chose half a dozen of the mandali for whom he ordered a feast to be served. The half-dozen were delighted to be given fresh and dried fruits, bowls of chocolates and the rich sweetmeats so much loved in India. But when they had already eaten heartily, cooked dishes appeared and the Master heaped their plates, and when these dishes were followed by still others, the disciples begged for mercy.

At times Baba's demand for strict obedience would lead one or other of the men into an awkward situation. Those who went to work each day might speak to their colleagues in the factory or office or to their fellow disciples, but were forbidden to speak to anyone else. One worker travelling home by train in the evening found himself face to face with an old school friend, to whose warm enquiries he could offer no answer but an embarrassed stare, which he maintained until he reached his station and could thankfully escape. Painful as such incidents were at the time, the mandali came to understand that every demand or instruction from Baba had a purpose. Unlike those who spend their lives in monasteries or convents, Baba's followers were being trained to live in the world yet maintain detachment from it. The breaking of social ties might be a necessity for one pledged now to live by different values. The ability to fast and go short of sleep, the capacity to travel around without money for fares or transport, would prove invaluable to them later on, developing qualities of determination and initiative without which they could never have faced their arduous life as Baba's close companions. From the physical point of view they underwent the equivalent of a rigorous military discipline and at times they came in for some tough handling as well.

> My body (Baba explained) was then very lean, but also supple, as I was constantly and energetically active. From four in the morning even in the severest cold I would move about in my thin mull *sadra* (robe). Those who did not know me well at that time might have considered me very quick-tempered, for suddenly with or without provocation, I would beat anyone at hand.
>
> In those days most of the *mandali* were hefty, robust young men. Several of them were good wrestlers and some were seasoned athletes. But when I would start for a brisk walk, the majority would have to run to keep up with me...
>
> One of the group had the physique of a giant, but once in a certain mood I knocked him down with a single slap.

> Another had to have a doctor treat his ear because of a blow I gave him. One of the *mandali* used to go into hiding on such occasions and would not emerge again without asking others if my mood had changed.[4]

Strange as such actions appear to Westerners, a similar fiery phase of activity is commonly understood and accepted by the followers of Eastern masters. Like the abuse they sometimes shower on their disciples or on one another, it is the outward manifestation of an inner purpose which is always beneficial, and a sharp blow from a Perfect Master – like the blow from a stone which Baba had himself received from Upasni Maharaj – is often the means of conferring spiritual enlightenment. So, too, a rebuke from a Master is accepted as a favour. Appreciation of this was shown by a Sanskrit research scholar whom Baba rebuked at a *sahavas*, or public gathering. Afterwards he said gratefully, "Ah, Baba must really love me, otherwise he would not have taken the trouble to correct me."

Two members of the mandali who continued with Baba throughout his life left memories of these early days. One, Sarosh,[5] was asked by Baba to join his ashram. With some hesitation he agreed to try it for year and 'see how I get on.' However, he was continually finding himself in situations in which he had somehow disobeyed the Master, and when he got back to the ashram would find his bedroll thrown out. Distressed, he would then plead with Baba to be allowed to bring the bedroll in and resume his place among the group. Eventually Baba would agree, embrace Sarosh, and all would go on as before – until again he found his bedroll outside the door.

Sarosh was a lively, good-looking youth with social interests, so this may have been Baba's way of forestalling any idea on his part of leaving the ashram. If so, it was well calculated, for Sarosh, who had signed on reluctantly for twelve months, remained for life. With Baba's approval he later married, founded a successful motor car business and became Mayor of Ahmednagar. With his wife, Viloo, he several times served as Baba's ambassador on official occasions, and their home has given a warm welcome to scores of Baba's followers from all over the world.

Dr Abdul Ghani Munsif was another disciple whom Baba once ordered to leave Manzil-e-Meem. A school friend of Baba's – his family and Baba's had been almost next door neighbours in Poona for about fifteen years and the boys were roughly the same age – Dr Ghani's wit and erudition often entertained Baba, and at times Dr Ghani would speak out more critically on some point in dispute, than anyone else around Baba dared to do.

> Once Baba became very angry with Dr Ghani and in the heat of the moment asked him to go away. Ghani like an obedient child got up, packed his things in preparation to leave and asked Baba where he should go. Baba told him he could go anywhere he liked and he should not show his face again. Dr Ghani quietly said that he did not know any place where Baba was not (Baba, as the Avatar of God, being all-pervading) and hence could not decide where to go. Baba's anger turned into laughter and in his unbounded compassion he forgave Ghani.[6]

Another early member was Meherjee (Meherjee A. Karkaria) who joined Baba as a boy of eighteen. He remembered Baba, who occasionally used to smoke at this time, giving him a single puff of a cigarette. When he had taken it, Baba told him to take another puff. He then ordered: "You are never to smoke again. But this," indicating a drink by a gesture of his arm, "is all right for you." Meherjee, who is sometimes troubled with his throat, considers this was a practical warning for the good of his health. He too married with Baba's approval, and later it became important for him to establish some kind of business. Baba told him to go into the making of filter papers for use in industry.

Meherjee hardly knew what filter papers were, and had no idea how they were made. Later, his factory, the only one of its kind in India, employed many workers and saved the country large sums in foreign exchange.

The house Manzil-e-Meem had been rented for a year. However, on the last day of March 1923, when there were still two months left to run, Baba called the mandali together. He told them the ashram was to be wound up. He would be leaving for Ahmednagar shortly, taking only a few of them with him. The rest should go to their homes, from which those who wished could join him later. But he warned them to think well before doing so since "discipline will be more strict and the mode of living more simple... you may have to do the work of masons, of coolies; in short, any kind of manual work."[7]

Meanwhile, for Baba and the few remaining with him, there ensued a period of continual travel. The little band was always on the move, ranging the country and travelling once as far as Persia. Often they went on foot; if by boat or train it was always in the lowest class, which Baba would insist on throughout his life. Apart from unavoidable privations of living on the march in a country of desert, mountain and forest with extremes of temperature, they were frequently under orders to fast; Baba himself fasted often, and once took nothing but liquids for two months on end – and this while walking across the continent with each man carrying his own bedding roll and equipment. The places where they put up were always the poorest and cheapest, and the men's tempers were constantly being tried by abrupt changes of plan. Hardly had they settled into some shelter, hoping to stay there for a while and recuperate, than they were ordered to pack everything up and be ready to move off next morning, or possibly in the middle of the night. They existed like soldiers on campaign – but without a soldier's usual reliefs of grumbling and getting drunk.

In the course of their travels, Baba led his band to a little walled village called Arangaon, not far from Ahmednagar. This was an ancient settlement, at that time decayed into ruins,[8] among which a number of peasants, mainly so-called 'untouchables', were living in poverty and degradation. 'Degradation' is no fanciful description since the filth of their clothes and persons was extreme, and their way of life almost brutish. They were accustomed, for example, to eating the bodies of any dead animals they found. Close by the old village was a dilapidated military camp, a hangover from the First World War. Yet this was the spot chosen by Baba to bear his name and become permanently associated with his life and work as 'Meherabad' ('abad' means flourishing). Like other places Baba chose, it had spiritual associations from the past. Here was the tomb of Buaji Bua, a Hindu saint who was said to have entered his grave while still alive. It had also been chosen for his burial place by a Muslim saint, Hazrat Shah, and when the saint's followers remonstrated with him for choosing a spot so desolate and barren, he replied: "You are wrong; this will blossom into a place of unique importance and thousands will visit it… So it is ordained, and so it shall be." It was here then, at a place sacred for both Hindus and Muslims, that in March 1924, twelve months after leaving Manzil-e-Meem, Baba founded his second ashram.

Life at Meherabad was just as strictly disciplined as in Bombay, and the diet equally sparse, but now in addition there was the heavy manual work he had warned them of a year before. The men had to clear the ground, put into order whatever buildings could be made serviceable, and start constructing new ones. The first to be built resembled the hut in which Baba had lived at Poona, being a small square room – solidly built of stone and mortar and rendered insect-proof with screens – to which Baba could retire for periods of solitude.[9] Apart from one paid mason, everything was done by the mandali, whose numbers had risen again to about forty, and who toiled away as labourers for six hours each day. After some months, under Baba's direction, they had covered the abandoned camp with a whole range of buildings. Looking back later on the scene, Baba recalled,

> ... it was like a small model town. In it lived about five hundred souls, working in the hospitals, the dispensary and the schools. There were also *ashrams* for boys, men and women, and shelters for the poor and for lepers... At that time nearly a thousand rupees a day used to be spent for the maintenance of the various services, while the *mandali* often lived on plain *dal* (curried lentils) and rice for lunch, and milkless tea or a thin soup of *methi* (bitter spinach) leaves and coarse bread for dinner... I remained generally on liquids or on limited meals taken once in a week or a fortnight. Weekly rations were issued to the most helpless of the Arangaon villagers. They were so needy that later, when the *ashrams* were shifted some scores of miles away to Toka, they used to travel on foot or by bullock-cart all that distance rather than miss the weekly quota of coarse grain.
>
> Hundreds of people from the villages near Meherabad benefited from the free hospitals, and thousands utilised the dispensary provided for out-patients. Boys of all castes and creeds including untouchables soon began to live, eat and intermingle freely.
>
> From dawn to dusk I would move about the place and take an active part in every phase including the cleaning of latrines.[10] Each day I spent three to four hours bathing the school children. When the number boarding became considerable, I allowed the *mandali* to share this service with me. All the *mandali* also had to grind grain for one to three hours each day, depending upon their assigned duties. I also shared in the daily grinding for an hour or more.[11]

An impression of the strict discipline under which the *mandali* lived during this phase has been given by Pendu, who was in charge of the free hospital while Padri, who had a wide knowledge of homoeopathy, looked after the dispensary.

Every day, and sometimes several times in the day, Baba would come round the hospital. He would look here and there, all round the place and in every corner, and would question the patients. Had they had their temperatures taken? Was the food all right? Had they any complaints? Always there proved to be something wrong, and every time there was any fault, Baba would give me a good buffet over the ear, and order me to put the matter right.

One day I had been over *everything*. I had swept the floor twice. All the patients had been fed and their temperatures taken. They were looking happy and everything seemed perfect. "He can't find anything wrong *today*," I told myself. "I shall surely be given congratulations and a pat on the back." Then Baba came along to the hospital, looking here and there, peering into all the corners. He spoke to the patients, but no one raised any complaint. Everything seemed to be fine… But then Baba went over to a shelf high up on the wall, rubbed his finger along it and wiped the finger on my white sleeve – a dirty mark appeared! At once he gave me a bang on the head and ordered me to keep the place thoroughly clean in future.

I was downcast, and when Baba had gone I thought to myself: "It's no good – whatever I do I can't please him. It's just impossible!" So I decided to leave. I put my few things together and started to walk away. But Baba saw me going out of the compound and sent someone after me.

"Come back! Baba wants you!"

So I went back and Baba said: "What are *you* doing, Pendu? Where are you going?"

"I'm leaving, Baba. Nothing I do is right. I try my best – but you always find fault. So now I'm off!"

Baba jumped up and gave me a big clout on the ear. "Come,

you fool! Go back to your place – and get on with your work!"

So I did, and I've been doing that ever since.[12]

The schoolchildren to whom Baba referred in his description of the 'model town' were attending a free primary school which was among the other new institutions. Starting with twenty boys, it had soon grown to include one hundred and fifty boys and girls, among whom were about thirty untouchable boys from poor and squalid homes, and it were these Baba spent so much of his time washing and bathing. At first they had been segregated, but it was not long before all differences of caste and creed were broken down and the children accepted one another freely.

Once when Baba was engaged in the bathhouse, some high-caste Brahmins called to receive his blessing. As they stood before him, Baba told them: "I am bathing untouchable boys. It is no use having my blessing unless you are prepared to do the work I do." The Brahmins set aside their code, according to which it is defilement even to be crossed by an untouchable's shadow, and joined Baba in his task.

If the Bombay ashram resembled a monastery, whose inmates were seeking enlightenment by living under discipline while working in the world, the ashram at Arangaon wore rather the aspect of a social centre whose efforts are directed towards serving the community. And if the motivation of the first was Eastern and spiritual, that of the second seemed practical and Western. Life in Bombay had been a form of seclusion with outside contacts strictly limited, but to Meherabad vast crowds were now starting to flock. Sometimes the stream flowed on all day, and on Baba's thirty-second birthday, 25th February 1926, some twenty thousand people gathered to receive his *darshan*.[13] Some were indeed seekers after truth, but most – as Baba observed to the mandali – were really intent, despite their protestations, on getting some material advantage. Baba spoke of these with humorous tolerance:

> Once an old man offered to dedicate everything he had to me, and then he would begin, he said, to lead a life of service and renunciation. However, on investigation, it was found that what would be dedicated to me was a wife and seven children to be taken care of.[14]

Another who came asking for divine guidance was advised to remain with Baba and lead the life of an ascetic. He did so for ten days, but then said he must be off. Enquiry showed that what he did not care for was the food. Baba let him go, with only a dry comment to the mandali: "Came for God, and gone for bread!"

A third who approached in tears declared: "For forty years I am in search of God. I do meditations; now I come to you!" Baba answered, "If you obey me, I will give you God-realisation. What about obeying?"

> "I will cut off my head," the man declared, "and lay it at your feet!"
>
> "You need not cut off your head, but be stark naked and walk about Ahmednagar."
>
> The man, who was well-dressed, objected: "Baba, that is very difficult, for I was brought up here. I know many people. What will they say?"
>
> "If you cannot do this," Baba replied, "why talk of cutting off your head?"

Despite the almost ceaseless activity of his daily life, it was at this period that Baba wrote a book, which has never been published and which no one, so far as is known, has ever read. He wrote it in various places, partly in his hut, partly in a low 'table house',[15] and partly at a seat under a neem tree by the roadside, and partly in a hut up on the hill in another part of the Meherabad settlement. To this book – which is said to contain Baba's message to the world, including spiritual secrets never previously revealed – Baba devoted some hours of each day for about a year, usually sitting down to write at six in the morning behind closed doors and sometimes continuing far into the night. At times he became so exhausted that he had to be massaged with oil before he could continue, and once he had a severe attack of fever lasting nearly a week, but he always went back to his task.

The book is said to have been written partly in English and partly in various Indian languages, all in Baba's own longhand. In the early days he took it with him everywhere. Housed in a steel box with chain and padlock, it travelled all over the subcontinent and possibly overseas as well. Meherjee, one of his mandali, recalls it many times being pushed under Baba's seat in crowded railway carriages. Later it was kept in a bank vault, from which it is known to have been collected in 1956 by a devotee now dead. No one, it is said, knows where the book is now. But somebody in fact must know, or be going to know, for when Baba was asked in the month before he laid down his body, where the book might be found, he replied: "It is all right, and you are not to worry. It is being looked after."

One day in October 1926, when the centre's activity was at its height, Baba called a special meeting of the mandali and put to them his proposal. All the work which had been built up with so much effort over the past two and a half years should now be wound up, and the buildings, with only two or three exceptions, levelled to the ground. The mandali naturally expressed concern at the prospect of up to four hundred people being left helpless and homeless, but it was soon clear that Baba had thought out all arrangements, and no person who needed relief would be left without it. However, a work seemingly of great value to the community, work on which much effort and money had been spent, was brought to an abrupt stop.

Few aspects of their work with Baba were more puzzling to the mandali than the rapidity – it sometimes seemed to them the capriciousness – with which Baba put a stop to one kind of activity and directed all their energies and his own into something different. Baba's own comment was: "Usually a temporary scaffolding is set up around a big building which is under construction, and when the building is completed, the scaffolding is removed. Often my external activities and commitments are only the outward expression of the internal work I am doing. The school, hospital etc. were but scaffolding for my real work… Hence, when my work is finished, I have no need of scaffoldings." Another time he declared:

> I have not come to establish retreats or ashrams. I create them for the purpose of my universal work, only to repeatedly dissolve them once that purpose has been served.
>
> The universe is my ashram, and every heart is my house…[16]

This is a mode of working difficult for most Westerners to comprehend. We are accustomed to think of hospitals and schools as 'absolute goods', which should continue indefinitely and if possible expand and multiply. But for Baba his model town, like other activities he would later start and then wind up, was only the shell for work of universal application. Its main purpose was invisible and symbolic, and for the mandali it also provided

Meher Baba. Location: Manzil-e-Meem 1922. © Meher Nazar Publications.

a lesson to be learned. But there were other lessons, and only so much time could be given to each. No one around Baba would be allowed to settle into a routine, even a routine as beneficent as handing out grain and bandages and washing the untouchables.

Notes

1. *Listen, Humanity*, p. 250
2. *Ashram* is an Indian word for 'a religious community under the direction of a Master'.
3. Padri, whose real name was Faredoon Naosherwan Driver, was known to all who visited Meherabad. He was tireless in Baba's service from the early 1920s till 14th March 1982, when – while he was engaged in dictating a letter – Baba called him away, or in Padri's own phrase, used of one who had preceded him, "gave him his visa". Pendu would receive *his* on 7th November 1986.
4. *Listen, Humanity*, pp. 250–1
5. His full name was Sarosh K. Irani. He died in 1973.
6. *Twenty Years with Meher Baba*, p. 14
7. *The God-Man*, p. 41
8. Today (1989) Arangaon, and Meherabad, have been extensively rebuilt and wear a look of prosperity, due to the work of the Avatar Meher Baba Trust (cf. map of Meherabad in Appendix).
9. Known as the *Jhopdi*, this room can be seen by the thousands coming to Meherabad every year.
10. In this way Baba was doing for the 'untouchable' children the very work of latrine-cleaning and refuse clearing which caused these children, and the caste from which they came, to be classed as 'untouchable'.
11. *Listen, Humanity*, p. 253
12. Told to the authors by Pendu while sitting on the verandah at Meherazad.
13. *Darshan*: Lit. 'sight of the Master'. Seeing, or being in, the

presence of the Master. *To receive darshan* is 'to express devotion to a Master often by bowing down'.

14. *Listen, Humanity*, p. 254
15. To be seen just below the main road and close to the current Post Office at Meherabad. It looks like a large packing case.
16. *The God-Man*, p. 273

Meher Baba with alphabet board. Location: Lower Meherabad, 3 June 1937. © MSI Collection.

Chapter 4

The 'Thunderous Silence'

When Baba drew to an apparent end the work at Arangaon – much of which would be resumed in one way or another before long – he inaugurated a new period, one of travel up and down the subcontinent, leading to a period of wider travel which would carry him and some of the mandali all over the world. But before considering that, there is another and a particularly mysterious aspect of Baba's life and work to be taken into account: from as far back as 10th July 1925, Baba had spoken no single word.

In June that year, Baba informed the mandali he would observe a long period of silence. This would begin on the 10th July and last for a whole year. At the end of this time he would "come out into the open", an expression which some took to mean a final manifestation after which there would be no further use for worldly goods or possessions. One went so far as to give away all his belongings and urge his family to do the same. The women disciples simply could not believe that Baba actually intended to keep silence for a whole year, and comforted one another: "At the most, he will keep silence for one month." And when, on the evening of the 9th July, Baba said, "Hear well my voice: you will not hear it for a long time," no one about him, man or woman, dreamed that the Master's silence would last, not for one year or five or ten, but for more than forty-four years and be still unbroken when his earthly life came to an end.

Why did Baba undertake his silence? Speech is the precious means of communication which above all distinguishes humans from animals. On speech and writing the whole of our intellectual development is based. To become dumb or deaf, and so cut off from easy communication with others, is considered among the greatest disasters that can befall one. Why did Baba bring this seeming disaster on himself?

It is true that after some years several of the mandali, in particular Eruch (Eruch B. Jessawala, whom Baba called "My right hand"), became so adept at interpreting Baba's meaning, that a few rapid gestures, illuminated by Baba's astonishing range of facial expression, enabled them to convey long explanations and instructions. Even a newcomer, watching Baba's face and hearing the quiet voice of Eruch close beside him, came away with the sense of having carried on a full conversation – and only later would recall that Baba himself had uttered no word. But during those first years when his voice would be most missed by his companions, Baba had to resort, first to a slate or writing pads, and then from January 1927, when he gave up writing as well as speech, to the laborious use of an alphabet board. This too, many years later in October 1954, would be discarded, after which only hand signs would be used. Surely, it might be argued, Baba was placing a needless burden on himself and a handicap on his work by the avoidance of speech. Certainly among Western intellectuals, who generally pride themselves on talking well, the idea of a Master who did not speak seems to arouse particularly angry disbelief, as though Baba were criticising all talkers by his silence.

It should be remembered, however, that silence has always formed an important part of religious discipline and practice, in the West as well as in the East. In India many pilgrims and holy men maintain complete silence. Baba's close companions would often be instructed to remain silent for varying periods, and one, Gustadji, maintained silence continually from 1927. In the Western world the Trappist monks provide the most familiar example of silence, but most monastic orders impose regular periods of silence as part of their rule of life.

Older people in Britain and one or two other Western countries can recall that, in the years between World Wars I and II, and again for nearly twenty years after the Second World War had ended, it was customary to maintain a Two-Minute Silence all over the country at eleven o'clock every 11th November (the anniversary of the date World War I ended) in memory of all those who had lost their lives in the two world wars. Traffic came to a standstill. In factories, offices and shops, in universities, colleges and schools, all work stopped. Everyone rose to their feet and stood motionless. The effect of such silence, though lasting for two minutes only, was profound. Today Baba-lovers all over the world keep 10th July, the day on which Baba began his silence, as a Day of Silence in his honour.

Of his silence Baba himself said:

> I have come not to teach but to awaken. Understand therefore that I lay down no precepts… Because man has been deaf to the principles and precepts laid down by God in the past, in this present *avataric* form I observe Silence. You have asked for and been given enough words – it is now time to live them.[1]

Baba's silence therefore served to impress upon the world that he had not come to add one more to the list of the great religions which man persistently misunderstands and distorts, using them to sanctify the self-interest, greed and hatred they were intended to help him overcome. Baba realised very well that if he put forward any 'new religion' it would before long go the way of all the rest. The very people who accepted the new teaching would take it over and 'interpret' it, so that inevitably it would be brought down by degrees to the level of the interpreters, and thus forced to conform to the attitudes and interests of mankind in general. With the 'teachers' would come 'organisers' who would codify and structure the new religion, place it on a sound financial footing and equip it with churches, temples and a priestly hierarchy. It would then compete for converts with other religions, measuring success by the hundreds of thousands who showed up at its services, the extent of references to it in newspapers or television programmes, and the number of noughts in its bank balance – turning it, in short, from a spiritual dynamic into a profitable business enterprise.

With none of this would Baba have anything to do. He was as scathing about church organisations as Jesus was about the scribes and Pharisees, or as he himself would be later on, about the "hypocritical saints and masters that now flourish everywhere like poisonous mushrooms", masters who travel in fleets of Rolls-Royces and accumulate vast tracts of real estate. Instead of putting forward a competing religion, Baba called attention through his silence to the underlying truth which is the same in all religions, and by means of which, he said, he would one day draw all religions and creeds together "like beads on a string".

We spoke above of speech and writing as factors on which "the whole of our intellectual development is based". And this may itself have been a powerful reason for Baba's keeping silent, since his message was not to our mind but to our heart, and the heart can only be reached when the mind is bypassed or compelled to abdicate its dictatorial role.

> External silence (Baba told Kitty Davy and other Western women who were with him at Nasik in early 1937) helps to achieve inner Silence, and only in internal Silence is Baba found – in profound inner Silence. I am never silent. I speak eternally. The voice that is heard deep within the soul is My voice... To those who are receptive to this voice, I speak.[2]

And to a great gathering of his Eastern followers at Poona in May 1965, Baba gave this message:

> This time of your being with me, I do not intend giving you a lot of words to exercise your minds. I want your minds to sleep so that your hearts may awaken to my love.
>
> You have had enough of words, I have had enough of words. It is not through words that I give what I have to give. In the silence of your perfect surrender, my love which is always silent can flow to you – to be yours always to keep and to share with those who seek me.
>
> When the word of my Love breaks out of its silence and speaks in your hearts, telling you who I really am, you will know that that is the Real Word you have been always longing to hear.[3]

At different times Baba gave other explanations for his silence, not conflicting with but related to those given above. He said he undertook it partly to assist him in carrying out his spiritual work, and partly because of the wars, upheavals and catastrophes which he saw coming upon the world and particularly on India, the land where he had chosen to make his home.

Neither of these statements can be easily understood since we have no conception of how a great Master carries out his spiritual work, far less than we can conceive – for example – what goes on in the mind of a great physicist or composer. But we can perhaps accept that Baba's silence, like the seclusion into which during the latter part of his life he withdrew for months on end, made possible a conservation of energy which he applied to far more potent effect than if he had dissipated it in words – of which already "you have asked for and been given enough". Energy retained he could make use of 100 per cent because he exercised 100 per cent control over it. Energy discharged in speech must depend on the use listeners made of it, we listeners who have already shown ourselves "deaf to the principles and precepts laid down" throughout eternity.

One consequence of Baba's silence, much feared by those about him, did not eventuate. A loss of contact and intimacy with the mandali and others close to him might have been expected when the Master no longer spoke directly to them. Yet surprisingly the opposite was true, for Baba did not retreat into lofty reserve or maintain a stony speechlessness. On the contrary, he gave himself through his ever-changing facial expressions; through his eyes which saw without illusion and yet radiated love; and through the forceful gestures of his hands and fingers.

Many who came in contact with Baba without knowing who he was remained quite unaware that he did not speak. An example of this occurred once when Baba was on his way with the mandali by train to Bombay. A gale had uprooted trees and caused breaches in the tracks so that there was no way of knowing when the journey would be resumed. Baba and his party were in a compartment just behind the engine, and when Baba wished for tea Eruch approached the engine driver for some water. This he readily provided, and then joined the party in their game of cards. "Baba had put on a coat and also a cap that covered His long hair. He played the game with such ease and grace that the engineer had not the slightest hint or sign that Baba was observing silence. But he did detect the silence of Gustadji and would refer to him as a *muga* – a dumb fellow."[4]

To those who came in contact with Baba knowingly, the very fact that he did not speak compelled them to concentrate their full attention in the effort to comprehend what he was seeking to convey. And the combination of silence with his dynamic visual expression produced on even casual visitors the awe-inspiring sense of a Being living simultaneously in the finite world and in the infinite.

Indeed a special closeness, a unique intimacy derived from Baba's silence so that communication with him seemed, in bypassing vocal chords, to flow from heart to heart direct.

"Why," Baba one day asked the mandali, "do we shout when we are angry? Do you know?"

One answered that we shout to dominate our adversary. Another, that we shout because he is probably shouting and we need to make ourselves heard. A third thought that we shout out of aggression. Eruch suggested that it is the explosive force of our anger which makes us shout.

"Yes," Baba replied, "but why should our anger express itself in *shouting*? We are talking quietly with a man when something arouses our anger and we begin to shout at him – why is this?"

No one could provide a satisfactory explanation.

"You shout at the man," Baba explained, "because in being angry with him you have pushed him far away from you. You have thrown him out of your heart and he is now far distant – so you have to shout to reach him."

"But now," Baba continued, "think about silence. When you are friends with someone you talk quietly to him or her. You show your affection by speaking softly. When you love someone you even whisper more softly still. Lovers take each other in their arms and are completely silent. So the real language of love is silence."

Yet when all explanations have been sought, there remains a profound mystery about Baba's silence, and a further mystery attaches itself to the statements he made from time to time about the breaking of it. These were full of promise, repeated in various words throughout his life, sometimes in general terms, at others with specific dates.

> I am silent. My Silence is not merely an observing of silence. My Silence has a purpose behind it. When I break it, all will know. The breaking of my Silence will be as forceful as thousands of atom bombs exploding together.
>
> (And again:) This idea of the self as a limited, separate entity will vanish. Co-operation will replace competition; certainty will replace fear; generosity will replace greed, exploitation will be no more. When I speak, I will reveal the One Supreme Self which is in every one.[5]

In September 1954, in the course of his "Final Declaration" to assembled lovers from both East and West, Baba declared:

> I am preparing to break my silence. When I break my silence it will not be to fill your ears with spiritual lectures. I shall speak only one Word, and this Word will penetrate the hearts of all men and make even the sinner feel that he is meant to be a saint, while the saint will know that God is in the sinner as much as he is in himself. When I speak that Word, I shall lay the foundation for that which is to take place during the next seven hundred years... my Word of words will touch the hearts of all mankind, and spontaneously this divine touch will instil in man the feeling of the oneness of all fellow beings. Gradually, in the course of the next seven hundred years, this feeling will supersede the tendency of separateness and rule over the hearts of all, driving away hatred, jealousy and greed that breed suffering, and happiness will reign.[6]

When, despite his statements about the Word of words which he would utter, Baba laid down his body without having broken his long silence, some of his followers expressed surprise. But those closest to him were confident that Baba's meaning would become clear in his own good time. Eruch recalled that in 1960 Baba had said that he would end his silence, but had not done so. Eruch had then said: "The delay that we feel to be made by Baba in carrying out His word is but the reflection of the delay within us in our preparedness to accept His Word of words."

And in June 1963, Baba's sister Mani wrote in her Family Letter: "We who are with Baba are understandably not excited when the Beloved pinpoints a time when He says He will break His silence. Those concerned most with Him, are somehow least concerned about *when* He will break it."

CB Purdom, in his book *The God-Man*, includes a perceptive section on 'The Silence' which contains these sentences.

> Those who have been in his presence know that Baba communicates through his silence. What proceeds from him is beyond words, does not need words, could not be contained in them. The inaudible sound is from heart to heart: silence that penetrates mind and heart. He sometimes reminds those who read or listen to what he 'says' that he uses another language from theirs, which should be remembered when his words are considered. That is, his standpoint is different from those who listen. He is on the level of the listener, but his standpoint is absolute, i.e. timeless and essential, while that of the listener is relative, i.e. in the terms of earthly life and history. Silence is not only a matter of non-speaking, but silence of the desires, passions, urgings and conflicts of body and mind. In those who practise it, silence brings about calmness and harmony in the body, making it a ready instrument: it is complete self-possession. Baba's silence places him among the intangible, the unrecorded and not documented, a positive sign that he does not wholly belong to the rational world of facts and events but to the inner world

of insight and intuition.[7]

Finally there are many followers who believe that Baba did in his own way 'break his silence', either shortly before or at the moment when he laid down his earthly body. They believe this because they experience his presence even more closely today than they did while he was visibly present upon earth. In Eruch's words: "He seems to have come into their hearts more forcefully than ever before. They feel His presence without seeing Him, and I can quite believe that, because I too feel that way. Although I miss Him, I feel His presence without seeing Him – the same as when Baba used to send me away on some errand, He being where He was."

To sum up, there is an apparent contradiction in Baba's repeated statements that he would shortly break his silence. Those who were closest to Baba worry about this least. Those who are now his followers either feel that he has spoken to them, or that he postponed his speaking for good reason, or that he used the word 'speaking' in his own personal language.

Perhaps every Avatar leaves a mystery for humanity to ponder. Buddha left a mystery in the manner of his death. Jesus left the mystery of his Second Coming, which his followers were expecting almost daily in the period following his Crucifixion, and then, when this did not occur, continued to

Meher Baba aboard the SS Bremen, New York City, May 1932, dictating on his alphabet board to Meredith Starr, Chanji, and his brother Beheram. © Meher Nazar Publications.

be confident that it would at least take place during their own lifetimes. Meher Baba has left the mystery of his long silence and his seemingly Unspoken Word.

Notes

1. From Meher Baba's "Universal Message", *The God-Man*, p. 343
2. *Love Alone Prevails*, pp. 166–7
3. *Family Letters*, Letter 64
4. Cf. *Glimpses, Vol I*, pp. 404–5
5. *Avatar*, p. 26
6. *The God-Man*, pp. 274–5
7. *The God-Man*, p. 410

Meher Baba with ashram boys by the crypt-room (later Meher Baba's tomb), on Meherabad Hill, taken March–May 1928. © Meher Nazar Publications.

Chapter 5

The Meher Ashram & Travel In the East

It was November 1926 when the work of healing and teaching was wound up at Meherabad, and almost all buildings, apart from Baba's little hut, were levelled with the ground. Baba and his followers set off for a neighbouring town in lorries, later travelling on to Bombay by train. But towards the end of December, after an absence of only a few weeks, Baba astonished everyone by ordering a return to the desolate and abandoned Meherabad. Nor was this all; a school was reopened for the village boys, and a second shortly after for the girls – though the other earlier institutions remained closed. In addition, a school of an entirely new kind was now established, known as the Meher Ashram, which would play a memorable part in the record of Baba's activities. This was a boarding school in which everything – board and lodging, books and even clothes – was to be provided free. Baba assigned five of the mandali to have charge of the school in which the standard of teaching was to be of the highest, though 'education' in the conventional sense was not the school's main purpose. "I want to impress upon all," Baba declared in March 1927, "the all-importance of spiritual training – this is the sole aim of the proposed institution."[1]

The opportunity of a free education for their sons quickly produced applications from parents and guardians, but many wanted to be assured that 'touchables' and 'untouchables' would be kept strictly apart, contrary to Baba's insistence that boys of all classes and creeds should live and work together:

> The education that will be imparted to the boys in the Ashram will also prove an advance towards the political salvation of India... These boys, at the completion of the course, will have no longer any bias or prejudice against any particular religion, as is the case these days, resulting in so much strife and slaughter all over the country.

For centuries differences of caste and religion have been India's curse, the cause of smouldering resentment between different peoples, a handicap to economic and social development, and an obstacle to India's assuming its true role of importance in the modern world. Twenty years after the founding of the Meher Ashram, these antagonisms would split the subcontinent, severing Pakistan from India in a violent partition, to be followed by massacres, boundary disputes and internal hostilities which have not yet been finally resolved. Politicians and leaders, despite lofty speeches about unity, have too often either encouraged partisan feelings or allowed themselves to be swept along on a tide of intolerance.

Boys for the Meher Ashram were chosen from all creeds and classes to receive an education in which spiritual and secular instruction were combined. The aim was to produce a group of educated men, utterly free from prejudice or hostility towards those of different origins, who could serve as a leaven in the life of the community and of the world – a parallel today[2] might be the founding of a school in South Africa whose pupils, drawn from all races, would be brought up without trace of colour antagonism. Looking for and accepting the best in one another, the boys would also learn to appreciate the truth in each other's religion and beliefs, so that the way would begin to be paved for the acceptance of that universal religion which will one day unite all religions "like beads on a string."

A basic condition which would later lead to much high drama was Baba's insistence that

> Once the boys are admitted they must remain in the institution till the completion of the full course whether it may take two years or seven years, and the option of granting leave to them... in case of emergencies during the course is solely left to his (Baba's) own discretion. Otherwise, Baba conveyed, his very purpose, which was *continued* close contact and moral training, would be defeated... But once the boys had passed through a long period under all the disciplines and restrictions in the institution, their character would get sufficiently moulded on ideal spiritual lines that they would remain unaffected, even when they mix themselves in the thick of worldly affairs afterwards. On the other hand, if the boys were allowed to go home and mix with worldly people in the middle of their training, there is every chance of the effect of the training being wiped out clean.

On 1st May 1927, the Meher Ashram was declared open at Meherabad with four Brahmin, three Maratha and three Mahar boys (all Hindus of different castes). On 17th July, with the arrival of fourteen boys from Persia, two Muslims and twelve

Zoroastrians, a Persian section of the school was also opened. English was the medium of instruction, with Persian and Sanskrit as second languages, and everything, down to details of the school uniform and the books in the library, had been planned by Baba with the minutest care.

On 1st September, classes of spiritual teaching were started, and

> ... the boys began to have explained to them the spirit of all religion and the lives of divine heroes in every nation... Within another month, the Master seemed all engrossed in the Ashram affairs and began to remain there for hours together, freely mixing with the boys to the extent of playing, and at times eating with them. In November quite a change came about in the atmosphere; mysticism was rampant everywhere, though at the same time the secular education of the boys was never overlooked or allowed to suffer in the least.

And by the middle of the month Baba began to convey to the boys, mainly by means of the alphabet board, "the importance of love, concentration and meditation, and thus directly to inspire the boys to divine aspiration."

Early in 1928 the Meher Ashram had grown to accommodate over a hundred pupils, with as many as twenty instructors taking part in the teaching. During that year the school changed its quarters several times, and at the beginning of 1929 Baba brought its activities to an end. The occasion, recorded in *Ramjoo's Diaries*, was the long struggle of Syed Ali, a Muslim boy, to remain at the Ashram with Baba against the wishes of his family. With hindsight, Ali's story might seem to offer an indication that Muslims were not yet willing to be reconciled to those of other religions.

Once again it might appear that a piece of valuable public

service had been launched, only to be closed abruptly before its task had been completed. It is impossible, however, to form any appreciation of Baba's activities unless one accepts a fundamental fact about his way of working. Baba was never concerned to establish institutions – which inevitably in time become diverted from their original purpose to conform with a general worldly pattern – but rather to carry out specific parts of his own spiritual work by means of 'models' or 'examples'. Once his purpose had been accomplished, the 'scaffolding' or organisation was immediately taken down, though in taking it down Baba always made scrupulous provision for those who would be affected by the decision. Why did he not leave the scaffolding up, it may be asked, since even one more school or clinic would be making *some* contribution to the country's social problems? The answer must be that their value depended on all that Baba himself put into them, and that, once his original intention had been achieved, his time and energy had to be put into something else – something which had become at that moment still more urgent. "The activities of the God-Man are not meant for immediate tangible results, but they are symbolic expressions of the inner work in which the *Avatar* is engaged."[3]

Every activity Baba undertook was thus a response to a particular need, which at times he alone could perceive, and until this had been met he gave himself to the task as wholeheartedly and spontaneously as he gave himself to those who came in contact with him. "I alone do my work," Baba often told his followers, and he alone was the judge of when a particular task had been accomplished.

For the mandali, and through them for ourselves, the lesson Baba conveyed was that the evils of the world are not put right by the founding of institutions, the establishing of societies or the promotion of religious organisations – but only through an immediate loving response to each situation as it arises. This response has to be from person to person and not through institutions, which may indeed serve a temporary purpose and act as a channel for combined effort, but which quickly lose their original impulse and become concerned with their own survival and importance. This is perhaps what Baba meant when he said at Nasik in 1937: "I never make plans, never change plans. It is all one endless plan of making people know that there is no plan."

Meantime from the beginning of 1927, shortly after his return to Meherabad, Baba had ceased to write as well as to speak, and from that time onwards he wrote nothing except a rare signature on a photograph or official document.

Though Baba's activity in connection with the Meher Ashram had been intense during the two years 1927–9, he had also spent periods of up to two months in seclusion and had fasted for as much as five and a half months at a stretch. During this prolonged fast he took nothing except liquids, weak tea, milk or cocoa. 'Fasting' for Baba covered varying degrees of abstinence, from going entirely without food or even water, to semi-fasts in which he took one simple meal every twenty-four hours. Sometimes the mandali, or a few members of it, would be instructed or allowed to share a fast, and sometimes not. Occasionally a fast which had been envisaged did not take place, and once or twice Baba suddenly ordered a special meal to be prepared in haste, of which when the time came he scarcely touched a mouthful.

Baba's explanation of his fasts was simple and surprising. He 'never fasted'. By this he meant that he never went without food in the way saints and yogis do, in order to deny their bodies and intensify their spiritual powers. Having no need for such exercises in self-denial, he never refused food when able and inclined to eat it. But the fact was, he explained, that at times when he fasted he was engaged in spiritual work which rendered it impossible for his physical body to accept food,[4] though the weakness and suffering caused by deprivation were just as acute as any ordinary person would feel. There may be a faint parallel to this in our common experience of inability to eat in times of intense concentration or powerful emotion.

An entertaining story in connection with his fasting was told by Baba many years later at the sahavas (gathering) in India during November 1955.

> This was also the period when I carried out one of my longest continuous fasts, which lasted five and one-half months (November 1927–April 1928). Once during this period I took nothing but a few sips of water for more than twenty-eight days. The remainder of the time I lived on cocoa in milk taken once in twenty-four hours.
>
> Even this was in scant supply as it happened. Lahu (a Baba favourite among the untouchable boys) used to carry my supply to me every day, and on the way he would drink half of it and then pass on the other half to me. I found out about this at the end of my seclusion when the women *mandali* assured me they had sent Lahu regularly, as I had originally instructed them, with the thermos bottle full of cocoa. When I questioned Lahu about this, he readily confessed pilfering half my cocoa every day. I pardoned the little fellow as readily as he had acknowledged the guilt.[5]

When not fasting, Baba's diet was sufficiently frugal to constitute the equivalent of a fast by Western standards. He lived mainly on rice and *dal*, a form of lentil curry. He was vegetarian, though not according to any rigid rule; some of the mandali recalled his having once on a plane journey sent for and eaten a whole tin of Spam when this was all that proved to be available. The mandali too were vegetarians, but to his followers in general he allowed freedom to follow their normal way of life. "I allow vegetarians to follow their own diet and non-vegetarians to eat meat; I do not interfere with any custom or religion. When faced with love for God these matters have no value."

Baba did not touch alcohol, but here too he occasionally overruled his own custom by taking a sip or two of wine and giving it to those about him. Occasionally this would have the air of a celebration or thanksgiving, as when Baba gave drink to those involved in the climbing adventure at Portofino in 1933. "When I give anything," he told them, "you should not hesitate to take. I give or not give for special reasons."[6]

At times the instruction to drink wine was a test of obedience. Eruch has recorded the case of a devout Brahmin who came to Baba offering to obey him in every respect if only Baba would help him to find God. But Baba's first instruction – that the man should disregard the strict dietary rules of his caste – was rejected, and Eruch recounts the sad end of the man's story.[7]

Today it surprises many of Baba's followers to learn that in his early days of youthful companionship Baba would smoke cigarettes with those who later became disciples, and though he never smoked after this time, he would allow others to do so freely... "When faced with love for God these matters have no value."

A special degree of tolerance about smoking was enjoyed by Dr Ghani, dating from the time of Manzil-e-Meem (1922–3).

> He was a chain-smoker and his daily diet included meat – both of which were not allowed in the Ashram... But denial of smoke dulled his spirits... and considering his long-standing habit Baba allowed him five cigarettes a day. But this was not sufficient for him. From his fertile brain he designed a plan. He began to join together four to five cigarettes and make one. Such five cigarettes of his own make he began smoking each day. When Baba came to know of this he was displeased and took Ghani to task for disobedience. But Ghani argued out his case convincingly stating that he was only smoking five cigarettes a day in obedience to Baba's order, the length of the cigarettes not being decided. Baba enjoyed the joke and

allowed him to smoke as he used to, an exception to the rule of the Ashram.[8]

And now, in April 1929, with the closing of the Meher Ashram, Baba began a period of journeying throughout India with the mandali, as if to prepare them for the much greater travels in which before long both he and they were to be involved. During these journeys the party visited cities all over India: Agra, Delhi, Lahore, Quetta, Bombay – partly on foot and partly by bus and train – also towns with special spiritual associations such as Nasik, Rishikesh and Srinagar. In many of these places large crowds flocked to greet Baba and from time to time he interrupted this life of contact with the people by spells of seclusion and fasting in remote, mountainous places. Near Panchgani in the mountains of the Western Ghat, where he had been invited by a devotee, Baba arranged for a cave fifteen feet deep to be dug[9] at a lonely spot near the head of the Tiger Valley, a haunt, as its name implies, of tigers, leopards and other wild creatures. To this cave Baba retired and fasted, a stay which was important, he explained, for his future working. Some of the mandali who were also fasting kept watch from huts above, below and beside the cave to ensure that no strangers came within two hundred yards, no easy task since word of a Master's seclusion in their area brought many people to the spot, some indeed hoping for his blessing but others out of idle curiosity. They would climb up to the cave in groups of as many as fifty, and the mandali – having of course no legal right, still less the physical power to disperse them – were sometimes hard put to induce them to go home and leave Baba undisturbed.

After a fortnight spent in this way, Baba summoned the group together one evening at eight o'clock and told them to make ready to leave at once. A bullock cart was found at a small town some miles away and brought up to carry the belongings, and at midnight the party set off on a four-hour descent of the mountains, before returning to Meherabad by bus. Later in the year, after a succession of other journeys, Baba and twelve of the mandali travelled by bus to Kashmir. Twelve miles north of Srinagar, in a tiny hut at an altitude of about 6,000 feet, Baba again retired into seclusion. Before doing so, however, he allowed all the people from surrounding villages to come and see him; they were mostly poor, and he ordered a feast to be given them.

The hut to which Baba now retired left space for only one person to lie down. Into this he locked himself, and two of the mandali, assisted by a third on night duty, kept watch outside, protected only by the hut's overhanging roof. Baba fasted throughout, taking nothing but water, which was passed to him through an opening at a certain hour daily in response to his knock; fresh water and food for the watchers were carried up twice a day from the village by other members of the mandali. With Baba locked in, the watchers outside – forbidden to speak and able to communicate only by signs – found their long vigil frightening. They had a stick to drive away scorpions and snakes and a fire was kept burning after sunset, but the pitch-dark nights were full of howls and cries. Sometimes they heard the roar of tigers and the padding of creatures not far off, against which a stick and a fire seemed scant protection.

Here too their stay ended without warning, and throughout the entire return journey to Meherabad, lasting for some days, the party took shelter in no rest house or home. They drove all day from early morning until late at night, stopping in mid-morning when the heat became intense for a meal and a wash, sleeping at night in woods or on the banks of rivers. At the time it must have seemed to some of the followers that much of their hardship was unnecessary, but later when Baba sent them out on long missions and journeys by themselves – in which difficulties and dangers were unavoidable – they looked back thankfully on the arduous training he had given them and the confidence in themselves which they had learned.

And now no sooner was Baba back in Meherabad than he declared he must set off for Persia. He went first to Bombay where word of his arrival brought thousands – Hindus, Muslims, Christians and Parsis – to gaze at him, and a great crowd assembled to see him off when he left by steamship. The captain and ship's officers were amazed that someone to whom such respect was accorded should be travelling third class with only a seat on a hatch for accommodation, and a wealthy Parsi merchant offered to arrange "a nice cabin in the upper class." Baba's answer was that he was happy where he was, and that "a fakir's place is always with the poorest."

The mandali observed on this tour that, though Baba's name was never mentioned and the tour itself kept private, people gathered in every town they reached. In addition there were persons at all levels of life, from government officials and army officers to the humblest workers, with whom some special contact seemed to be made, or possibly renewed. These experiences started already on the voyage. A member of the engine room crew, a Muslim, used to come up and stand gazing at him with tears, for minutes at a time. Throughout the five days of the voyage, no word was exchanged, but on the final day Baba beckoned the man over and gave him his handkerchief.

At Bam, a town where Baba put up at a quiet rest house on the outskirts, several strange incidents occurred. A man in imposing military uniform came requesting to see "the Holy Master who has just arrived". Told there was no such person in the rest house, he persisted that the Holy One be informed that "a beggar has arrived, begging for alms from him." Admitted on Baba's instructions, he saluted, laid down his sword, and fell on his knees to kiss Baba's hand. Asked who he was, he replied: "Your humble slave."

"What is your rank?"

"Nothing, beside your Holiness."

"I mean your military rank."

"A general of the Persian Army." He later added words strange from the mouth of a high-ranking officer: "I humbly believe that the salvation of this country lies not in its military power but in its spiritual rebirth through an understanding of life, brought about by the benign grace of great saints of your exalted dignity, and I humbly pray on behalf of my country for the great gift of your Grace."

"That is why you see me here," was Baba's acknowledgement and the general withdrew, walking backwards step by step.

In the street just opposite the rest house was the seat of a saint held locally in high reverence. On Baba's coming out with the mandali for an evening walk, this man rose from his seat as a mark of respect, and to those who visited him declared that "the Emperor of all Fakirs" was now present in their midst.

From Persia the party returned to India overland in a journey lasting many days.[10] Back in India Baba made his headquarters for a time at Nasik, a Hindu city of many temples and immense antiquity on the banks of a river 120 miles to the north-east of

Meher Ashram schoolboys at Upper Meherabad water reservoir in 1927. © Meher Nazar Publications.

Bombay. From here and from Meherabad over the next two years, Baba journeyed to South India, twice up to Kashmir in the far north and once again to Persia. At the end of 1930, perhaps as a result of continual travelling in conditions of great hardship, frequently while fasting, Baba's health broke down. It was not long, however, before he recovered to begin an entirely new period of travel on a far wider scale.

Notes

1. This and following extracts: "Pawar's Diary" in *Ramjoo's Diaries*, pp. 409–13
2. 1980s (Ed.)
3. *Glimpses, Vol II*, p. 157
4. Cf. *The Silent Word*, p. 256. "He explained to the mandali that the particular work he had been doing required him to breathe in the opposite way to which a man usually breathes, and an empty stomach was a great help for such work."
5. *Listen, Humanity*, p. 255
6. *Love Alone Prevails*, pp. 105–7
7. *The Ancient One*, pp. 93–5
8. *Twenty Years with Meher Baba*, p. 12
9. Presumably into the hillside, not directly down into the ground.
10. A full account of this eventful journey is given in *The Perfect Master*, pp. 141–152.

L-r: (unknown), John Cousins and his younger son, Dorothy Cousins, Baba, Minta Toledano, Adi Sr., Ann Powell. Location: Combe Martin, Devon, England, April 1932. © Meher Nazar Publications.

Chapter 6

Travel To the West

Ever since 1922 Baba had been warning his followers: "War will break out again, and it will be the worst holocaust the world has ever seen. Almost all the nations will be drawn into it either militarily or economically." And now, in 1931, he started an intensive period of world travel, as though he were intending to make as many visits to the West as possible before the clouds came down. Also, in striking contrast to previous journeys – usually made incognito with strict orders to the mandali not to reveal his name – these visits were publicised and reported. Baba showed himself eager to meet people at all levels; he attended parties, gatherings, theatres; he gave interviews to newspapermen and was photographed for magazines and newsreels.

His first visit to the West came at a crucial moment in world history and in the history of Britain, where Baba made his first stay. In mid-July he sent a cable: "Love calls me to the West. Make preparations." But during August the date of his sailing was repeatedly put off, so that he finally left India on 1st September, travelling by sea from Karachi to Marseilles in the *SS Rajputana*, accompanied by three followers. Also on board the *Rajputana* was Mahatma Gandhi, lately released from gaol and on his way to the Round Table Conference, which would prove so important a milestone on the road to India's independence.

Gandhi was now at the height of his prestige; as sole representative of the Congress Party at the London Conference, he was in effect the voice of Hindu India. Nine years previously Baba had foretold that on his first trip to the West he would travel with and meet Gandhi, so the mandali were not surprised to learn that the Mahatma was on the same boat, and to receive a message that he would like to come to Baba's cabin for a talk; he had in fact been sent a cable advising him to contact Baba. When he appeared, accompanied by his secretary, Gandhi said he had only come because of the cable and could spare no more than five minutes. However, he remained for three hours and came back again next day.

"Baba," he concluded, "it is now time for you to speak and to let the world hear. I feel within me that you are something great; I did not feel the same when I visited Upasni Maharaj."

"Why?" Baba asked.

"When I went to Upasni Maharaj he was wearing a piece of rag round his loins: he removed it and showed his private parts and said, 'You may be a great man; what is that to me? Why have you come here?'"

Baba's reply showed his power to assume authority regardless of whom he was addressing. "Now you really know that I am great, with the authority of that greatness I tell you that Maharaj was a Perfect Master."

But Gandhi was bewildered: "No, Baba, I do not understand

it at all." He did, however, return later for a third discussion.[1]

When Baba arrived in Marseilles on 11th September, he was met by two Englishmen, Meredith Starr and Herbert Davy, who went with him from the boat to a hotel. "You have never seen such a Being!" Herbert Davy reported to London over the telephone. Later the two travelled on with Baba by train, first to Paris and then to London, where they were met by Kitty Davy and taken to the Davy family home in Kensington. Here he was to stay before travelling down to the West Country and the village of Combe Martin in North Devon, where Meredith Starr had established 'The Retreat', a centre for meditation and spiritual exercise.

A detailed and illuminating account of Baba's 1931 visit has been given by Kitty Davy in her book *Love Alone Prevails*. In the course of the visit Baba contacted a number of those to whom special tasks would be entrusted, and who would remain his devoted followers throughout their lives. In Britain, besides Kitty and Herbert Davy, he met Delia de Leon, Margaret Craske, CB Purdom, Will and Mary Backett and Kim Grajera (then Kim Tolhurst).

No event in Baba's life was the result of chance, and special significance must have attached to the timing of his first visit to the West. Historians and political commentators looking back over the twentieth century now see 1931 as one of the turning points in world affairs. It was a year of economic collapse and political disillusion, in which cherished hopes for international cooperation, leading to disarmament and peace through the League of Nations, were seen to be illusory. Another world war began to seem inevitable, and men's hearts sank at the prospect of a second so soon after the first, and at the destruction, death and chaos which loomed ever more ominously from now on.

All over Europe throughout the summer of 1931, the great Wall Street crash of two years earlier was producing its delayed effects. In Germany and Austria the breakdown of the banking and financial system had led to industrial collapse and massive unemployment, thus playing into the hands of the National Socialists and their leader Adolf Hitler, whose grip on Germany tightened with every fresh calamity. Hitler was not only bent on war, he had already outlined his plans for it in his book *Mein Kampf*.

Economic disaster on a similar scale to that in Germany threatened Britain also at this moment. The number of unemployed had risen to three million out of a work force far smaller than today's, and with a social system far less able to withstand the strain. "What threatened was not a mere financial crisis – but a complete commercial collapse which would engulf employed and unemployed in a common ruin."[2] A hastily-formed National Government had presented an 'Economy Budget' on 10th September, and its drastic measures were being discussed throughout the country just as Baba was on his way from Marseilles to London.

As for what was happening at this moment in the world at large, a single example must serve; on 18th September, the Japanese moved into Manchuria, following which action peace would not return to the Far East for fifty years, and perhaps not within the twentieth century at all. Wherever men turned their eyes, the process of destruction which, Baba tells us, must inevitably precede construction, was visibly underway.

On 3rd October, Baba left England for Constantinople, where he stayed nine days, moving on from there to Milan and Genoa, from which port he sailed for New York and his first visit to the United States. Here, as in England, Baba made contact with a number of men and women, some of whom later became his workers and remained devoted to him throughout their lives. Among them were Malcolm and Jean Schloss (Jean Adriel, author of *Avatar*); Nadine Tolstoy, daughter-in-law of Count Leo Tolstoy; Norina Matchabelli, wife of Prince Georges Matchabelli; and Elizabeth Patterson, future founder of the Meher Spiritual Center at Myrtle Beach. Of her first meeting with Baba, Elizabeth

Patterson has recorded: "When I looked at Baba, I recognised Him... It was absolute recognition... My experience was that of meeting someone I had always known, it was one of recognition from the recesses of forgotten time and at the same time, a portent of the future."[3]

Baba's first visit to the West was brief, as though it were a reconnaissance for the longer ones to follow, and in March 1932 he again set out from India on what was this time virtually a world tour, taking in England, France, Switzerland, the US, Honolulu, China, and returning through France, Italy and Egypt. In all, between first leaving the East in the *Rajputana* and October 1937, Baba made no fewer than nine[4] visits to the West, two of the journeys being world tours. The countries chiefly visited were Britain, America, France, Switzerland and Italy, but he made a fairly long stay also in Spain and went twice to both Egypt and Ceylon.[5]

It was early in April 1932 when Baba and his party arrived in London for this his second visit, and he gave a number of press interviews. Among those who came to see him was James Douglas, then editor of the *Sunday Express*. Douglas, an able and experienced journalist, had taken much trouble to prepare himself for the meeting.

> I had prepared a questionnaire with the help of Sir Denison Ross, the Oriental scholar. It was designed to trap the teacher, but he smilingly threaded his way through it without stumbling. His mastery of dialectic is consummate. It was quite Socratic in its ease.
>
> He frequently put questions to me which startled me by their penetration. But he never evaded a direct question. His simplicity is very subtle.
>
> "I am a Persian," he said. "I was born in Poona, but my father and mother were Persians."
>
> *"Are you divine?"* He smiled.

"I am one with God. I live in Him, like Buddha, like Christ, like Krishna. They knew Him as I know Him. All men can know Him."

"Have you solved the problem of evil?"

"There is no evil," he said. "There are only degrees of good."

"What is your secret?" I asked.

"The elimination of the ego," he replied…

"Have you a Scripture, a Bible, a Koran, an inspired book?"

"No, I teach. I am a teacher."[6]

"Do you believe in Buddha and the Eight-fold path?"

"Yes. All religion is ascent by stages to perfect union with God."

"What God do you believe in?"

"There is only one God for all men."

"What religion is nearest to yours?"

"All religions are revelations of God."

"Is there a future life?"

"Yes. The soul does not die. It goes on from life to life till it is merged in God."

"Nirvana?"

"Yes. But not loss of the self."

"Does the self survive?"

"Yes. But it is merged in God. The soul is not the brain. It functions in the brain. The brain is its instrument."

"Is God a Person or a Power?"

"God is both personal and impersonal. He is in art, in literature, everything."

"Are you a Pantheist?"

"No," he smiled. "When you know God it is plain. The Self is one with Him at the height of experience."

"Why am I not happy?"

"You have not grown out of self," he smiled.

He had said he would give me a minute, but the minute

lasted an hour.

"You are lucky," said a disciple. "He likes you."

He is serenely certain that he can redeem mankind... I wonder.[7]

Not all interviews, however, were as sympathetic as this, or as another which had been published the day before (9th April 1932) in the *Daily Mirror*. *John Bull* was a weekly magazine founded by Horatio Bottomley, a barnstorming politician of the First World War, and a financial trickster who thrived for a time in the years which immediately followed. *John Bull*, as its name implied, posed as a fearless defender of the public whose safety it ensured by denouncing small-time crooks – absconding Christmas Club secretaries, broken-down clergymen or schoolmasters in trouble – once they had been safely convicted by the courts. It also specialised in 'free insurance' schemes to attract readers, to whom it promised compensation for such misfortunes as being struck by lightning, carried off by flood, or losing both arms and legs in a railway accident.

John Bull now published an article in which it declared Baba to be "a fraud". Some of his followers wrote indignantly in his defence, but when Baba heard of this he ordered them to stop, first because opposition to him was no fault, and second because, "People who speak ill of me should not be condemned. They, too, are unconsciously serving my work, because they often think of me."[8]

He repeated this in May when he reached New York. His statement ended with the words: "My work will arouse great enthusiasm and a certain amount of opposition – that is inevitable. But spiritual work is strengthened by opposition, and so it will be with mine. It is like shooting an arrow from a bow – the more you pull the bow-string towards you, the swifter the arrow speeds to its goal."[9]

Baba's visits to London, New York and Chicago had been

met with an outburst of publicity which built up to his arrival in Hollywood, described as a "meteoric advent that crashed the front-page headlines of every paper in the land." Hollywood at this time was at its peak, the centre of the first world entertainment industry, with a reputation as fabulous as that of Baghdad or Atlantis. Its producers and directors handled budgets larger than those of many countries' exchequers; the influence of its productions was worldwide; its stars were more famous and admired than kings and queens, more idolised perhaps than any men and women have ever been idolised in history.

The 'King' and 'Queen' of the Hollywood court at this time were Douglas Fairbanks and Mary Pickford, who gave a reception in Baba's honour. He spent part of the evening talking to Mary, who was a student of Eastern philosophy, but also spoke individually to all the other guests. Later he was received at the principal studios: Fox, Metro-Goldwyn-Mayer, Warner Bros., Paramount, and met many of the stars at work. Of the directors, he spent time with Ernst Lubitsch and Von Sternberg, then directing Marlene Dietrich in *The Blonde Venus*. Marlene Dietrich was described as being offhand, but Tallulah Bankhead, who returned one evening for a longer interview, became deeply attached to Baba. There are delightful photographs of them together, Baba in an elegant white suit, with flowing hair and open-necked shirt, talking to Tallulah by means of his alphabet board, both entirely concentrated on the interchange. Another with whom he got on happily was Marie Dressler, whose humour delighted him. In the middle of lunch she declared she would like to take Baba out into the woods for a dance, adding that if for once he liked to "speak just a few words" she would not let anyone know he had broken his silence.

In all Baba remained in Hollywood six days, which included another evening reception in which he shook hands with each of the guests as they filed past him. Baba, who was at home with the untouchables at Arangaon or among the travellers camped on a ship's deck in the Indian Ocean, was equally at ease in the luxurious, competitive world of Hollywood. At 'Pickfair', home of Douglas Fairbanks and Mary Pickford, he gave a message which revealed his knowledge of the cinema and its importance at that period as a medium of communication, and of the spiritual guidance and inspiration which entertainment, often indirectly, gives mankind.

> He who stimulates the imagination of the masses can move them in any direction he chooses, and there is no more powerful instrument for stimulating their imagination than moving pictures... Both the press and the radio influence thought, but lack the power of visible example which is the great stimulant to action, and which the moving pictures offer better now than any other medium...[10]
>
> Plays which inspire those who see them to greater understanding, truer feeling, better lives, need not necessarily have anything to do with so-called religion. Creed, ritual, dogma, the conventional ideas of heaven and hell and sin, are perversions of the truth, and confuse and bewilder rather than clarify and inspire. Real spirituality is best portrayed in stories of pure love, of selfless service, of truth realised and applied to the most humble circumstances of our daily lives, raying out into manifold expression, through home and business, school and college, studio and laboratory... producing everywhere a constant symphony of bliss.
>
> This is the highest practicality. To portray such circumstances on the screen will make people realise that the spiritual life is something to be lived, not talked about, and that it – and it alone – will produce the peace and love and harmony which we seek to establish as the constant of our lives.[11]

Baba had let it be accepted that he would break his silence

in the Hollywood Bowl on the 13th July 1932, when a great crowd was expected to gather. But he now said that he must first visit China, and before leaving for Honolulu he sent home his Western followers. Then after two days in Honolulu Baba cabled that he was sailing for Shanghai and would not return to Hollywood. The breaking of a silence which had lasted already for seven years had been much publicised, so the disappointment was correspondingly great. It gave a shock from which not all Baba's Western followers recovered; for many it was their first experience of those abrupt 'changes of plan' familiar to his Eastern followers who had come by now to accept that "there is no plan".

In China Baba visited Shanghai and Nanking. This time his visit was not publicised, rather he travelled incognito, blending in with other people. Herbert Davy, who was at that time a professor at Nanking University, was host to him during his visit. He has left an account in which he stresses what others frequently noted, Baba's insistence on making contact with people in the mass as well as with individuals.

> Baba was dressed in a European suit and a panama hat. I had booked rooms in a hotel overlooking the Bund, the busy street and waterfront of the Whangpoo River (in Shanghai).
>
> Immediately we had had tea, Baba said that he wished to go round the city and mix with the Chinese crowds. I had had very little experience of Baba's ways and was still rather awkward in his presence. I took them along the Bund, and from the French settlement by tram through the British to the war-stricken districts near the North station, thinking it would interest them. Not at all. There were not enough people. We took a tram back and saw Nanking Road, the now brightly lit Chinese stores, Chungking Road, Racecourse, along Tibet Road. The streets were densely packed with long-gowned clerks and short-coated coolies, endless rickshaw-

pullers with cheerful faces and poverty-stricken appearances beseeching us to ride not walk; the narrow streets were hung with lanterns and waving banners of Chinese characters. Baba was delighted as we threaded the narrow, perfumed alleys and the Chinese turned to stare at us in a not too friendly manner. Baba was delighted and liked them.

(A similar impression was recorded on Baba's visit to Spain a year later. Here too Baba wished to come in contact with the masses.) All day we walked along the crowded streets of Madrid until our feet were tired... Baba particularly loved to stand in the central square, Puerta del Sol, the Gate of the Sun, among the crowds. Every day and several times a day he came here. Sometimes as we walked, despite his normal appearance, European clothes and Spanish beret which concealed his hair, they would turn and stare at him as if drawn by something they could not understand. That night we went to the East End, to a cabaret, a rather low-class dance hall...[12]

Again and again in the cities of the world Baba would insist on being taken to places where many people gathered with their outward attention concentrated, leaving – it would seem – their inner natures free to be contacted by his silent influence. Baba was little concerned what the spectacle might be which had drawn the audience together, whether plays such as *White Horse Inn* and *The Ten Commandments*, or a cabaret, or a "low-class dance hall". Though at times he enjoyed entertainment, particularly if it was funny, he would frequently leave after only a short stay, saying his work at that place had been completed.

From Madrid, during the same visit of 1933, Baba went on to Barcelona, arriving exactly on the day of celebration for the newly formed federal state of Catalonia – all too soon to be abolished when the Spanish Civil War broke out. No one with Baba was aware beforehand of these celebrations, which involved a long procession among applauding crowds, but his companions had often noticed how Baba's arrival in a place would coincide with some important public event that resulted in mass gatherings. There was a similar occasion a year later when Baba reached London on the night of a royal wedding,[13] and his party drove past Buckingham Palace and through packed West End streets.

In contrast to the work which Baba accomplished among masses was that which required solitude in a particular setting. Throughout his travels Baba made a point of visiting shrines or holy places connected with great saints or spiritual figures. In Europe the four most holy places, he explained, are at Assisi, Avila, St Mark's in Venice, and a spot on the Ligurian coast of Italy; in each of these Baba spent some time, though it was not always easy to arrange. In addition, Baba paid special visits to Egypt and Ceylon. In Egypt, where he spent five days in 1932, his objective was the Coptic Church in Cairo. This, he told his companions, contains a cave in which Joseph and Mary sheltered with the infant Jesus on their flight from Herod. The custodian of the Coptic Church made difficulty about opening the cave, but yielded to Baba's insistence, and he remained there for some time alone.

In Ceylon a somewhat similar experience was met with.

> He (Baba) went with three of his disciples for a short stay at Bandarawela in the hills. One day he expressed a desire to find a place where he could retire into seclusion for twenty-four hours. The party walked up by a narrow path to a Buddhist temple. The novice who was looking after the temple was not anxious to allow them to enter, so they descended some steps into a small courtyard adjoining the temple. A door opened, and an old man came out who appeared to be at least one hundred years old. He seemed to recognise Baba, and communicated with him by signs. Baba also talked by signs, telling him that he wished to retire into a room for twenty-

four hours without being disturbed. The old man understood, and ordered the novice to open the temple and to show Baba the room adjoining, which Baba used.[14]

The purpose of these spells of solitude in places with sacred associations from the past, such as caves or shrines, was explained by Baba to some of his followers who were with him earlier at Assisi: "It is the spiritual atmosphere, the quickening vibrations, that give value to the shrines of saints. They are not present in the more subtle body, nor is there any special virtue in the dust and bones of their physical bodies."

L-r: Adi Jr., Quentin Tod, Baba, Beheram, Tallulah Bankhead, Chanji, Kaka Baria. Location: Hollywood, USA, 1932. © Meher Nazar Collection.

Notes

1. Cf. *The God-Man*, pp. 94–5
2. *Britain's Locust Years, 1918–1940*, by William McElwee, Faber & Faber 1962, p. 171. (Out of print — Ed.)

3. *Love Alone Prevails*, p. 31
4. Because on his second journey he came back through Europe from China on his way home to India, some accounts speak of Baba's *ten* visits to the West. Three of these involved visiting the US.
5. 'Sri Lanka' (Ed.)
6. Baba's actual words were: "I awaken."
7. From an interview in the *Sunday Express*, 10th April 1932.
8. A highly critical account of Meher Baba appears in *A Search in Secret India*, by Paul Brunton, 1933 (reprinted by Random House, 2013 – Ed.); a second, less antagonistic one in *God is My Adventure*, by Rom Landau, 1933 (reprinted by Landau Press, 2008 – Ed.). Cf. *The God-Man*, p. 128.
9. *The God-Man*, p. 103
10. Noted down by a young actor, Quentin Tod, who travelled with Baba across America and introduced him to many film people.
11. In London three years later Baba was taken to see Gary Cooper in *Mr. Deeds Goes to Town*. He was delighted with the picture, quoting it as an example of the way films can combine entertainment with spiritual truth. Its story, some may remember, is of one man's battle for the poor against the rich and powerful.
12. *The Perfect Master*, pp. 177–8 & 217
13. This was the wedding of the Duke & Duchess of Kent (Princess Marina) on 30th November 1934.
14. *The God-Man*, pp. 113–4

Standing l-r: Minta Toledano, Kitty Davy, Kaka, Baba, Delia de Leon, Chanji, Herbert Davy, Enid Corfe, Margaret Craske (next to Delia). *Seated:* Quentin Tod and Mabel Ryan. Location: St Mark's Square, Venice, Italy, August 1932. © Meher Nazar Publications.

Chapter 7

Bringing East and West Together

Throughout his life, almost indeed from his schooldays, Baba had emphasised with words and action the need to bring East and West together. To bring together individual Easterners and Westerners had been one of the purposes of his period of world travel, and again and again in prepared statements and informal talks he stressed the need for a fusion between the contemplative spirituality of the East and the practical energy of the West.

> I have come to help people realise their ideals in daily life... My work and aims are intensely practical. It is not practical to over-emphasise the material at the cost of the spiritual. It is not practical to have spiritual ideals without putting them into practice. But to realise the ideal in daily life, to give beautiful and adequate form to the living spirit, to make Brotherhood a fact, not merely a theory, as at present – that is being practical in the truest sense of the word.[1]

Back in 1928, after the establishment of the Meher Ashram, Baba had made efforts to include some English pupils, sending a special representative over to Britain to arrange this. Though this particular project did not materialise, numbers of Westerners had at different times come over to stay at Meherabad and other places which served as his headquarters. For his journeys to the West Baba took with him members of the mandali who, besides making personal contacts, also became familiar with Western attitudes to life, experiencing at first hand that energetic handling of practical problems and material difficulties which Baba so often praised. But it was not only in work that Baba brought the two worlds together. More than once while in Europe he took combined parties of Westerners and Easterners to stay with him for some weeks in holiday surroundings. There was such a stay at Santa Margherita in Italy during August 1932, of which Herbert Davy kept the following account.

> These Italian days with Baba were very happy times. Warm sun, blue sea, a wonderful coastline, and behind the hotel green hills and shaded walks through vineyards and forests. In the morning we trooped down to the rocks, bathed, dived, splashed or basked in the sun, Baba in our midst...
>
> Baba's room led out on to a private balcony. When we swam before breakfast we would see his white-clad figure watching us from the balcony. Often at night we would sit there listening

> to music on the gramophone; Baba's favourites were Indian and Persian spiritual songs which he would explain to us, Spanish dances and Paul Robeson's spirituals. On the terrace we would act charades or get up entertainments. Under the name of Thomas, Baba would also take dancing lessons with one of us who was a skilled dancing instructor. Thus, and in innumerable ways, Baba entered into our lives as playmate, friend, child and father.[2]

But Baba also made use of these holiday times to teach important lessons. Some of the Westerners were over-concerned about correct behaviour and the maintaining of outward appearances.

> One day, (Herbert Davy recalls) Baba wished to walk to a distant beach for bathing. The large party got strung out along the road. Baba did not like this, and called us back. He suddenly stopped and indicated that He wished to get down on to the seashore. I looked over the embankment wall and saw that it was a private beach, the owner had left cushions and his beach tent, and would obviously return in a moment. I protested to Kitty that Baba could not risk the indignity, and trespass with our motley crew on someone's private terrain. Kitty insisted that Baba's slightest whim must be obeyed and so we descended the steps. I went further along the beach and refused even Baba's commands to return. My feelings were churned up. After some time I gave in and came back very sheepishly to the tent. Baba severely reprimanded me in the presence of the others. During my absence I had failed to meet an old Italian man who had stood, gazed respectfully at Baba and bowed. This man was the twin in appearance of an agent in Warsaw that I had to identify in a month's time. We never saw the Italian man again, a fact which led to considerable difficulty for me later in Warsaw.
>
> I admitted my error in disobeying but said, "Surely we

should use our common sense and warn You when You are likely, in the West, to put Yourself in a false position." Baba agreed. "It was your duty to warn Me, but should I still insist, you must give way." When harmony was restored and we were still seated round, but not actually inside the tent, the rather indignant owner came down the steps with two large dogs and reminded us that it was a private beach. Feeling a little small, we gathered our belongings and, like a band of gypsies, moved on. Such storms and stresses usually punctuated the pleasure. Baba brushes away the annoyance, and afterward is even kinder to the victim, but the occasion is unpleasant.[3]

One of the points of difference between Baba's Eastern and Western followers was that the Easterners gave obedience without question to any instruction from the Master, whereas the Westerners were inclined to 'use their own judgement' as to when and how they would carry out any task, and the instinct to 'please ourselves' or to 'do it our way' still often carried the day. Again and again the need for instant and sustained obedience had to be emphasised. Baba was due to leave Venice and return via Egypt to India with his companions Chanji and Kaka on 20th August 1932.

The last day before Baba left us (Kitty Davy records) was not altogether a happy one. Baba was testing us. He requested us all to remain close to Him all day, as He had special work to do through us and He repeated this order many times. Of course, we all said that we would. None for a moment thought they would be tempted to leave the side of Baba, it being His last day with us. Well, we started to walk around the shops. What was the result? Some of us lagged behind to look at the lovely things displayed in the windows. We lost sight of Baba. He had to send one back to find us. This

> happened more than once and He had to remind us what we had promised – not to leave Him.
>
> That day was a scorcher and we suggested going to the Lido. Some asked to bathe and Baba again reminded us that this was His last day and He wanted us near. On arrival at the Lido, though, the sight was too much. Some of us went off to bathe, leaving Baba for nearly an hour. When they returned to where they left Him, He was gone, with only Delia and Margaret who had obeyed... On our arrival (back at the hotel) we found a sad party; Delia and Margaret were almost in tears. Baba looked miserable. He was a wonderful actor and this time even the boys (Chanji and Kaka) were taken in... He said how the Easterners were ready to sit at His feet but that the Westerners wanted Baba at their feet. He said that He wanted the West to work for Him, but that now He would have to change His plans and not make use of us...
>
> We were all terribly upset but Baba used the moment and through such a crisis brought us to a fresh awareness of His love and ultimate forgiveness.[4]

In a later passage in the diaries he kept throughout this period, Herbert Davy records Baba's explanation of his way of working with those close to him. "We had faults, egoism and weaknesses; these scenes were manufactured in order to stir up the feelings and, according to the way we bore them, Baba would work on our characters, and perhaps in some way He could use the energies and emotions liberated for His work." To this Kitty Davy adds the footnote that "when the Master showed emotions such as annoyance, disappointment, anger etc., it meant that He was using a special form of energy for certain deep-seated sanskaras (mental impressions) with which He was dealing for the benefit of the devotee or person. It did not imply that his inner serenity was disturbed at all as when an ordinary person shows any of these emotions."

In July of the following year Baba returned to Europe, bringing Chanji, Kaka, Adi Sr., and Pendu. At Portofino a large house had been rented to which a number of Baba's Western followers were invited, but this time they were given various tasks, such as typing and dealing with correspondence. It was at Portofino that a dramatic incident happened, which again, it seemed, Baba was able to make use of for his inner work.

> After tea one afternoon, fifteen or sixteen of the group went for a walk with Baba along the cliffs. He took them down a rather dangerous ravine to the sea. A number lagged behind, despite Baba's repeated admonition to keep together. Several fell out by the wayside... By the time they reached the sea-washed shore only two men (Herbert and a youth from the villa) and two girls (Anita and Vivienne[5]) had kept pace with Baba.
>
> Instead of returning the way they came, Baba elected to climb back another way. Nimble and light-footed as a deer, he made his way up the smooth rocky surface while behind the four tried to keep up with him. At particularly difficult places Baba would stop to help the women with his gentle but strong hands. But suddenly they found themselves stuck! Above them was a sheer surface of rock and thin trees while to their right was a precipice which fell almost perpendicularly into the sea. They searched for the main path not realising that it was more than one hundred and fifty feet above them. One of the men, Herbert, crept around corners, climbed up cliffs, hung on to the roots of bushes... Thirty minutes passed as he tried futilely to find the main path. He spied a steep cleft that seemed to have been used as a rubbish dump, but it proved insecure footing and fifteen feet up it was blocked by a very large boulder. Yet it was apparently the only possible way out.
>
> Baba, wiry and sure-footed, climbed ahead, scattering

a little earth behind him. He clapped his hands as a signal for them to follow and then disappeared from view. Herbert followed, but got stranded on the boulder for some minutes, while the two women and the youth were waiting anxiously below. Above was a steep gully, filled with loose earth, rusty metal and broken glass; a foot moved meant the descent, on the women below, of stones, possibly a small avalanche of rubbish. With a final wriggle Herbert got past the boulder. By hanging on to the roots of bushes he could crouch on the loose earth but could not move up the remaining forty feet. Baba had completely disappeared. The youth, who weighed but one hundred pounds or less, came next. With a slight hand-grip from Herbert, he was safely past the boulder.

Baba's last signal had been "Come up". Herbert called to Vivienne to follow, but she too foundered on the boulder, with her strength slowly ebbing away. The others shouted to Baba for help, but received no apparent response... Herbert was gradually slipping downwards. Any desperate move meant a torrent of earth on Vivienne's face, just below him. She hung there for ten to fifteen minutes. Two fingers of her right hand clung to a small hole in the rock, her body rested against the boulder and her left knee was wedged in the rock at the side.

The majority of the group had by this time returned to the house. They were surprised that after two hours the others had not yet returned. Meanwhile Baba was mounting still higher up the cliff and clapping his hands to attract attention. But being a mile or more from the house no one there could hear him. Tino, however, an Italian boy who worked on the estate, had met a priest – or, so he seemed – who told him that someone was signalling for help. Tino then ran to Baba, who gave him signs to fetch a rope. He rushed back to the house kitchen. Kaka, Adi and Pendu, who were cooking the evening meal, instantly left their pots and ran to Baba...

At length shouts were heard from the top. Pendu appeared with long ropes and a rescue party. Baba, quite evidently pleased at the scent of danger, came down the gully. Even he found it extremely difficult to keep his footing on the loose earth. Herbert bent down a long-stemmed bush and held its root-end firmly with his right hand, while Baba's right hand held the other end of the stem. Then Herbert leaned down to pull Vivienne up over the boulder with his left hand.

Pendu, who was very muscular and agile, took the rope down to Anita, who was still standing below. By means of the rope they all climbed to safety, and their exciting adventure was over.

To celebrate its safe ending, Baba called the group together in the library, retold the story for the benefit of those who had not participated in it, and gave each a sip of Italian wine with His own hands. (This in itself indicated how momentous and significant the experience had been, because wine is only used by Baba for sacramental purposes.) The Italian servants who were present, knowing well the danger that had been involved, wept with joy at the group's safe return. Baba's delight continued to be evident. He said that he had done important work through this experience; that the energies released, the feelings aroused, and the courage displayed had been utilized by him for his spiritual work.[6]

Despite the hard lessons taught on such occasions, a holiday spirit prevailed throughout the gathering at Santa Margherita and Portofino, and again at Cannes in 1938, when Baba once more called a number of his Western followers to stay with him for several months. This visit differed from previous ones, however, in that Baba brought a number of women mandali with him from India as well as some of the men. The intention evidently was that the Eastern and Western women should get to know one another better before entering upon a shared life under Indian conditions. "When Baba took us to Cannes," Kitty Davy records, "none of us knew what was to follow; whether we would return to India or to the West, for an indefinite period of time or for good. Perhaps in Cannes we were on probation." And again, "Cannes was the final preparation for the strictness and discipline we would experience at Meherabad. Previous trips to India also had been stepping stones towards this final move."

On one of these 'previous trips', between the holiday stays at Portofino and Cannes, Baba had called a group of fifteen Westerners, both men and women, to stay with him at Nasik, a Hindu holy place on the banks of the river Godavari, some 120 miles north-east of Bombay. "This," Kitty Davy wrote, "from beginning to end was a training in discipleship."

The group had been warned to be prepared to stay in India with Baba for a period of from one to five years. They had to arrange for their own travelling expenses, and undertake to live strictly in accordance with his instructions. "All possible arrangements have been made to make the physical life easy for you Westerners," Baba told them. "And though it won't be a crown of thorns, it won't be a bed of roses either."[7]

While at Nasik, the Western women paid visits to Meherabad, where eventually they and the Eastern women were to share a fully communal life. Jean Adriel, who was one of the visitors, records:

> In the Western group was a former dancer in the Russian ballet (Margaret Craske); a woman with her own insurance business in New York (Elizabeth Patterson); an actress who had held salons in many of the large European cities (Norina Matchabelli); two other actresses (Delia de Leon and Ruano Bogislav); an artist (Rano Gayley); and one who had devoted a number of years to social work in the slums, alms-houses, prisons and hospitals of New York, Philadelphia and Pittsburgh (Jean Adriel). Practically all were women who

had travelled extensively and seen much of what is popularly termed 'life'.

(Despite their background of sophistication, it was the Western women who felt overawed by these meetings.) Because we Westerners were still far from the conscious inner freedom which these holy women enjoyed, many of us suffered acutely on the Meherabad trips. I felt as if I were being required to function in a kind of mental vacuum... It was like being dropped into a fair country where language is neither spoken nor read, but where people go about their affairs with serene, happy faces, communicating with each other by some inner means which one does not yet know...

Their 'House on the Hill', in which they lived their quiet, gentle lives, was surrounded by a wall twelve feet high. This enclosed a compound of about forty feet square upon which two houses faced. The larger one consisted – at that time – of a single room about thirty feet by twenty. The chief appointments of the room were six iron beds, each with its mosquito-netting canopy. Beside each bed was a small wooden trunk, in which were kept the few belongings of the women, and a straight wooden chair. There were no ornaments, no gadgets, no books. The most austere convent would be luxurious by comparison...

Though on the surface their lives were acutely circumscribed, monotonous and meagre, their faces bore the unmistakable imprint of a happier, more contented life than we Westerners with our so-called full, colourful lives had ever known... Having no need to disburden themselves of mental impressions, and feeling no inclination towards gossip, they spoke but little. But one could see that they lived deeply, consciously; each one a distinct *individual*.[8]

Among the six who formed the women mandali at that time were two uniquely close to Baba, both of whom would become well known in later years to his followers throughout the world. One of these was his sister Mani, described by Jean Adriel at this time as "a beautiful young woman about eighteen... very versatile in her creative gifts. She writes, paints, sings, dances and acts with charming spontaneity and grace." Mani, who acted as secretary to Baba, later wrote the *Family Letters* sent out regularly every few months from 1956–69 to keep Westerners in touch at a time when Baba was spending long periods in seclusion. The other was Mehera (Mehera J. Irani), Baba's chief woman disciple; 'The Beloved's Beloved', a beautiful, stately and gentle woman. While still a young girl, she with her mother, Daulatmai, had been among the first to join the ashram at Meherabad when women were allowed to do so. Since then her life had been one of entire devotion to Baba, passed mainly in strict seclusion.[9]

The intention had been that after three months in Nasik, the Western women would share the much more austere life of Meherabad, but in fact they remained the whole time in Nasik. Here disagreements and upsets arose, until finally a crisis developed in the group, and by the end of July most were sent home. Later in the same year, however, following the holiday in Cannes, three Western women returned with Baba's party to India, to be joined later on by three others who had gone home first to see their families. And now the shared life of the two groups really began. A second storey had been added to the 'House on the Hill' in Meherabad, forming a dormitory with cubicles separated by curtains, corresponding to the large room shared by the women mandali below. All the women were given arduous tasks to perform, partly in the running of the women's hospital which had been opened.

When the inevitable conflicts and even quarrels arose, Baba did not seek to damp them down. On the contrary, he would allow them to develop and then call those involved together and face them with the situation, often compelling them to speak out and say what they thought of one another. Only then, when everything had been brought out into the open, would he resolve the conflict. "If you cannot love each other, then learn to give in," he told them, and in the course of giving in they found that they had come to love each other, so that fifty years later some from both East and West were still sharing a common life and a common devotion.

Of this period at Meherabad Kitty Davy later wrote:

> Two things impressed me deeply when I came to live with the Eastern group on the Hill: (1) their implicit obedience to Baba in the tiniest details – thinking more of Him than of themselves, having Him as their constant companion and guide throughout the day in their thought, speech and action; (2) a sublime, childlike quality and attitude in their love for and faith in Baba, their Master. The words of Jesus seemed so exactly to fit: "Except ye become as a little child..."
>
> Something of this same quality we caught from them, I am sure, for we also felt that we were and still are Baba's children. As was His wish, it was to Baba we went for all our needs. To Baba we told our problems and secrets. To Baba we went if not feeling well. He was always approachable, always full of understanding, as ready to forgive as to rebuke, to encourage and to explain. When we were hesitant to come to Him, not for wants but needs, He would smile and spell out on His board, "You have given all to Me, all I have is yours. We are all one. To whom else would you go?"[10]

What must we suppose to have been the purpose behind these persistent efforts to unite two groups of women who in upbringing and outlook were at first such poles apart? Did Baba give so freely of his time and energy in order that some half-dozen Western women should learn a deeper outlook on the world, and that an equal number from the East – albeit those closest to him – should assimilate the experience, and develop that capacity to cope with the material world, which distinguishes the West?

It was Baba's way, and is said to be the practice of all Perfect Masters, to work out in their lifetimes, on a small scale, models for developments which will later become worldwide. Throughout his life Baba constantly emphasised the importance of woman and the values associated with her, love, tenderness, service to others, stressing these not as something to be demanded of woman by man for his enjoyment or advantage, but as qualities he must cherish in her and learn to develop in himself.

So in bringing the groups together with such patience and determination, Baba was perhaps – for all attempts to interpret are only guesswork – achieving three aims at the same time, possibly among many others. He was sowing the seeds of unity between East and West. He was stressing the importance of woman for the coming age; and he was developing a pattern for the kind of woman she would be – one in whom the energy

Meher Baba dressed as Lord Krishna, with His Gopis, *l-r:* Khorshed, Margaret Craske, Princess Norina Matchabelli, Mehera, Baba, his sister Mani, Delia de Leon, Kitty Davy. Location: Meherabad Hill, 1937. © MSI Collection.

and practical capacity of the Westerners will be blended with the devotion and spirituality shown by the women mandali.

Woman has to be liberated, not in order to become either man's imitation or his enslaver, but in order to become something new, something more than she has ever been till now – and in so doing to inspire man to become more than he has ever thought of being, more than he has ever been willing to become.

Her role, derived from that of Baba himself, is to awaken.

Notes

1. *The Perfect Master*, pp. 169–71
2. *The Perfect Master*, pp. 180–1
3. *Love Alone Prevails*, p. 80
4. *Love Alone Prevails*, pp. 83–4. All quotes by Kitty Davy are from this book. (Ed.)
5. This is spelt Vivian by Jean Adriel in *Avatar*, and Vivienne by Kitty Davy in *Love Alone Prevails*.
6. *Avatar*, slightly condensed from pp. 160–3, with some addition from *Love Alone Prevails*, p. 107
7. *Love Alone Prevails*, p. 143
8. *Avatar*, pp. 188–191
9. Mehera would live on more than 20 years after Baba laid down his body. It was 20th May 1989 before her own earthly life came to an end.
10. *Love Alone Prevails*, p. 229

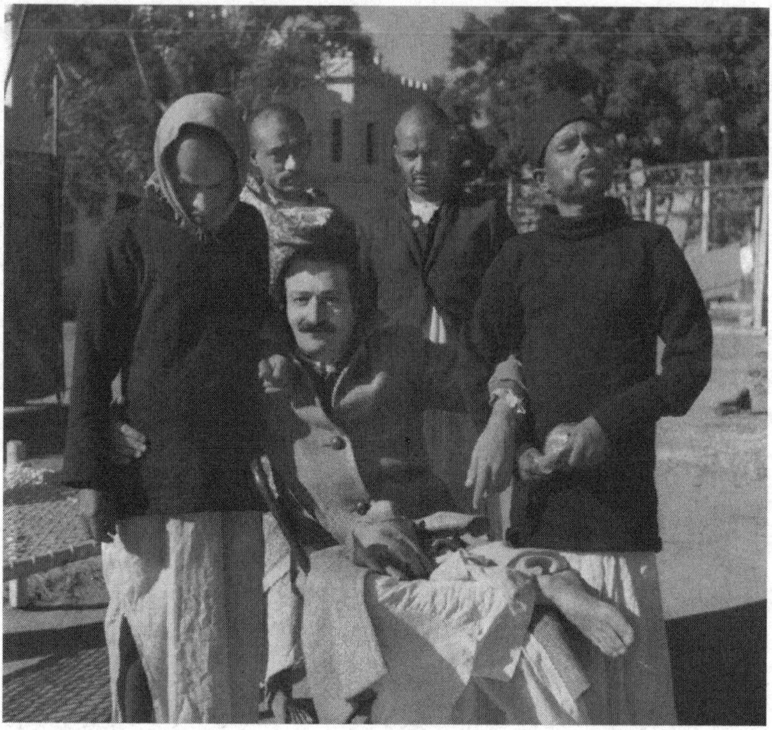

Standing l-r: Mohammed, Lakhan Shah, (unknown), Shariat Khan. *Seated:* Meher Baba. Location: Bangalore Mast ashram, 1939. © MSI Collection.

Chapter 8

The 'God-Intoxicated' (1)

Six years had been spent by Baba in forging links with the West. At times his world tours wore almost the aspect of social visits; film-stars, writers, musicians, artists, bankers, businessmen, politicians – Baba had been happy to meet everyone and had time for everyone. His engagements might have been, and sometimes were, chronicled in newspapers and gossip columns. But now, for a period extending over nearly thirteen years, he focused his attention upon a group of beings unknown outside their own localities, virtually inaccessible to normal contact, and only contacted by Baba himself at immense cost in physical and inner effort. And, incidentally, at great financial cost as well. "Money came to me in waves," he remarked in 1954, "and as waves it rolled away." One of the waves which rolled it away was the cost of searching out and caring for the 'God-mad' or 'God-intoxicated'.

To the Western mind this aspect of Baba's work is at the same time fascinating and perplexing. It also appears to be unique, having no parallel in the life of any other spiritual Master. But its importance is shown, first by the fact that Baba devoted to it more than one-sixth of his entire earthly life, and, secondly, by the period at which this activity was taking place. For these years, 1936–49, coincided with the approach, onset, duration and aftermath of the Second World War, the supreme crisis for both the Eastern and Western worlds. This culminated in the dropping of the atomic bomb, the establishment of the 'Iron Curtain', and the tension over the Berlin Blockade, which was within an inch of leading to war between the Western powers and the then USSR. The same period also included the Chinese revolution, the achievement of Indian independence after centuries of foreign domination, with the tragic migrations and slaughter of refugees consequent upon partition.

So that throughout those years, when the sane and practical peoples of the world were almost entirely occupied with the madness and waste of war, Baba was concentrating his efforts and resources upon a few hundred persons whom these same practical peoples would consider to be mad. Today, almost half a century later, Baba's work with the God-mad may seem less strange, for in an age when all barriers are collapsing and classifications dissolving into one another, the distinction between 'mad' and 'sane' is dissolving too, so that the more aware any of us become of our own natures, the more reluctant we are to claim sanity or impute madness.

As was often his way, Baba found his own word for the God-mad; he called them *masts*.[1] Of his work among the masts, and of the strange individualities of the masts themselves a contemporary record happily exists. It was compiled, surprisingly, by a Westerner, Dr William Donkin, who in 1938, having then only recently qualified, gave up his career in England, his family and country, in order to be with Baba, as he said "till the end".[2] Baba many times suggested that Donkin was free to return to England if he wished, but he always insisted on remaining. He was one of very few Westerners who ever formed part of the mandali, and the only one to belong to it throughout these years and during the succeeding period of the 'New Life'. What makes Dr Donkin's book *The Wayfarers* so overpowering is partly the nature of its subject matter, and partly the fact that the author was at the same time doctor and writer. He had both the interest to study and the sympathy to penetrate the confusion in which the masts, like the mad, are shrouded, with the capacity to express what he saw and understood. His little-known book, from which virtually everything in this and the following chapter has been taken, is one of those, largely ignored in their own age, to which further stages in humanity's development are certain one day to bring appreciation and acclaim.

What is a mast, and how is a mast distinguished from a common madman?

Masts are of many types – actually, Baba said, of no fewer than fifty-six[3] and he explained to his followers some of their distinguishing characteristics and stages of development. But there is one characteristic shared by all. They are dead to the world and living inwardly in bliss, to which the nearest parallel most of us could imagine would perhaps be the early stages of happy intoxication, physical or emotional. But for the mast this state is permanent. The mast, in Baba's words, "loves and knows only God. He loses all consciousness of self, of body, and the world. Whether it rains or shines, whether it is winter or summer, it is all the same to him. He is dead to himself..." And of a particular mast, Baba said:

> He has no body consciousness. He remains in the same position for hours together without moving his limbs in the slightest degree... He is not mad; but looks like it. He is also childlike. If you make him stand up, he will remain standing until you tell him to sit down again.[4] His mind does not function as the mind of an ordinary human being; yet his mind is not blank. Intense love and longing for God has made him like dust. This mast does not belong to this world, though he is in it.[5]

To be in the world, yet not belong to or be dominated by it, has been recognised by every religion as a principal aim of man's life on earth, and the mast has achieved this condition. But he has achieved it at the cost of losing his awareness of external reality and even of his own body and its functions. To the outward eye therefore the mast is no more than a madman, a fragment in the tide of derelicts who drift up and down the Indian subcontinent or squat stranded by its dusty roadsides.

In the West we have no tradition and no conception, not even any myths or fairy tales, concerned with the God-mad – and no wonder, for in our society no creatures of the sort exist. We Westerners do indeed 'go out of our minds'. We 'become beside ourselves' with the strain of competition, through fear of failure, financial deprivation, or through emotional distress. But we do not go out of our minds through love of God. In India, however, spirituality is the most widespread and powerful preoccupation, and great numbers of men, women, and even children, apply themselves to spiritual development with the passionate determination we apply to making money, following sport, gratifying desire, or trying to alter the world and other people through political action.

Though we have no conception of the 'God-mad' or 'God-intoxicated' – and indeed a 'God-intoxicated' clergyman could hardly expect to remain long in office – we do have the expression 'divine madness', and we recognise certain exceptions, or half-exceptions, to the materialistic order. Artists, musicians, writers are expected to show eccentricity of behaviour and indifference to money values, even to be willing to starve in garrets and endure a lifetime of suffering in the hope of possible recognition after they are dead. Philosophers and thinkers, we consider, should be 'unworldly', forgetful of everyday requirements, inwardly absorbed. The eccentric artist and the absent-minded professor are perhaps our nearest equivalent to the God-mad. And the familiar lines of Dryden –

Great wits are sure to madness near alli'd,
And thin partitions do their bounds divide –

would never have become so popular as to be generally misquoted if they were not held to contain a profound truth.[6]

Throughout the Muslim world, however, madness is commonly associated with spiritual development and what may be a blinding awareness of God's presence. Madmen are seldom confined. They are treated with tolerance, almost reverence, and it is a religious duty to contribute to their needs. Masts are frequently Muslim by religion, though there are also many Hindus; they are found, Baba explained, almost entirely in India, though there are a few also in Egypt and Arabia, and a very few in Iran and Tibet. There are none at all in Europe and the Americas, though there are saints, mystics and devout followers of God. It is India's pervasive climate of spirituality which accounts for the flowering of so many of the God-mad, who themselves in turn intensify that climate.

There are, of course, many false masts and sham *sadhus* (holy men). Baba himself, in the course of his search for masts and advanced souls, visited Allahabad in February 1948 for a great fair held only every six years, to which thousands of sadhus come together from all over India to bathe at the confluence of two sacred rivers, the Jumna and the Ganges. At this fair, among something like a million persons, there were estimated to be 30,000 sadhus. The estimate is more than a guess, since sadhus of many sects attend, and each sect has its own territory reserved for it. In the course of a morning, Baba went around all the territories, contacting some 4,000 sadhus. He afterwards told the mandali that among these four thousand there were no more than *seven* advanced souls.

However, the fact that among many so-called 'holy men' the vast majority are less than holy does not affect the picture of India in general. There are in the capitalist West many dishonest financiers and incompetent industrialists, but in financial and industrial development the West nonetheless leads the world. Similarly, in previously Communist countries there were many high officials whose main interest was private gain, but the preoccupation of these countries as a whole was with political development on Socialist lines. It is not the honesty or otherwise of individuals which creates a climate, but the concentration of interest in the minds of ordinary people, and in India that concentration is far more than elsewhere upon spiritual matters.

A remarkable instance of this was shown in Madras over a mast named Mohammed Mastan. Two members of the mandali had come upon him in a back street, and were concerned that Baba should have the opportunity of sitting with him in seclusion. The only place which offered privacy was the office of a small private bank, into which the two followers went and put forward the request on their Master's behalf. Without question or argument, the banker ordered his clerks into the street and himself followed them out, leaving his office littered with money and papers, so that Baba should be able to sit there with the mast for a short while undisturbed.

Equally surprising to us as an example of Indian respect for spiritual values, shown even at official levels, is the case of the mast Buddhi contacted by Baba at Gulbarga in July 1945. "He looked restless in his activities but had a mild temper. Because of his lovable nature he was much respected by all, and his fancy for travelling by any class in any train was not objected to by the railway authorities."[7]

Apart from being constantly in a state of God-intoxication, what are the other characteristics of a mast? One which Westerners have difficulty in accepting is that they are frequently found in sordid surroundings, in a state of neglect and even filth. Baba, who devoted hours each day for months on end to washing and bathing masts, has explained their condition.

> From general standards of society, religion, health, morality and so forth, cleanliness of body and mind are indispensable. It is, however, very easy to keep the body clean; but cleanliness of mind is very difficult indeed. The more one gets attached to body cleanliness for merely selfish reasons, the less are the chances of having a clean mind.
>
> If, however, one is given up wholly to mental cleanliness, which means becoming free from low, selfish, impure desires and thoughts of lust, greed, anger, backbiting, etc., the less is one's mind attached to bodily needs and bodily cleanliness... You will find that the majority of ordinary mad people have very little consciousness of their bodies. So if an ordinary mind, when mad, does not pay attention to bodily cleanliness, then... (masts) who unconsciously or consciously know all the universe to be zero, body to be a shadow, and whose minds are absolutely unattached to the body, cannot be expected to keep their bodies and surroundings clean... For these souls, good or bad, cleanliness or dirt, a palace or a hut, a spotless avenue or a filthy gutter are all the same, and they are driven

into any of these places according to circumstance.[8]

Moreover, Baba explained, the squalid and sordid surroundings in which masts are often found may actually assist them in their total absorption with the sublime.

> To live in dirty surroundings, such as in or near a latrine or urinal, is one way of utterly forgetting one's bodily existence. And the beauty of it is that when the body is utterly neglected or forgotten – because the consciousness is aware only of love for the Divine Beloved – it does not deteriorate but takes care of itself automatically. The minds of ordinary people are constantly busy looking after their bodies, but they find that, in spite of taking every kind of precaution and care, deterioration can never be avoided altogether.
>
> Kabir said,
> Discard the body, it remains,
> Preserve the body, it goes;
> And so the astounding fact emerges
> That the (uncared for) corpse eats up death.[9]

However dirty the mast may be, and however scanty or unsuitable his diet, he remains physically healthy, resistant to exposure and extremes of climate far beyond the endurance of normal men, and frequently lives to a great age. Of one such Baba said:

> Divine love is the fire which not only eliminates all kinds of cold, but also all sorts of imagined heat. For example, amongst the very, very few who possess such love is the mast known as Dhondiba at Kolahpur. Though exposed to the rigours of heat, cold and rain through all the seasons, his body remains healthy, well-fleshed and strong. The fire is burning within him unknown to those in his surroundings. His mind has no

> link with his body. Love pervades him from head to foot.[10]

Another mast who possessed this resistance to an eminent degree was Chatti Baba, a prince among masts, who remained for two years with Baba. Of him Dr Donkin writes:

> In Quetta, where the weather was still colder, he used to pour icy water on his bedding, and sit on it. One day, there was such a monstrous hail-storm that the hail-stones took three or four days to melt, and on the night following the storm, Chatti Baba sat stripped to the waist on the hail, from four until seven in the morning.[11]

A violent temper[12] is characteristic of many masts, or else its opposite, extreme passivity. Common to many is also a childlike capriciousness; they will ask for something and on receiving it immediately hand it back or give it away. In their detachment from all worldly values, their restless fancy lights upon chance objects, rags, old papers, pieces of rubbish, which they collect and hoard – or else give away. Baba, who kept no possessions, treasured the 'worthless' objects given to him by masts. All these and similar eccentricities may be equally typical of ordinary madmen, and Dr Donkin records that – despite all the expertise which certain members of the mandali developed in the recognition and handling of masts – they made mistakes and brought along persons of little or no spiritual development. So that in the last resort a man was accepted as a mast because Baba said he was one.

Dr Donkin adds, however, two interesting perceptions of his own, first that, "However strangely they (masts) may behave, they make one feel unmistakably happy in their company. They do not exhale any of that subtle antipathy that seems to emanate from the insane, but actually kindle a sense of harmony in one's self."

His second observation is that animals are attracted to masts and masts to them, and he records instances of masts whose abodes were shared by a pack of stray dogs, cats or other animals, adding that such masts invariably fed their animals before taking anything themselves.

Masts live in literal accord with the instruction of Jesus to "take no thought for the morrow" – indeed they take no thought for today. Yet there is always someone to feed and care for them to the degree they will allow. Sometimes this is a personal attendant or disciple, drawn by devotion, respect or the hope of spiritual progress. Sometimes it is a relative who assumes the task as a duty, and Dr Donkin records the extraordinary case of a Bombay family in which two brothers were masts and seven sisters *mastanis* (female masts), all nine being looked after by their eldest brother who alone was leading a conventional life.

Sometimes a group will adopt a mast as a kind of patron saint. The great mast Ali Shah of Ahmednagar was so adopted by a group of bus drivers, men who – in India as elsewhere – are of a type little given to sentimental gestures. People in well-to-do circumstances – civil servants, stationmasters, senior clerks – sometimes allow a mast to settle on the verandah of their bungalow and see that his modest needs are met, much as some Western businessmen or their wives support a favourite charity. This can make heavy demands on a host's goodwill as Dr Donkin records in the case of Aghori Baba, near Simla.

> A very high mast... He is a very impressive and powerful-looking man with fiery eyes, and he sits covered only with a piece of sack on the verandah... All about him he has collected piles of rubbish and rags, and the owner of the house – a Sikh – is now unable to enter his house by way of his own verandah, for not only is it chock-a-block with the rags and rubbish belonging to Aghori Baba, but also if he ventures to enter by this route, the mast rebuffs him with abuse. The Sikh,

therefore, has set up a ladder by means of which he bridges over the territory upon which Aghori Baba dislikes him to trespass, and so reaches his house in this way.[13]

Baba has summed up for us the difference between a God-mad and a lunatic in a couple of sentences. To the outward eye both seem alike; the difference is within.

> The mind of an ordinary madman has failed to adapt itself to the problems of the material world, and has fled permanently into the realm of make-believe to escape an intolerable material situation. But a God-mad man, although he has lost the balance of his mind, and the insight into his abnormal state, has not come to this condition by failing to solve his worldly troubles, but has lost his sanity through continually thinking about God.[14]

Unlike the madman, therefore, who is in a state of confusion, anger and despair, the mast is in a state of unalloyed, intoxicated bliss.

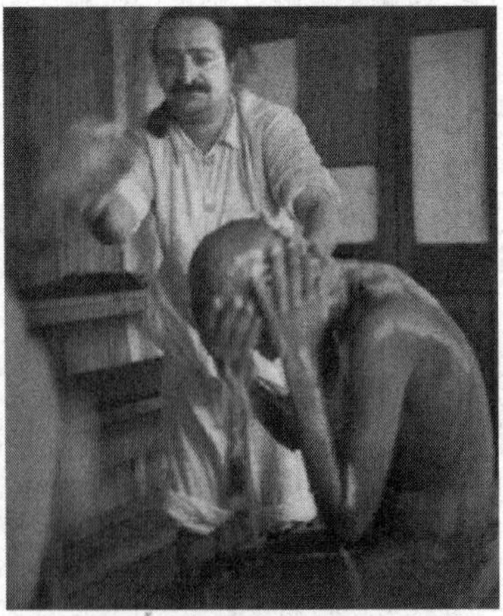

Meher Baba bathing Lakhan Shah at Meherabad, June 1939. © MSI Collection.

Notes

1. *Mast* (pronounced 'must') may be derived from a Sufi expression, or else from a Persian word meaning 'overpowered'. However, the use Baba made of it was, as always, his own.
2. Dr Donkin died in August 1969, little more than six months after Baba himself laid down his body.
3. The number fifty-six evidently carries a special significance, for it may be noted that there are always, at all times and in all ages, fifty-six God-realised souls present in human form on earth. Cf. *God Speaks*, p. 161.
4. The condition Baba himself was in after his initiation by Babajan.
5. *The God-Man*, p. 303
6. William Blake (1757–1827) is one of the English poets and artists who were actually at times insane, or regarded as being so.
7. *Glimpses, Vol I*, p. 101
8. *The Wayfarers*, pp. 33–4
9. Quoted in *Glimpses, Vol II*, p. 15. Kabir, a 15th century teacher and poet, was, with Hafiz, Baba's favourite among the Eastern mystic poets.
10. *Listen, Humanity*, p. 21. It is this same mast who, when offered anything for his material needs, would refuse it, saying, "I cannot bear comfort."
11. *The Wayfarers*, p. 69
12. This is not due to personal antagonisms, but arises from a fierce resistance to any interruption of the mast's inner bliss. Passivity is another way of avoiding such interruption.
13. *The Wayfarers*, p. 358
14. *The Wayfarers*, p. 23

Meher Baba contacting a mast in the street. Location: Poona, 22 May 1951. *L-r:* Baidul, Shastri Kher, (mast), Meher Baba. Photo taken by Padri (Faredoon Driver) / © MSI Collection.

Chapter 9

The 'God-Intoxicated' (2)

Baba's work among the masts was carried on principally in two ways, both being means to the same end. In one, groups of masts were concentrated in ashrams or communal dwelling places temporarily established at convenient spots, where Baba with the help of the mandali tended and took care of them. Mast ashrams in six centres[1] strategically placed all over India occupied much of Baba's time and attention from August 1936 to October 1940. Some years later two more ashrams were established for brief periods, December 1946–January 1947 and June–July 1947. The six years in between, roughly from 1941–6, were the years of the great 'mast tours' in which Baba ranged from end to end of the subcontinent seeking out and contacting advanced souls. In all he travelled no less than 75,000 miles, from Ceylon up to the Himalayas, from Bombay in the west to Calcutta in the east, with innumerable shorter journeys. He was in every province except Assam, in every great city and many smaller ones, as well as in hundreds of remote villages – making, his followers reckoned, some 20,000 contacts in his search for masts and spiritual pilgrims.

Mast ashrams were accommodated in houses or bungalows lent or temporarily rented. Usually these included outbuildings or servants' quarters which would be adapted to provide the simple accommodation the masts preferred. For Baba there was either a cottage or hut, or else one would be constructed in which he could sit in private with each mast. An odd addition to the Bangalore Ashram was a 'mast hotel'. Masts enjoy frequenting tumbledown teashops, so to make them feel at home, one was "constructed with diligent negligence, everything a trifle awry, with low roof, crooked pillars and limping tables and chairs." Here they were served with tea, cigarettes, beedies (locally-made cigarettes of the cheapest kind, looking more like matchsticks than cigarettes) or *pan*[2] as often as they asked, for Baba made it a rule that a mast was to be given at once whatever he asked for.

Since masts are absorbed in inner contemplation, it is painful for them to be brought sharply down to earth as can be done when their wishes are crossed. Masts would sometimes fly into rages or, if of the submissive type, burst into tears over seeming trifles, and it was to avoid such distresses that Baba gave orders for their wishes to be indulged. How far he would go himself to meet a mast's demands was shown in the case of Moeinuddin of Hyderabad, for whom Baba had to wait three hours before he allowed himself to be fed. When Baba had eventually succeeded in feeding a substantial meal to him, Moeinuddin called for mincemeat, then for a chapatti, tea, sweetmeats – and lastly for a special kind of bread hard to obtain. All were brought and, after his every whim had been satisfied, Moeinuddin finally agreed to cooperate.

When a new mast was brought into the ashram, a first task was to bathe and shave him, which Baba did himself. Bathing for some was a simple matter, but other masts would refuse point-blank, and had to be coaxed gently but persistently into consenting; others were in such a state of neglect that a first bath lasted hours. After a while some masts began to take pleasure in the bath and insist on prolonging the enjoyment; one of the greatest, Chatti Baba, used to call for 150–200 buckets of water, and would sit "chuckling and gurgling happily" while all this was poured over him. Once bathed, the incoming mast was given clean clothing and then fed by Baba, usually by hand as one feeds a small child. In addition each mast was given a coin. Since embarking on his silence, Baba never touched money, but he made an exception for the masts. The gift was not charity so its value was unimportant. What mattered, Baba explained, was that, being metal, the coin served as a medium of contact.[3] Only when this had been accomplished would Baba sit with the mast in silent conference.

These conferences afforded the spiritual contact to which everything else led up. They might take place by day or night, at any hour, but always in secret, consequently no eyewitness account of what took place exists. Dr Donkin records, however, that when Baba was working with a high mast who cooperated fully, the effort and drain on his vitality were immense, so that he would emerge from a session "pale, and apparently exhausted, his clothes often drenched in perspiration out of all proportion to the heat of the day." Nothing made him so happy, however, as a successful session with such a one as Chacha of Ajmer, of whom Baba said that he was "as good as a hundred ordinary masts." Working with Chacha he would become so engrossed as utterly to forget meals, sleep, the mandali – "and, it seems, the whole wide world." And Dr Donkin gives this glimpse of Baba in February 1940, as he saw him in an interval of his mast work:

> … he was looking radiantly noble, with hair let down for once, and really glistening, he was a fine sight to look at, his phenomenal strength of character, and his sort of mysterious spiritual beauty and radiance very much visible as he sat on his couch. Baba's face in repose is such a fusion of spiritual bliss and serenity and a sort of dragging sadness which gives such dignity and grandeur: his face really surpasses all scenery of nature, both in its amazing hold on the onlooker, and in its rapid changes of mood.[4]

No doubt the main reason for Baba's insistence on absolute seclusion during his sessions with the masts lay in the nature of his spiritual work. But Dr Donkin suggests as a secondary reason the physical danger, both to the mast and to any intruder upon spiritual proceedings at this level, and he instances the experience of Eruch – Baba's 'right hand' – who once, after Baba had been closeted with Chatti Baba for about two hours, heard sounds of movement and went forward to release a door catch. Chatti Baba, emerging from the session, brushed past him, causing "a palpable and excruciating shock" which made Eruch feel as though he was being electrocuted.

Whenever an ashram closed because work in that area had been completed, great care was taken to ensure the well-being of all masts. Usually they were happy to return to their own town or village, and the people would eagerly welcome back their 'patron saint'. The mast would be given a parting gift of blanket or clothing, and a member of the mandali would escort him home. Where necessary a sum of money would be handed over to someone in his neighbourhood to look after him and feed him twice a day. Only when all such arrangements had been completed would the party set out for its next objective. Usually the journey was by bus, its roof piled high with bedding rolls, cooking pots, baths – all the gear and impedimenta of perhaps thirty people. One particular journey half up the Indian continent from Bangalore to Meherabad was made by rail, and gives a glimpse of what such journeys could be like.

> The mandali, twenty odd madmen, five or six masts, a gazelle, a peacock, a sheep, a white rabbit, some geese, five dogs, three monkeys, and two pet birds were all crammed into this one compartment,[5] and sat cheek by jowl with tin trunks, packing cases, tables, chairs, and the inevitable medley of domestic and culinary equipment... As soon as the train started, Shariat Khan – one of the masts – tied bells round his ankles, and danced to a rhythm beaten out by Punjia on his kerosene tin. Punjia danced as he drummed, and made Eruch and Baidul join in. Once or twice stray strangers tried to get in, but changed their minds after one glance through the window.[6]

The work on mast tours consisted partly in contacting masts for the future, and partly it was similar to that done in the ashrams, but far more exhausting since it was carried out on the move. In everything he did, or that was done for him, Baba insisted on the most careful planning. "I have that bad Avataric habit," he once said, "of supervising every detail myself," so that every tour was precisely planned and preceded by a preliminary survey in which two or three members of the mandali would be sent over the ground beforehand, meeting and observing likely souls.

The three most experienced 'mast discoverers' were considered to be Baidul (Rustom J. Irani), Eruch and Kaka Baria, and Dr Donkin reported:

> If you corner Baidul or Kaka in moments of expansiveness, and provoke them to describe some of these journeys, you will hear tales of tramping on foot across arid sands, through dark forests, or over mountain and valley; of riding on camels, mules, ponies and asses; of bumping over mile after

> mile of purgatorial tracks in bullock carts and tongas; of enduring nights and days in the dusty and sweaty turmoil of overcrowded third class railway carriages… in the mere preliminary reconnaissance of almost every one of Baba's mast tours.[7]

These hardships, however, were insignificant compared with those accepted as a matter of course on the tours themselves. Here Baba set the pace and – like that at which he often walked – it was one which tested his and their endurance to the utmost.

> After two or three days of work from dawn to dusk with little or no food, and after two or three nights with little or no sleep, (Dr Donkin records) the world simply becomes unreal, and one lives a kind of reflex life in which the parts of one's body move and work; but the zest of living, and that sense of well-being, dependent, one supposes, upon a nervous system refreshed by sleep, and upon tissues nourished by adequate food, are simply no longer there. But mast tours do not last just two or three days, they go on for two or three weeks, and this tempo of work goes on and on, Baba ever spurring those with him to the very limits of their powers. On one of the tours in 1946, Baidul estimated that, in eight days, they had a *total* of fourteen hours' sleep… Finally, add to all these things the infliction of a tropical climate, and the drain on one's vitality through constant perspiration, and you will get an approximate answer to what a mast tour is like…
>
> Thus, you see Baba and three or four disciples set out on a mast tour, looking strong and fresh, and when they enter the garden gate two or three weeks later, you go to welcome them back, and help bring their luggage into the house; and you see their tired, unshaven faces, and Baba's face; and their tired eyes, and Baba's eyes; and you see their clothes, and Baba's clothes too, dirty, with dirt worked into the fabric of

> the cloth, and fixed there by days of perspiration; and you see places where the clothes are torn, memorials and little outer signs of the weird days and nights of moving and working, working and moving – days and nights when the Master submits himself to the sordid limitations of physical existence, not for his own sake, but for mankind…
>
> And when the mandali who went with him add their tribute of description, you hear how, throughout all these hardships, Baba remained the freshest of all, and how, after each contact with a really good mast, he seemed particularly radiant, as if some great work had been achieved, or some heavy burden lifted.

On one tour when the party dossed down on a railway platform, they were so exhausted that a petty thief crept in and shared Baba's blanket unnoticed by anyone. Questioned in the morning, he admitted to being a thief but said he had only come there for shelter, and Baba told the mandali to let him go.

Besides the hardships of travel, there were endless problems with the masts themselves. The fact that a mast had been approached by one of the mandali was no guarantee that he would still be in the same place, or in the mood to come forward when required. Sometimes a mast had disappeared; some made difficulties over being brought to Baba, as if sensing they would be called on for some supreme effort or sacrifice. At times their reaction on meeting Baba was ambivalent, as though in self-protection. Bhayya Baba of Kishangarh was first met with in an eating house. Asked to sit near Baba, he objected: "I know what your work with me is, and I won't come." When Baba wanted to feed him, he said shrewdly: "Give me food, I will eat it myself here." However, with persistence and persuasion – and it must be remembered that Baba himself could never speak – Bhayya Baba at last yielded and gave Baba his cooperation.

In the approaches to masts Baba never allowed his name to

be disclosed. Masts had to come of their own free will to meet 'the Master', or at least with reluctant consent, not impelled by the authority of his name. How powerful this authority was for them emerged in their talk. In the ashram at Ajmer, the attendant whose special task it was to look after Chatti Baba became so exasperated one day that he felt like walking out. "You want to leave, don't you?" the great mast rebuked him. "But what's the good of it? All the world's in Baba's power, where will you go? Serve him now, he is the ocean, because one day when lots of people throng to see him, you may never get the opportunity..."

The same metaphor was used by other masts. Khala Masi, a woman mast, said to Baba: "You are the Ocean. Give me a few drops from it to drink." Another, refusing to come, gave as his excuse: "My boat will be drowned in that Ocean." Pir Fazl Shah, a pilgrim, spoke of a flood: "No one, until you came, has touched my heart with the arrow of Divine Love. You have the power to destroy and flood the world; no one fully knows the limits of your greatness; you are the spiritual authority of the time, and if I were to die I would take another body to be close to you." Another mast being brought to Baba said, on reaching the gate: "We have come to the garden of Paradise." When Baba came out, he gazed at him, laughed with tears of joy, and then embraced him. "Look at this man's face and forehead!" he exclaimed to those about him. "They shine as if the sun were there. Can't you recognise who he is?"

What was the purpose of Baba's work among masts? It would seem to have been partly for humanity at large, and partly for the masts themselves. In the foreword to Dr Donkin's book, Baba himself has given a full explanation, of which we can here include no more than a short summary:

> Because of his being stationed on the inner planes, which are free from the limitations and handicaps of the gross world, a mast can be, and often is, in contact with a far greater number

> of souls than is possible for an ordinary person... A mast can therefore be a more effective *agent for spiritual work* than the most able persons of the gross world. The mast mind is also often used directly by the Master as a medium for sending his spiritual help to different parts of the world.[8]

However, Baba explains, because of the inward bliss which the mast continually enjoys, he tends to become totally absorbed in contemplation, and then his power is not being released and utilised for the benefit of others who are in need of spiritual help.

> Some masts get stuck on the inner planes. They are overpowered by the onflow of grace and love, and get into a state of divine stupor... Some masts find their insurgent powers uncontrollable, and are faced by new and insurmountable temptations. They can make no further advancement through their own unaided efforts, and have to avoid the possibility of a precipitous fall through *the indiscriminate use of occult powers*. In short, in spite of having attained a high spiritual status, many masts on the inner planes need real guidance and help from a Perfect Master.
>
> The Master has a direct and unerring insight into the exact working of the minds of masts... He gives masts effective guidance and a spiritual push, and he facilitates their onward march on the path, so that they become more and more fit as vehicles for the expression of the Divine Will. They become more efficient agents for the promotion of God's plan on earth.
>
> When a mast gets walled-in by his own self-sufficiency and desirelessness, only the Master can draw him out of the isolation of his choice, by awakening within him an expansive love that breaks through all limitations, and prepares him for shouldering the important responsibility of rendering true service to others who are in need of spiritual help... Very

> often, when the Master is helping a mast, he is also helping the world through him at that very time.

So the Master's activity with masts is twofold, helping mankind through the masts, and – in reward for cooperation, as it were – helping the mast himself to advance further along the spiritual path.

Exactly how Baba helped mankind by means of the masts is, of course, his own secret. But it has been suggested that the masts serve as what might be called 'spiritual powerhouses'. We are familiar with the idea of contemplative orders in the Christian religion, monks and nuns who do not involve themselves in charitable work, believing they achieve more for their fellow men and women through prayer than by attempts to relieve distress directly. Masts, particularly those who have attained high levels of development, have freed themselves from desires and ambitions which clutter the minds of normal human beings, and in so doing have turned themselves into spiritual channels, through which divine power and love can flow into the world. At times, however, it is not so flowing because, in becoming 'God-intoxicated', the mast has not only lost consciousness of himself but of the needs of humanity at large. If this is a true picture, Baba's work with masts can be compared to the clearing of spiritual irrigation channels.

"I love them, and they love me. I help them, and they help me," was Baba's own simple statement. But years later, at the great sahavas or gathering in India in 1955, he expanded this.

> My love for the *masts* is similar in many ways to that shown by a mother who continues to look lovingly after her children regardless of their behaviour. To make her child clean a mother does not even mind soiling her hands with the child's excrement.
>
> I am the mother of the masts. They also are like parts of

> my body. Some are like my right and some are like my left limbs and fingers. Some are nose, ears and eyes for me. I am helpful to them and they are helpful to me. The *masts* alone know how they love me and I alone know how I love them. I work for the *masts*, and knowingly or unknowingly they work for me.[9]

It has been suggested – though not by Dr Donkin – that through these 'spiritual powerhouses' Baba exerted his influence on events in the external world: "The Mad Ashram was one of the activities in Baba's spiritual programme to restore normality to a war-crazy world."[10] And CB Purdom, in his book *The God-Man*, has sought to establish a correlation between world events and specific phases of the mast work. Whether such correlation can be established or not, it is apparent that Baba's periods of most intense work among the masts coincided with the crisis of the war and the years of 'near-war' which followed.

Finally, there appears also to have existed a special relationship, inexplicable by our notions of cause and effect, between individual masts and particular countries. An example of this was the great mast Chatti Baba and his connection with France. Though literate, Chatti Baba never to anyone's knowledge saw a newspaper or had any means of information about current events. Yet, in the early part of 1940 at the Meherabad Ashram, he repeatedly told his attendant that the people of Europe were undergoing great suffering, but would survive to enjoy happy days again. One day, pouring earth over his head, he said that there would be much anguish and privation, and many would perish of starvation, but that Baba would finally assuage the suffering of the world.

However, on the night of 9th June 1940,[11] Chatti Baba became suddenly violent and abusive. Rushing from his room in a frenzy, he went to Baba's room, saying that he had come for shelter since his own home was utterly destroyed. Baba at once gave orders that they were to be left alone together, and Chatti Baba could be heard arguing and expostulating with him for some hours. At last he became quiet, spent the rest of the night alone with Baba, and in the morning returned to his own room, which, far from being 'utterly destroyed', was just as neat and orderly as it had always been.

Baba then explained to the mandali that it was Chatti Baba's spiritual connection with France, and the disaster then overwhelming that country, which had filled him with despair.

Baba washing the feet of a poor woman at Kharda, a district of Ahmednagar, India, taken during one of three programmes held in February 1948. *L-r:* Baidul, Meher Baba, unknown woman, Sailor. Photo by Padri (Faredoon Driver) / © MSI Collection.

Notes

1. They were at Rahuri, Ajmer, Jabalpur (Jubbulpore), Bangalore, Meherabad, and Ranchi, and a glance at the map will show that they were indeed 'strategically placed'. The two later ashrams were at Mahabaleshwar and Satara, both

of them close to the Meherabad headquarters.

2. *Pan,* familiar on the trays or baskets of Indian roadside sellers, is a bright green leaf, which is dexterously folded and secured with a clove as a pin. Inside are spices. The whole little bundle is put into the mouth and chewed. One result is a scarlet saliva which stains gums, teeth and lips, and often dribbles in rivulets from the corners of an addict's mouth.
3. This is perhaps partly the significance of the gold ring in marriage. It is said, too, that an initiate into Freemasonry has to have all metal removed from his person, special clothing being worn in which tapes are used to avoid having metal fasteners. This would carry the opposite meaning, the severance of previous contacts – thus a form of purification.
4. Unpublished diary of Dr William Donkin: Entry for 19th February 1940. (This has since been published: *Donkin's Diaries*, p. 83 [Ed.].)
5. It must surely have been a whole railway coach, not what we understand by a 'compartment'.
6. *The Wayfarers*, p. 103
7. This and following extract: *The Wayfarers*, pp. 161–3
8. This and following extract: *The Wayfarers*, pp. 8–10
9. *Listen, Humanity*, p. 260
10. *Meher Baba on War*, p. 120
11. It may be recalled that the collapse of the French Army began about 5th June 1940, and the Germans entered Paris eight days later.

Meher Baba seated by the Blue Bus with Gustadji, Baidul, Pendu, Eruch. Photographer: Padri (Faredoon Driver). Date: February 1952. Location: Meherazad. © MSI Collection.

Chapter 10

The New Life

During 1948 it became plain to those with Baba that a new phase of his work was about to begin. In June–July he called upon all followers throughout the world for special abstinence "because spiritually this is a period of crisis". On New Year's Day 1949, he sent them all a warning that a great personal disaster was coming upon himself; that the mandali would be faced with severe trials which only a few might be able to endure; he called upon "all men and women who believe in me" to observe a full month's silence during the coming July, and he repeated his ban on political activities. Meanwhile Baba continued his mast tours as strenuously as ever until June when he went into seclusion. He is described at this time as having "the bearing of one who had succeeded in a great campaign. There was a great peace about him, his gaze penetrating and glowing, his mien alert, his hair short and manageable, with a pigtail."[1]

Baba had entered upon many seclusions and would enter upon many more, but this of June–July 1949, because of the work to be accomplished, was regarded by him as 'The Great Seclusion'. It took place at Meherazad, not in any building, but inside the body of that renowned blue motor bus in which so many tours had been conducted. Worn out with years of journeying, overloaded, over every kind of road, it had been removed from its wheels and mounted on oil drums built in with brick and lime.

The seclusion was for forty days (22nd June–31st July 1949). At times Baba fasted completely, at others took only liquids or food once a day. A continual watch was maintained outside the bus with total silence, and it was noticed that whereas normally Baba would sleep for an hour or an hour and a half each night, he appeared now never to sleep for more than a few minutes. Of the first spell of seclusion he said later: "No one except God and myself knows what I went through during those nine days." Yet when the full forty days were up he emerged at the hour fixed "the picture of health and radiance."

A New Life was to begin, he told his followers. To all who accepted Baba as the Avatar its keynote must have sounded strange: "I shall be absolutely helpless in the true and literal sense of the word on account of some personal disaster to me." Meanwhile Baba would cease to apply himself to any material affairs: "Everything I possess including ashram buildings, fields and houses, etc., both here and elsewhere, and all furniture, cars, power-plants, cattle, chattels and in fact everything that belongs to me, is to be disposed of. Nothing is to remain as my property and in my name except the Meherabad Hill premises on which the tomb for my bodily remains has already been built..."

A deadline of 15th October was fixed by which all arrangements had to be completed. "I want to be absolutely free from everything and everybody. There will be no compromise now about anything. I am becoming *ghutt* (hardened), *naffat* (callous), and penniless. Remember the proverb *Naga-se-Khuda bhi darta hai* (even God is afraid of the 'naked')."[2]

To the mandali three alternatives were offered. To go with Baba, face all the difficulties of their choice and literally beg their bread with him from day to day; or to earn their own living in the world and spare what they could for the support of dependent families, while continuing to obey all Baba's orders; or to leave him and go their own way. Everyone had been warned to be absolutely honest in giving his opinion. "Don't be vague. Say exactly what you think and how you feel. You should not say 'Baba, your will'." A similar choice was set before the women mandali, with one difference, that they might if they wished leave all decision to Baba. But even in abdicating decision they must take responsibility for such abdication, since every man or woman was obliged to accept responsibility for his or her course of action upon oath before God.

Sarosh, that same Sarosh who as a young man had so often found his bedding roll thrown out by his Master, was now a prosperous businessman, besides being one of the mandali. He at once offered to maintain indefinitely all men and women who remained with Baba. Baba smiled his approval of the offer, but told Sarosh he had 'missed the whole point' of his instructions. Proceeds from the sale of all properties were to be set aside to support those *not* going with Baba, but for those who chose to remain with him no provision whatever must be made. "I and those who are going with me are going to suffer. We are going to start without any protection. We shall have to go a-begging."

At a solemn ceremony on the 18th August (1949), Baba offered a prayer, read out from his dictation on the alphabet board: "May God help Baba to definitely make this step, which he is taking to give up everything and to go away, irrevocable, so that from the 16th October when he enters the new life, there will be no turning back." This was the first prayer from Baba to God for help which the mandali had heard for twenty-eight years, and they were so astonished that no one could even say 'Amen.'

Eruch, in a later interview, suggested a reason for this 'human' prayer: "Baba during the New Life did not want his companions to accept him as the God-man. To them he was one of the companions. When he came down from the highest level to the level of a Perfect Person he invoked the blessings of God as any ordinary man would."[3]

At a further ceremony on 31st August, in the presence of thirty-two persons – the only ones he had chosen out of 1,200 who in past times had sworn to follow his instructions – Baba himself took a solemn oath to lead the New Life till the end. Once again he warned those present that their decision would be binding for all time, and that anyone not prepared for a life of absolute obedience and sacrifice would do better to remain behind. All present then withdrew to make up their minds, and three hours later, when all decisions had been handed in, it appeared that sixteen men and four women were resolved to accompany Baba into the New Life.

Meantime, Baba's instructions for the disposing of all property were being literally carried out.

> Everything in Meherabad which was not personally used by Baba had to be sold... Brass pots, pans, kettles, tea-sets, cutlery, glassware, carpets, presents given by the Western disciples or by Eastern devotees, were brought out and packed to be sent to Bombay by truck. Some might mumble, 'You'll not be able to get another kettle like this one, or knives like this,' to be hushed by others with 'It doesn't matter, we never used them anyway.' Mehera and some of the others gave costly silk sarees and any jewellery they had. Furniture, beds, cupboards, everything went into the jackpot. From Meherazad also articles were sent – the brand-new refrigerator that Elizabeth (Patterson) had ordered from America and her

two De Soto cars which she had given to Baba and a small car which Nariman (Nariman M. Dadachanji) had presented.[4]

Excitement mounted as the day fixed drew near, and at last in the earliest hours of the morning of the 16th October under the driving rain of the monsoon, the party started off. Partly on foot and partly by bus and rail they made their way across India, arriving early on the morning of the 15th November at the holy city of Benares, where an old house with a large garden had been taken for the party. Divested of all belongings, they had now to support themselves by begging, and trust, like the disciples sent out by Jesus, that their needs would be provided for. Like those disciples also, they were sent out in pairs and under stringent orders. They were to accept nothing except food, and any money must be refused. On receiving a gift they must come away immediately; if rejected they must go to the next house. When both had received *bhiksha* (alms) they should return directly to headquarters. They were not allowed to beg from acquaintances or from shops. Moreover, when they moved on from place to place, no food must be put aside for the next day: "Every day will be a new day for us in this New Life." On a number of days Baba himself shared in the ordeal of begging, barefoot and bareheaded, dressed in white, carrying a brass bowl and a cotton bag, with an ochre satchel over his left arm.[5]

Benares is a city of beggars. Since the mandali were clearly not ordinary paupers, yet were forbidden to mention Baba's name or offer any explanation, they had a far from easy time. One well-dressed man rounded on two of the disciples, telling them they should be ashamed to be seen begging and ought to go and find themselves a job. Two other disciples, stout to begin with and looking stouter because they were wearing all the clothes they had, were ridiculed: "You look like wrestlers – go and work for your living!" On the other hand a poor village woman, having said she had no food in the house and nothing to cook with, urged the disciples to wait, borrowed what she could from a neighbour and prepared vegetables and bread which Baba himself shared out among them all.

On the 1st December, the party moved to Sarnath, a few miles north, where they lived in two small bungalows. All spare clothing and last vestiges of the 'old life' had now been discarded, but something else had been acquired, a small horde of animals – a white horse, a camel and camel-cart, a caravan pulled by oxen for the women, a bullock cart, two donkeys, two cows and a calf which, when tired, had to be carried on someone's shoulders. All inevitably had to be fed, and before leaving Sarnath all the party except three were asked to surrender their wristwatches to raise money, which they immediately did.

As the party set off from Sarnath in what Baba called "the walking *fakiri* (poverty)" the men were wearing white *kafnis* and green turbans and the women blue cotton saris. Watching them was Padri who had come from Ahmednagar to hand over the caravan. He was under orders not to take a photograph, not to talk, just to be at a distance when the party started out. Later Padri told Mani that it was an unforgettable scene, indelibly printed on his mind.

> You could not have known it because you were in it, but it was really out of this world, a most wondrous sight that greeted my eyes as I silently watched that long procession passing by while the dawn was still young.[6]

One of the most difficult tasks for the party was to remain cheerful under all conditions as insisted on by Baba.

> I am expecting of you in this New Life something which is superhuman in some aspects (he told them). I am in the soup too along with you. To keep cheerful under all circumstances is superhuman. Let us therefore do our best to help each

> other. I help you, you help me in order to uphold each other's oath. The most important point that would carry you through safely with me, is to have no moods... Even if moods sometimes come and anger is stirred, never express them in any manner, covert or overt. It is all the play of the mind and the mind, with a little conscientious effort, can be made to adapt itself.

Mani, Baba's sister, who was one of the four women companions, has left a vivid picture "of those days when the discipline and privations were extreme, as was the feeling of freedom and inner satisfaction." She tells of

> seemingly nonstop walking day by day, and of nights spent in a disused barn or schoolhouse or stable, or again (as so often) under the trees in a mango orchard with far from sufficient covering to ward off the bitter cold and heavy dew... Baba would usually walk ahead with Eruch, we women a little distance behind, with the rest of the procession following last. Baba never appeared to be walking fast, just to be walking on air with that strong, graceful stride, while our pace was too obviously hurried. And as the miles would vanish, miles of often beautiful countryside, we lesser companions would not unnaturally find our thoughts dwelling more on food than nature's beauty.[7]

Eruch, in the interview previously quoted from *The Glow* magazine, gives the picture as the men saw it:

> ... we had absolutely no shelter over our heads, our food rations were inadequate, we walked in the rain, under the sun and were exposed to the elements. Moreover, we had a moral responsibility of looking after the women and then again the fear that Baba would send us back if we

> showed any emotion or broke his orders. It will indeed be incomprehensible to those who have not been through this New Life, to visualise the tremendous suffering each one had to undergo, but this suffering was largely nullified by Baba's benign presence... during the New Life we addressed Baba as our Elder Brother and Baba's identity was never revealed to anyone. He played the role of the elder brother to the hilt. He was our guide, our friend and above all our companion. During this companionship we loved each other, helped each other, despite the fact that each one of us had a different temperament. Baba brought us together into a cohesive whole; free of selfishness.

At the start of the New Life, Baba had publicly put aside his condition as God to become man among men, the 'Son of Man', the companion of his companions. He refused to allow anyone to bow down to him or pay marks of respect. He himself bowed down to the humblest, washed their feet and gave them alms from what he had, as testimony to the brotherhood of all men, and in humility before the Divine spirit which lives on in every creature, however degraded and unaware of its presence we may be.

An intense devotion was aroused in the little band by their sense of Baba's presence continually among them, and his loving comradeship.

> The elder companions – Gustadji, Patel and Anna 104,[8] never once took a lift but walked all the way. Anna was known as 104 because once when he was ill at his home he kept telling everyone that his temperature was 104 and Baba gave him this nickname... all day he would walk with the others and at night would sit outside Baba's tent to keep watch. He rested a while in the evening, but that hardly meant any rest. He said sitting and keeping watch and repeating Baba's name to

himself was rest enough.[9]

This intensely exacting New Life was continued throughout the year 1950. Sometimes the begging regulations were relaxed or suspended for a short period and a degree of modest comfort permitted; sometimes they were intensified. Some of the companions left Baba for a while to go back to their homes or take up various employments. Enormous distances were covered – 3,500 miles by train and on foot between 21st October and 6th December 1950 – and many masts and holy persons contacted. These contacts, Baba explained, were different from those made during the 'old life' since there was now no special work to be done with them. He contacted the masts to take their darshan, which had significance for him, but what this significance might be he did not explain, except to say that it had "nothing to do with spirituality."

On occasions collections were made among the followers in India and overseas and considerable sums raised. In general these were used for distribution to the poor, to sufferers from famine and to victims of the disastrous floods. But once, when searching for poor people, Baba learned of a man who had inherited several million rupees, wasted it all, and was now living with his wife in a hovel, a sick man. Baba sought him out, washed his feet, and gave him 300 rupees. The man was so overcome that he collapsed, and Baba sat with him till he recovered consciousness.

If we should attempt an explanation of the inexplicable, we might say that the New Life was a living demonstration of the unity of all life, and of our mutual dependence on one another and upon God. To the acceptance of this unity – which unites not only man to man, but also man to God and God to man – all belongings constitute a barrier. Wealth and possessions tie us to the superficial world, and so come between us and reality. To find 'treasure in Heaven' we must first, as the young man was told many centuries ago, 'sell all that thou hast and give to the poor', which is literally the way the New Life began for Baba and the mandali.

How then are we to live when we have given everything away? The answer supplied by faith, and demonstrated over and over again by Baba and his mandali, is that God always provides for those who make themselves utterly dependent on him by taking no thought for the morrow. "If you worry about yourself," Baba told two of his followers during the New Life period, "God does not worry about you. And why should He? If you stop worrying, God has to begin to worry for you. Remember Him wholeheartedly; leave your worrying to Him and be free to remain cheerful."

And Eruch has recorded how it felt to live from day to day in a state of total dependence upon God and the charity of one's fellow men.

> We had really left the world completely and we felt ourselves released. We didn't know if we would get food for the next day or not, but we didn't care because we had set out on a life of complete helplessness and hopelessness, and we were completely determined to continue in this way, come what might... The greatest of spiritual truths also were absolutely insignificant to us, because our wholehearted attention was focused only on Baba's personality and wishes. We never gave a second thought to all those things... (And, despite all that they endured) nobody fell ill during that period of hardship, not even the four women who were with Baba. There was not even a cold or cough, although we felt the sting of the bitterly cold winter days and our nails turned blue and our fingers became stiff.[10]

However, it is not only material possessions which constitute a tie. We are tied by our desires and ambitions; even our hopes and spiritual aims can constitute fetters. In the New Life *everything* had to be given up – "No spiritual benefit" Baba insisted in each of the alternatives put to the mandali. Hopelessness and helplessness had to be literal and complete – even the hope of being alive tomorrow or of seeing Baba again must be abandoned. "I am going to see who is out to die for no reason by going with me." And he told the women mandali and all those followers who were left behind that they must wholeheartedly and sincerely give up hope of ever seeing and meeting him again. All trouble comes from hoping; where there is no hope there can follow no disappointment. "Being with Baba and following him," Eruch records, "meant renunciation which even renounced renunciation. The very concept of renunciation had to be renounced... our sole object was to follow Baba to where he took us and to obey his every command."[11]

If the purpose of the New Life was to demonstrate the *unity of all life* and of our dependence upon one another and on God, what was the reason for its timing; and why was it launched precisely at that moment?

These years of the late 1940s and early 1950s were ones in which, following the ravages of World War II in Europe and Asia, and as a consequence of partition and famine in India, millions of people had been uprooted from their homes, rendered 'helpless and hopeless' in the most literal sense, and forced to depend for their mere existence upon charity. Over much of Asia this took the form of begging each day's bread; in Europe charity took the form of refugee camps dependent on overseas aid, particularly help from America under the Marshall Plan, and from the United Nations under the organisation known as UNRRA (United Nations Relief and Rehabilitation Administration). In the mysterious way in which he operated, Baba was, perhaps, taking upon his own shoulders and those of the mandali the condition of all the lost and unhappy people of the world.

In February 1951, his journeyings over for the present, Baba once more went into seclusion accompanied by fasting. In the middle of the year he called his disciples and devotees together, including those from the old life, and declared that a further step had been decided upon. This would not be a step back from 'helplessness and hopelessness', but a step beyond, into complete mental annihilation, and Baba would, he said,

> in the natural course of events be facing physical annihilation as well, without my actually seeking it... Anyone who wants to go through this dying process with me can join me; but I want every one of you to understand fully the magnitude of the mental preparation needed to stand by such a decision... If you choose to accompany me from mere emotional impulse, it will prove disastrous... I shall have absolutely no responsibility and might have no concern whatever for anyone accompanying.[12]

Despite these stern warnings, twenty-one men volunteered to go with Baba into the mental annihilation which he called *manonash*, and from them he chose eight for consideration before finally deciding upon five. All Baba's followers throughout the world were asked to participate in this further undertaking, first by a day of total silence on the 10th July, the anniversary of Baba's starting his own silence, and later, from the end of December to mid-February 1952, by repeating the name of God as used by their own religion with wholehearted devotion for half an hour each day.

On the last day of the year 1951, Baba dictated a statement which included the following:

> To try to understand with the mind that which the mind can never understand, is futile; and to try to express by sounds of language and in forms of words the transcendent state of the soul, is even more futile. All that can be said, and has

> been said, and will be said, by those who live and experience that state, is that when the false self is lost the Real Self is found; that the birth of the Real can follow only the death of the false; and that dying to ourselves – the true death which ends all dying – is the only way to perpetual life. This means that when the mind with its desires, cravings and longings, is completely consumed by the fire of Divine Love, then the infinite, indestructible, indivisible, eternal Self is manifested. This is *manonash,* the annihilation of the false, limited, miserable, ignorant, destructible 'I', to be replaced by the real 'I', the eternal possessor of Infinite Knowledge, Love, Power, Peace, Bliss and Glory... We are all in this shoreless Ocean of Infinite Knowledge, and yet are ignorant of it until the mind – which is the source of ignorance – vanishes for ever; for ignorance ceases to exist when the mind ceases to exist.[13]

To most of us this will appear a shattering statement. It is not ignorance but knowledge which, in our view of the world, "ceases to exist when the mind ceases to exist." Mind, to us, is the source of all progress and development. We honour a person of great intellect, and there can be few actions more praiseworthy, we believe, than for a man or woman to develop his or her own mind by study, or the minds of children through education. And indeed Baba himself insisted many times on the importance of mental effort and application. How then can it be said that the mind is the source of ignorance and has to be annihilated?

The mind is the enemy of ultimate reality because, through the mental processes, our whole picture of life and our own place in it has been constructed on a false premise, that of each person's total separation from their neighbours. For every man and woman, through the operation of mind and the impressions it gathers in, life becomes 'myself as distinct from everybody and everything', which is all too easily distorted into 'myself *before* everybody and everything, and myself *against* everybody and everything.' It is the mind which has separated the human race into classes, castes, tribes and nations through the network of prejudices, customs, taboos, laws which maintain division and uphold separation – divisions and separations which we assume to be 'part of our nature', but are so far from being innate that they have actually to be taught to children, since children naturally accept all other children regardless of colour, nationality or creed.

It is the mind which is responsible for mistrust and hostility between one people and another, and between one religion and another, causing us on the long journey to God to forget the goal and start fighting among ourselves – even to the final blasphemy of claiming to be fighting each other *in the name of God*.

It is the mind which drives us to accumulate wealth and possessions far beyond our needs, and even beyond our capacity to use them effectively. The mind is the source of competition and rivalry between individuals, groups, organisations, political parties, peoples. In the successful striving ruthlessly to acquire more and more, it breeds self-preoccupation and a callous disregard of others; and in those who are unsuccessful it produces envy, hatred and violence.

At the national level it is mind which continually invents, acquires and heaps up armaments for 'protection', but which, by the threat these offer to neighbour states, impel them to do the same. This results in a seemingly endless, increasingly costly, struggle to 'go one better'. In this way resources which should feed the world's hungry and provide shelter for the homeless are dissipated on means of destruction, which the rulers of each country have sworn never to use, yet continue to develop and accumulate.

Conditioned to see life in terms of dualism and separateness, the mind can admit no other viewpoint – just as a bird's eyes being set on each side of its head present it always with two separate unfocussed views. Setting itself up as the sole judge of 'reality', mind regards everything which cannot be proved by its own system of tests as illusory, allowing nothing which cannot be weighed, measured, demonstrated and repeated or reproduced to order, to have 'real' existence. And it is this claim to absolute authority which makes mind, in Baba's words, "the source of ignorance", since from the spiritual standpoint, those factors which can be weighed and measured are precisely those which have least importance, so that, in the words of the great Christian saint Thomas Aquinas, "The slenderest knowledge which may be obtained of the highest things is more to be desired than the most certain knowledge obtained of lesser things."

Moreover the basic spiritual truth of the *unity of all life*, on which Baba continually insists, is one which the dualistic mind, through its very nature, cannot accept. So far from being completely separate individuals, we are all eternally one and indivisible; and every form of life down to the rocks and stones, and the gases from which solid matter originally took shape, is a form of spirit, linked indissolubly with every other form.

> Reality (said Baba) is beyond human understanding, for it is beyond reason. Understanding cannot help because God is beyond understanding. The moment you try to understand God you 'misunderstand' him; you miss him when you try to understand him. Reason must go before knowledge dawns... Only manonash (annihilation of mind) takes one to reality. There is a way to annihilate the mind. The way is love. Just consider ordinary human love: when a man or woman is deeply in love with his or her partner, nothing comes between them. They get totally lost in love for one another. There is neither admiration nor fault-finding. There is total absence even of exchange of thought: love prevails without thoughts. Mind becomes defunct for the time being: for in such intense human love mind does not come into play... If ordinary human love can go so far, what should be said of the

> height of love divine?[14]

Manonash, the elimination through love of mental domination and self-interest, was the culmination of the New Life. And the New Life, in which all are companions, loving and serving one another, and dependent for each day's food and shelter upon God and the charity of fellow men, has provided perhaps a glimpse into that New Age which Baba has foretold will succeed the present one. This is an age in which intuition has superseded reason; love has conquered fear and greed; sharing has replaced competition and self-seeking; and all men – whether as individuals or nations – depend confidently on one another's generosity and love.

And the animals that accompanied Baba and the mandali into the New Life – what were they doing? That camel, the bullocks and cows, the calf that was always having to be carried, the white horse? They stand perhaps for the animal creation which must, since the whole universe is linked by spirit, share in and benefit from that raising of the spiritual climate brought about by the New Life, taught and demonstrated to us by Meher Baba. As indeed must also benefit, in one way or another, the whole of our misused, exploited, eroded and polluted planet.

When we wrote the above paragraph for our book *Much Silence* it was speculation. But since then Bal Natu has recorded that, years after this period,

> Kaka Baria, one of the companions, commented that through the animals taken with them in the New Life, Baba gave fresh impetus to the work done for the animal kingdom in His past Advents. The white horse... represented the work accomplished by Zoroaster and the cows that by Krishna. The donkeys were the medium for recharging the spiritual push given by Jesus and the camel that by Prophet Mohammad.[15]

Begging during the New Life, outside Dr Nath's house. Location: Benares, 25 November 1949. *L-r:* Adi Sr., Baba, Babadas in hat. © Meher Nazar Publications.

Notes

1. These and quotes in the following narration: *The God-Man*, pp. 160–8
2. Baba once explained: "To be empty means to be rid of all desire, and concerns the heart. To be naked concerns the mind, and means not to care for the opinions, criticism, or censure of others in one's pursuit" (of the True Goal).
3. Eruch Jessawala interviewed in *The Glow*, February 1973
4. Condensed from *Tales from the New Life*, p. 137
5. There is a photograph of Baba setting off for a morning's begging with Eruch, dressed in this manner. It is used on the cover of *Tales from the New Life*.
6. *Tales from the New Life*, p. 179
7. *Family Letters*, Letter 23

8. Gustadji N. Hansotia, Sadashiv Patel and Anna Jakkal
9. Eruch in *The Glow*, February 1973
10. *Tales from the New Life*, condensed from pp. 18, 21 and 116
11. *The Glow*, February 1973
12. This and following extract: *The God-Man*, pp. 191–5
13. N.B.: The word 'mind' does not mean the physical mind.
14. *The God-Man*, p. 315
15. *Glimpses, Vol. II*, pp. 156–7

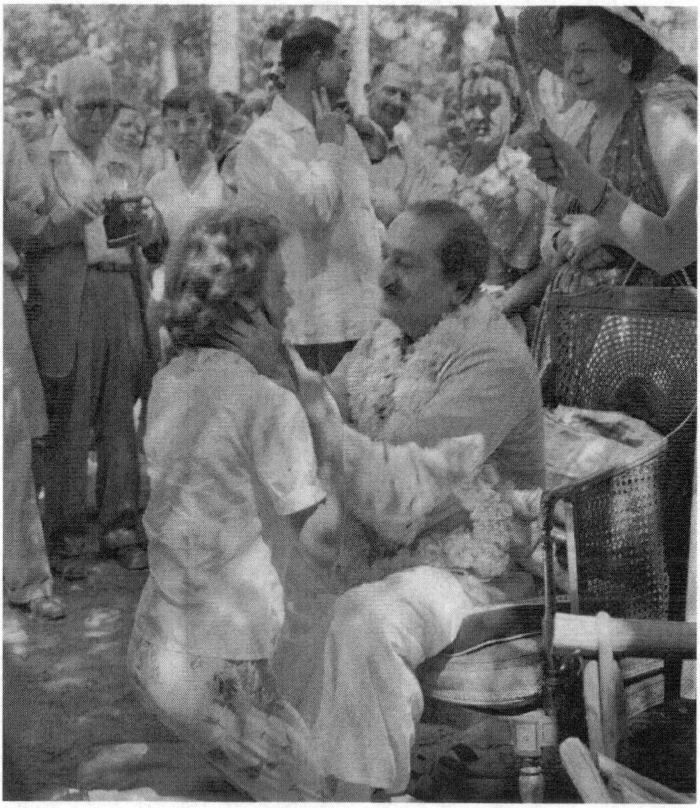

Meher Baba greeting sahavasees. Location: Myrtle Beach, USA, May 1958. *L-r behind Baba:* Ben Hayman with camera, Eruch Jessawala looking away from camera, and Delia de Leon in spotted dress. © Meher Nazar Publications.

Chapter 11

The 'Great Personal Disaster'

At the end of the four-month period of manonash, which was the culmination of the New Life, Baba dictated a statement summing up what had been achieved; divinity and humanity were now completely merged.

> For these last four months, according to ordinary human standards, and by ways and means known to me, I have tried my utmost for the achievement of manonash,[1] and I can say in all truth that I feel satisfied with the work done. This satisfaction is due to the feeling I have, of having regained my old-life Meher Baba state – yet retaining my New Life ordinary state. I have regained the Knowledge, Strength and Greatness that I had in the Old Life, and retained the ignorance, weaknesses and humility of the New Life. This union of the old and new life states has given birth to Life that is eternally old and new.
>
> Life for me now means:
>
> 1. Free and obligationless life.
> 2. Life of a Master in giving orders; and of a Servant in all humility.
> 3. The feeling of absolute conviction that we are all eternally One, Indivisible and Infinite in essence; and with it a feeling of separateness from the real Omnipresent Self, through ignorance.
> 4. Life of God in essence; and of a man in action.
> 5. Life of Strength born of inherent Knowledge of Oneness; and of weakness born of binding desires.[2]

Between the last day of 1951, when the above statement was dictated, and 16th February 1952, Baba was in seclusion. Following that seclusion there began a new phase of his life and work. This was divided into three periods, in each of which freedom was stressed and for each of which fixed dates were given. These dates were to prove deeply significant, particularly in view of the warnings he had recently expressed of some great danger he was facing.

Back on New Year's Day 1949, before he embarked on his 'Great Seclusion', Baba had sent out from Meherazad a circular to all devotees and followers giving warning of "a great personal disaster" to himself. In August of the same year, when preparations for the New Life were in hand, Baba had told the mandali that at some time after 1st October, "I shall be absolutely helpless in the true and literal sense of the word on account of some personal disaster to me." And again on 28th June 1951, shortly before the start of the four-month manonash period, Baba had caused a statement to be read out in the presence of many disciples and devotees. In this he spoke of his coming mental annihilation, and added that he would "... be facing physical annihilation as well, without my actually seeking it."

The three new periods now announced in February 1952 were named the 'Complicated Free Life'; the 'Full Free Life'; and the 'Fiery Free Life'. The first of these would last from the 21st March to the 10th July – that is from the vernal equinox when days and nights are of equal length throughout the world, to the anniversary of that day on which he had first entered on his silence. But for Baba, with his Persian background, the 21st March had a further significance, being the start of the Irani New Year, Persia's oldest festival, which dates back several thousand years and is observed in every home with great rejoicing.

During this first period, Baba said, "bindings will dominate freedom". What did this mean? 'Bindings' carries a special significance for Baba followers. Bindings are the *sanskaras* or 'attachments' resulting from our experiences over a long sequence of lives, modified or it may be intensified by further experiences in our present life. All our ambitions, hopes, fears; all our capacities, limitations and innate tendencies – in short everything which constitutes the 'personality' with which we entered upon our present life is the result of our sanskaras.

Every parent or teacher who has watched small children grow up has wondered how it is that one child is brave and another timid; one loving and another self-occupied or withdrawn; one eager to travel while another stays at home; one is musical or artistic and another cares only for material success. The truth, Baba tells us, is that all talents have been worked for; all so-called 'gifts' earned; all tendencies, whether for good or bad, have been acquired and cultivated; and all handicaps in some way brought upon ourselves.

The sum total of all our sanskaras constitutes our predisposition, our inborn attitude to life, which continues to exercise a powerful influence over each one of us from birth to death. Indeed the influence of sanskaras, Baba tells us, persists through many lives until they are weakened by time,[3] altered by change of heart, or until, if we should be so fortunate, they are unwound and dispelled by the help of a Perfect Master.

Did Baba's words then mean that between March and July destinies from the past would be working themselves out in a manner that would 'dominate' freedom in the present, and thus lead to the 'Free Life' being 'Complicated'? And, since Baba as a Perfect Master had long since liberated himself from his own sanskaras, did this imply that during these months he would be voluntarily identifying himself with his human aspect and undergoing suffering in the body, in order to ease the burden on humanity of its bindings from the past?

From the 10th July to the 14th November, 'freedom would dominate bindings' in what Baba called the 'Full Free Life', a period perhaps of identification with the divine aspect of himself. Then, on the 15th November, would begin the 'Fiery Free Life' in which both aspects would be united, and for this Baba gave the following explanation:

> The consuming of freedom and bindings (which is characteristic of the Fiery Free Life) means that there is a complete blending of the God-state and the man-state, so that the one does not live through opposition to the other, and there can be no question of the one encroaching upon the other.

> Spiritual freedom is essentially a positive state of conscious enjoyment of divinity. It does not have to maintain itself through the overcoming of any bindings, for these are not bindings of the soul in its essence, but temporary bindings of the body and the mind, which can in no way curtail the Bliss, Power or Understanding of conscious Divinity... After the annihilation of the limited mind, the infinite consciousness of the soul, with all its Knowledge, Power and Bliss, remains unaffected by any weaknesses or diseases to which the body may yield as a result of natural laws...
>
> Side by side with other activities of the Fiery Free Life, there will be one constant feature of that life, wherever it takes me. I shall bow down to the saints whom I adore, the *masts* whom I worship, and the poor, to whom I am wholeheartedly devoted. Nothing makes me more happy than to bow down to God in all these forms.
>
> In the Fiery Free Life, all the frailties of the ego-life are completely consumed; and there is complete emancipation from all wants, desires and temptations. And the result of this Fiery Free Life will make the world understand that Meher Baba, and everyone, is one with God.[4]

The phrase "wherever it takes me", used by Baba, clearly indicated that the Fiery Free Life would be one of travel, bringing many new personal contacts. It was therefore significant that he had already sent out Eruch and Pendu on a far-ranging tour of India and Pakistan in order to make preparations.

The 21st March 1952 was the date fixed for the start of that Complicated Free Life in which 'bindings were to dominate freedom', and in April Baba set out for the United States. "My work in the West will be done by women,"[5] he had once declared, and in the same way that he had sent two men throughout India to prepare for his Fiery Free Life, he had long since sent two women with a special charge to America. These were Elizabeth

Patterson, a successful American businesswoman who had devoted her whole life to Baba since first meeting him in 1931, and Princess Norina Matchabelli, the Italian-born American wife of a Georgian diplomat, famous for having played the Madonna in Max Reinhardt's production of *The Miracle*. For the past few years, on Baba's instructions, they had been establishing the Meher Spiritual Center at Myrtle Beach, 500 acres in a beautiful setting on the coast of South Carolina. This was now complete and Baba, who arrived in New York with five members of the mandali and four women disciples on the 19th April, came here with his party after only one night's rest. With them also were three women disciples from the West – Kitty Davy, Rano Gayley, and Delia de Leon who had come out from England to join the others.

Kitty Davy has recorded Baba's first sight of Myrtle Beach and how, after embracing Elizabeth and Norina, he spelled out on his board

> I have had many homes this time. I have laid My head on the ground (bowed down) in palaces and on concrete floors of humble homes. (Then Baba gestured over all the Center and continued,) Of all the homes I have visited, this is the home that I love the best, because it was given to Me and built for Me with such love... I never leave. Remember, I do not leave because this is My home.
>
> (Later he remarked,) Ages ago this was a place where I moved about and stayed, and the combination of the lake, the ocean and the woods gives it a unique atmosphere.[6]

After a stay of one month in the new Center, Baba sent some of the mandali on ahead to Meher Mount, a small estate over on the West Coast in California where the party would remain for a while. He himself and the others were to follow in two cars. Before setting out, Baba went up to Elizabeth who was sitting in the driver's seat and asked if she had her insurance policy with her. Hearing that it was at her house, he told her to stop there and pick it up. With them in the car were three of the women mandali who had chosen to follow Baba into the New Life (in which he would see, he had said, "who is out to die for no reason by going with me"), Mehera, Baba's sister Mani, and Mehera's niece Meheru R. Irani. The fourth, Dr Goher R. Irani, was in a station wagon driven by Sarosh, together with Kitty Davy, Delia de Leon and Rano Gayley.

Three nights were spent at different stops on the long journey westward, and on the morning of the 24th May, Kitty Davy records:

> We were up early as usual... After breakfast the group stood waiting in front of the motel for Baba's signal to step into the cars. This morning Baba delayed starting, however. He came out of His room and stood quite still for some minutes on the doorstep, withdrawn, sad and unusually still. No last minute questions, no haste to be off. Elizabeth sat at the wheel awaiting His signal. Ten minutes elapsed before Baba walked to the car, followed by the Eastern women. The rest of us got into Sarosh's car as before. After a short distance, Baba's car stopped suddenly and Baba got out and paced up and down on the right-hand side of the road. We too got out and stood by the car. No word was uttered...
>
> (Elizabeth Patterson now continues the account.) It had rained the night before and Route 64 was slippery, oil slick. The shoulder of the road was not wide and there were ditches on either side. As we came up over the crest of a small hill a car came along driving on the left-hand side of the road, going at a good clip. I started to slow up. The car continued without slowing up right at us on the left-hand side of the road. At any instant I expected him to turn... At the last instant he saw us and put on the brakes, whirling around to take up the

> entire side of the road. The point of contact was my bumper which made him whirl all the more.[7]

Baba, sitting in front, was flung out by the impact. His arm and leg were fractured, his head cut. Mehera and Meheru were also thrown out and injured. Elizabeth at the wheel was badly hurt, arms and wrists fractured and some ribs broken. Only Mani, who had been sleeping, had minor injuries. Baba, who had previously said that he must shed blood on American soil, was the only one who actually did so, a much worse disaster being averted by the fact that the ditch into which they were flung was unusually soft. Of the three people in the oncoming car not one was injured. "We learned later," Elizabeth writes, that the driver "was a Korean veteran, a double amputee, who was driving for the very first time that day a car made especially for him; also he was used to driving on the left-hand side in Japan... My one feeling was, 'Don't go in the ditch!'... Just before it happened Baba stretched out His hand and pointed at the oncoming car."

Delia de Leon recalls: "Baba had warned in India that an accident would befall him, but none of us gave it serious thought, though he kept warning us that we must keep with his car and not get lost, or he would never forgive us." During the morning the party in the following car stopped for a cold drink, and then put on speed to catch up. Delia continues:

> We could see no sign of His car and were beginning to get worried. It was about 10.05 a.m. We heard an exclamation of alarm from Sarosh. We turned our heads to the right. At first we could not take in what had happened; we could not see clearly from the car. We saw people standing round Baba, who seemed to be lying on the ground. The women were lying in various directions. Sarosh exclaimed, "Oh God, there's been an accident!"
>
> With lightning speed we jumped out of the car and rushed

> forward. The anguish of that moment is unforgettable... Baba's face with blood pouring from His head, the extraordinary expression on Baba's face, His eyes just staring straight ahead as if into unfathomable distances... Elizabeth was in the car doubled over the wheel. Her first question had been, "Is He alive?"

The first person to bring help was a man on his way into the little town of Prague, Oklahoma, seven miles away, where he was taking his wife to have a baby. He ordered out two ambulances which carried the injured to a small private hospital run by a Dr Burleson. Here they were excellently cared for, but it was two weeks before the party could leave, travelling by ambulance the 1,500 miles back to Myrtle Beach where they slowly recovered. In a letter dated 3rd June 1952, Dr Burleson wrote to Baba: "From you and your party we have seen a demonstration of most of the teachings of Christ. Many Americans preach these things but we have never observed so close an application of them. The profound devotion to you which is demonstrated by all your party convinces us that you deserve all of it. Such devotion cannot be forced, it can only be obtained by love; and to have that demonstrated affection from so many wonderful people is almost unbelievable. We are not accustomed to dealing with people who appreciate our efforts as you do, and the manifestation of this appreciation leaves us very humble..."

On the 13th June, Baba dictated a message to his followers.

> The personal disaster for some years[8] foretold by me has at last happened while crossing the American continent, causing me through facial injuries, a broken leg and arm, much mental and physical suffering. It was necessary that it should happen in America. God willed it so...
>
> It brings to fruition the first part of the circular which said

> that until July 10th (in the Complicated Free Life), weakness would dominate strength, and bindings would dominate freedom; but from July 10th, in my Full Free Life, strength would dominate weakness and freedom would dominate bindings; and then, from 15th November, in my Fiery Free Life, both strength and weakness, freedom and bindings, would be consumed in the fire of Divine Love.[9]

When sufficiently recovered, Baba returned to New York where he attended a number of meetings and gave interviews. From there on the 31st July he flew to London, staying for six days at the Hotel Rubens near Victoria, and giving interviews in, of all surprising places, one of those private rooms at the Charing Cross Hotel whose normal use was for small company meetings or salesmen's conferences. It was here that many of his British followers, including the two writers of this book, saw Baba for the first time. He was still in pain, with his leg encased in plaster, but he was cheerful and full of energy, seeing everyone

Meher Baba. Location: Locarno, Switzerland, August 1952. © Meher Nazar Publications.

who wished to see him. A number of entertainments had been arranged before Baba's injury was known, and he insisted on going through with the programme in case his companions might be disappointed. Among the shows to which he was taken were the circus, a 'spectacular' on ice, and the musical *South Pacific*. Baba's own interest, one may imagine, being mainly in the large rapt audiences and the opportunity to make contact while their outward attention was absorbed. On the 6th August, the party left for Switzerland, flying back two weeks later to Bombay.

Notes

1. *Manonash*: 'the elimination through love of mental domination and self-interest'. Cf. Chapter 10.
2. *The God-Man*, pp. 195–6
3. Cf. "If the fool would persist in his folly he would become wise." William Blake (1757–1827).
4. *The God-Man*, pp. 198–200
5. "Memories of '52" by Filis Frederick, *The Awakener Magazine*: vol. XIV, no. 2, p. 13
6. *Love Alone Prevails*, p. 386
7. This and remaining extracts from *Love Alone Prevails*, pp. 397–9
8. It had originally been foretold as far back as 1928.
9. *The God-Man*, pp. 203–4

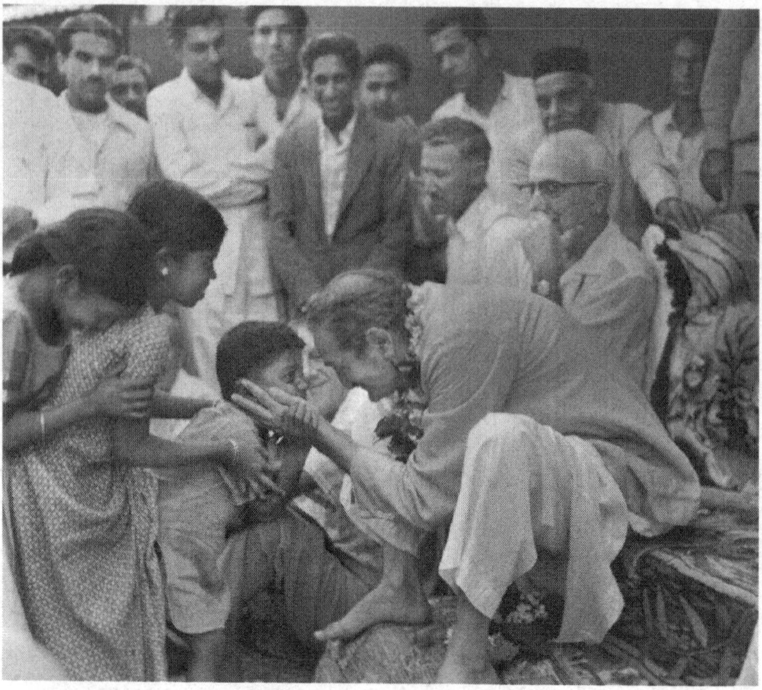

Darshan programme at Khushru Quarters, Ahmednagar, India, 26 September 1954. Baba is holding Suresh Panday (the son of the photographer Manohar Panday). *Behind Baba, l-r:* Krishna Nair, (unknown), Bhagirath, Thade, Beheram R. Irani, Frank Hendrick, Pappa, Kumar, Ben Hayman. © Meher Nazar Collection.

Chapter 12

'What Am I?'

During the years following his injury, Baba held a number of gatherings, mainly in India but also in the United States, and in addition paid shorter visits to Europe and Australia. At these gatherings, known as *sahavas*,[1] he made a series of statements plain enough for a child to understand, but with a power and authority unheard for two thousand years, covering the whole field of human life and of our relationship with God. These were made partly through prepared discourses read out by the mandali to groups of his assembled followers, and partly in answer to questions from his audiences. In both, certain themes continually recur.

Humanity's need is to get rid of the *false* self (ego), and liberate the *true* self (spirit) which is in every one of us. It is the ego which keeps us in a state of conflict and separation, while spirit seeks always to unite. The way to achieve liberation from the ego is through love. Love, in the word's true meaning, is not a mere emotion, nor is it something which appears naturally in us like eyesight. It has to be ardently sought and diligently developed, in the first place through service to others: "Emotion is not bad, but love is quite different."

Baba's demand is for honesty towards ourselves, towards others, and towards God – "God forgives everything except hypocrisy" – and for obedience among those claiming to be his followers. "Obedience is more than love. Love is a gift from the Beloved to the lover, whereas obedience is an offering from the lover to the Beloved."[2]

Above all, he spoke of the role of the Avatar or God-Man, which is *to awaken in us the knowledge of our own true nature*. By arousing love and a passion for service in our heart, the Avatar helps us to draw closer and ever closer to the divine within us, and so, over countless centuries and through many lives, to become 'God-realised' – oneness with God being the sole purpose of life.

In September 1953, the Fiery Free Life, in which would come about "a complete blending of the God-state and the man-state", reached its climax. At Dehra Dun – centre of country sacred to Siva – on the 7th September, reputed anniversary of the birth of Zoroaster,[3] he made an explicit statement of his own position as the latest, though not the last in the succession of Avataric appearances on earth:

> When God manifests on earth in the form of man and reveals his Divinity to mankind, he is recognised as the *Avatar* – thus God becomes Man…
>
> The *Avatar* is always one and the same, because God is always One and the Same, the Eternal, Indivisible, Infinite One… This Eternally One and the Same *Avatar* repeats his manifestation from time to time, in different cycles, adopting different human forms and different names, in different places, to reveal Truth in different garbs and different languages, in order to raise humanity from the pit of ignorance and free it from the bondage of delusions.
>
> Of the most recognised and much-worshipped manifestations of God as *Avatar*, that of Zoroaster is the earlier – having been before Rama, Krishna, Buddha, Jesus and Muhammad. Thousands of years ago, he gave to the world the essence of Truth in the form of three fundamental precepts – Good Thoughts, Good Words and Good Deeds. These precepts were and are constantly unfolded to humanity in one form or another, directly or indirectly in every cycle, by the *Avatar* of the Age, as he leads humanity towards the Truth.

Baba went on to declare that he was not one of the countless sadhus, saints, mahatmas, yogis of whom the world is full, and that if he is not to be included in their ranks, the question inevitably arises –

> then what am I? The natural assumption would be that I am either just an ordinary human being, or I am the Highest of the High…
>
> Now, if I am just an ordinary man, my capabilities and powers are limited – I am no better or different from an

ordinary human being. If people take me as such they should not expect supernatural help from me in the form of miracles or spiritual guidance; and to approach me to fulfil their desires would also be absolutely futile.

On the other hand, if I am beyond the level of an ordinary human being, and much beyond the level of saints and yogis, then I must be Highest of the High...

If I am the Highest of the High my Will is Law, my wish governs the Law, and my Love sustains the Universe. Whatever your apparent calamities and transient sufferings, they are but the outcome of my Love for the ultimate good. Therefore, to approach me for deliverance from your predicaments, to expect me to satisfy your worldly desires, would be asking me to undo what I have already ordained...

Know you all that if I am the Highest of the High, my role demands that I strip you of all your possessions and wants, consume all your desires and make you desireless rather than satisfy your desires...

Mere intellectuals can never understand me through their intellect. If I am the Highest of the High, it becomes impossible for the mind to gauge me nor is it possible for my ways to be fathomed by the human mind. I am not to be attained by those who, loving me, stand reverently by in rapt admiration. I am not for those who ridicule me and point at me with contempt. To have a crowd of tens of millions flocking around me is not what I am for. I am for the few who, scattered amongst the crowd, silently and unostentatiously surrender their all – body, mind and possessions – to me. I am still more for those who, after surrendering their all, never give another thought to their surrender...

From my point of view, far more blessed is the atheist who confidently discharges his worldly responsibilities accepting them as his honourable duty, than the man who presumes he is a devout believer in God, yet shirks the responsibilities apportioned to him through Divine Law, and runs after *sadhus*, saints and yogis, seeking relief from the suffering which ultimately would have pronounced his eternal liberation.

To have one eye glued on the enchanting pleasures of the flesh and with the other expect to see a spark of Eternal Bliss is not only impossible but the height of hypocrisy…

I declare to all of you who approach me, and to those of you who desire to approach me, accepting me as the Highest of the High, that you must never come with the desire in your heart which craves for wealth and worldly gain, but only with the fervent longing to give your all – body, mind and possessions with all their attachments. Seek me not to extricate you from your predicaments, but find me to surrender yourself wholeheartedly to my Will. Cling to me not for worldly happiness and short-lived comforts, but adhere to me, through thick and thin, sacrificing your own happiness and comforts at my feet. Let my happiness be your cheer and my comfort your rest. Do not ask me to bless you with a good job, but desire to serve me more diligently and honestly without expectation of reward. Never beg of me to save your life or the lives of your dear ones, but beg of me to accept you and permit you to lay down your life for me. Never expect me to cure you of your bodily afflictions, but beseech me to cure you of your ignorance. Never stretch out your hands to receive anything from me, but hold them high in praise of me whom you have approached as the Highest of the High.[4]

This was the most explicit and commanding public statement Baba had yet made about himself. On 1st March 1954, at Rajamundry, to a gathering of his workers from Andhra State, which began at nine in the evening and continued until three o'clock the following morning, Baba urged uncompromising honesty towards his claims.

Do not propagate what you do not feel. What your heart says and what your conscience dictates about me, pour out without hesitation. Be unmindful of whether you are ridiculed or accepted in pouring out your heart for me, or against me, to others.

If you take 'Baba' as God, say so; do not hesitate.

If you think 'Baba' is the Devil, say it. Do not be afraid.

I am everything that you take me to be, and I am also beyond everything... Of myself I say again and again, "I am the Ancient One – the Highest of the High."

(At Kakinada three weeks later, in a large hall filled with people, Baba declared) It has been possible through love for man to become God; when God becomes man it is due to his love.

If people were to ask me, "Have you seen God?" I would reply, "What else is there to see?" If they were to ask me, "Are you God?" I would reply, "Who else could I be?" If they were to ask me, "Are you *Avatar*?" I would reply, "Why else have I taken this human form?"[5]

These explicit and forceful statements had been made in India and to Indians. But now, in June 1954, Baba sent out invitations to select people from the West, as well as from India and Pakistan, to attend a 'meeting of meetings' at Meherabad during September. This was to be all-male, with no one present under sixteen years of age. From the East about a thousand assembled, and from the West a handful of seventeen men. They were present at a mass *darshan* at Wadia Park in Ahmednagar, where, to a gathering of some ten thousand people, Baba's message, now known as 'Meher Baba's Call', was broadcast, in English and Marathi.

Age after age, amidst the clamour of disruptions, wars, fear and chaos, rings the *Avatar*'s call: "Come all unto Me."

Although, because of the veil of illusion, this Call of the

Ancient One may appear as a voice in the wilderness, its echo and re-echo nevertheless pervades through time and space, to rouse at first a few, and eventually millions, from their deep slumber of ignorance. And in the midst of illusion, as the Voice behind all voices, it awakens humanity to bear witness to the manifestation of God amidst mankind.

The time is come. I repeat the Call, and bid all to come unto me… I tell you all with my Divine authority, that you and I are not 'We', but 'One'… There is nothing but God. He is the only Reality, and we are all one in the indivisible Oneness of this absolute Reality…

Awaken from your ignorance, and try at least to understand that in the uncompromisingly Indivisible Oneness, not only is the *Avatar* God, but also the ant and the sparrow, just as one and all of you are nothing but God. The only apparent difference is in the states of consciousness. The Avatar knows that that which is a sparrow is not a sparrow, whereas the sparrow does not realise this, and, being ignorant of its ignorance, remains a sparrow.

Live not in ignorance. Do not waste your precious life-span in differentiating and judging your fellow men, but learn to long for the love of God. Even in the midst of your worldly activities, live only to find and realize your true Identity with your Beloved God.

Be pure and simple, and love all because all are one. Live a sincere life; be natural and be honest with yourself.[6]

To those attending the sahavas Baba showed concern for every detail of their health and comfort, urging them to be completely open and to speak their minds.

If the food does not agree with you, say so. If there is anything you don't like, say so… Don (Dr Donkin) is in charge of your health. If you have any difficulty of any kind, tell him… After

> all, you have come a great distance to attend these meetings, and I want you to receive as much as you possibly can from them. When they are over, I want you to go home as quickly and directly as possible, so that you can carry with you, still fresh, what you have received.

The visitors from the West were with Baba for some three weeks, during which time he gave them an intimacy of personal contact: "I am your Master, but I am also your friend. I am one of you, and one with you." He talked to them about his early life, about the nature of the universe, about the differences between states of trance and true God-realisation. At times he revealed an almost childlike aspect of himself. Following a profound explanation of the nature of the ego, and of what is meant by purity of heart, he remarked:

> Sometimes I feel, why explain anything? Just come, sit down, you all here, be quiet, and be in company with Baba. Sometimes I feel like explaining things. I wonder which is better. What shall we do? Shall we go on explaining, or shall we be quiet?

At times his humour gleamed through unexpectedly. When one of his devotees read out in Sanskrit a passage from the *Bhagavad Gita* in which Krishna speaks of the coming of the Avatar, "Age after age, from time immemorial, for the destruction of ignorance, for the preservation of Truth, I have taken human form," Baba remarked when he had finished: "You say this as if you were swimming in mid-ocean and attacked by sharks." He then added wryly, "I have created everything, and yet I don't know Sanskrit. I just nod my head as if I knew."[7]

As the final act in this 'meeting of meetings', at 3 p.m. on Thursday, 30th September 1954, Eruch read out Meher Baba's "Final Declaration":

I have not come to establish anything new – I have come to put life into the old. I have not come to establish retreats or ashrams. I create them for the purpose of my universal work, only to repeatedly dissolve them once that purpose has been served.

The universe is my ashram, and every heart is my house; but I manifest only in those hearts in which all, other than me, ceases to live.

When my universal religion of love is on the verge of fading into insignificance, I come to breathe life into it and to do away with the farce of dogmas that defile it in the name of religions and stifle it with ceremonies and rituals.

The present universal confusion and unrest has filled the heart of man with greater lust for power and a greed for wealth and fame, bringing in its wake untold misery, hatred, jealousy, frustration and fear. Suffering in the world is at its height, in spite of all the striving to spread peace and prosperity to bring about lasting happiness…

(Baba went on to make the statement which would cause intense discussion among his followers.) The time has come for the pre-ordained destruction of multiple separateness which keeps man from experiencing the feeling of unity and brotherhood. This destruction which will take place very soon, will cause three-fourths of the world to be destroyed. The remaining one-fourth will be brought together to live a life of concord and mutual understanding, thus establishing a feeling of oneness in all fellow beings, leading them towards lasting happiness…

To affirm religious faiths, to establish societies, or to hold conferences will never bring about the feeling of unity and oneness in the life of mankind, now completely absorbed in the manyness of illusion. Unity in the midst of diversity can be made to be felt only by touching the very core of the heart. That is the work for which I have come.

I have come to sow the seed of love in your hearts so that, in spite of all superficial diversity which your life in illusion must experience and endure, the feeling of oneness, through love, is brought about amongst all the nations, creeds, sects and castes of the world.

(And Baba continued by making one of his mysterious references to the end of his silence and the Word which he would speak.) In order to bring this about, I am preparing to break my silence. When I break my silence it will not be to fill your ears with spiritual lectures. I shall speak only one Word, and this Word will penetrate the hearts of all men and make even the sinner feel that he is meant to be a saint, while the saint will know that God is in the sinner as much as he is in himself.

When I speak that Word, I shall lay the foundation for that which is to take place during the next seven hundred years. When I come again after seven hundred years the evolution of consciousness will have reached such an apex that materialistic tendencies will be automatically transmuted into spiritual longing, and the feeling of equality in spiritual brotherhood will prevail. This means that opulence and poverty, literacy and illiteracy, jealousy and hatred, which are in evidence today in their full measure, will then be dissolved through the feelings of the oneness of all men. Prosperity and happiness will then be at their zenith.

The full "Final Declaration",[8] which was read out in English, and then translated into Hindi, Marathi, Gujerati and Telegu, was received in complete silence. Following it, the whole company broke up and went to their own homes.

During the weeks following the sahavas, Baba's statement that "three-fourths of the world will be destroyed", and about the Word which he would shortly speak, caused much discussion among his followers. At Satara in November, Baba gave a "Clarification and Confirmation of the Final Declaration", in which he said:

> It is really very difficult for anyone to believe and understand what I say, because none can grasp the meaning underlying my words... Everyone is free to interpret my words in any way they think and feel. But one thing I tell you, that whenever I say a thing, I naturally use my own 'language', and whatsoever is said by me is truth. But, my 'language' is such that none can understand or grasp the underlying meaning

Meher Baba having a lunch break from the Dashan programme with Saint Gadge Maharaj sitting to his left and Sarosh Irani (standing) talking to Baba. Location: Darshan programme, Wadia Park, India, 1954. © Meher Nazar Publications.

of what I say; therefore, when I want to say a thing I have simultaneously to make use of your language also, knowing well that you would understand nothing whatsoever if I were to make use of my 'language' alone.

(To this Baba added that what he had dictated on the alphabet board during the meeting at Meherabad concerning) the breaking of my silence and my uttering the one Word of words: was said in my own 'language' and simultaneously in yours, (and that what he had dictated about) the destruction of three-fourths of the world: was said in my own 'language' alone.[9]

Notes

1. *Sahavas*: Lit. close companionship. A gathering where there is the intimacy of give and take between the devotees/lovers and the Beloved.
2. *The God-Man*, p. 303
3. Zoroaster: Founder of the Zoroastrian (or Parsi) religion into which Baba had been born.
4. For the whole of this all-important declaration cf. *The God-Man*, pp. 210–4.
5. *The God-Man*, p. 218
6. *The God-Man*, pp. 222–4
7. *The God-Man*, p. 263. The languages Baba spoke were Persian, English, Hindi, Gujerati, Urdu and Marathi.
8. Given in *The God-Man*, pp. 272–5
9. *The God-Man*, pp. 277–8

Meher Baba 'You and I are not we but One.' Location: Ganeshkhind, Pune. Date: April, June, or August 1957. Photographer: Meelan / © Meher Nazar Publications.

Chapter 13

A 'So-Called Tragedy'

For three months, in the middle of 1955 Baba was in seclusion, but towards the end of that year he gave sahavas at Meherabad. One of those present, Don Stevens, an American devotee now resident in Europe, has written a full and illuminating account in his book *Listen, Humanity*.[1] At these sahavas, given largely for his Indian followers, Baba stressed the importance of living in the world and not retreating from it. Among those attending was one, Mouni Bua, who had been keeping silence for many years. Baba ordered him to speak, which he did, just as on other occasions he had ordered a holy man to eat or to take a drink.

From the start of the sahavas Baba emphasised the importance of obedience.

The three most important things on the path to God-realisation are love, obedience and surrender. There is no possibility of compromise about these three.

Love is a gift from God to man, obedience is a gift from master to man, and surrender is a gift from man to master. The one who loves, desires to do the will of the beloved, and seeks union with the beloved. Obedience performs the will of the beloved and seeks the pleasure of the beloved. Surrender resigns to the will of the beloved and seeks nothing…

In spite of the difference between a keenly intelligent person and a very unintelligent person, each is equally capable of experiencing love. The quality which determines one's capacity for love is not one's wit or wisdom, but one's readiness to lay down life itself for the beloved, and yet remain alive. One must, so to speak, slough off body, energy, mind and all else, and become dust under the feet of the beloved. This dust of a lover who cannot remain alive without God – just as an ordinary man cannot live without breath – is then transformed into the beloved. Thus man becomes God…

Love God and become God. I have come to receive your love and to give you mine… If you love me you will find me. Unless you love me, you can never find me.[2]

On the following day Baba returned to the theme he had already broached – that truth is to be found by living an outwardly normal life, and not through ascetic practices or religious routines, the path followed by so many Eastern seekers and holy men.

The whole of creation is a play of thoughts: the outcome of the mind. It is your own mind which binds you, and it is also the mind which is the means of your freedom…

Every human mind is a gigantic storehouse of accumulated and fast-changing impressions. How can one gain an adequate idea of these impressions left by innumerable actions – and particularly those born of anger, lust and greed – during the lengthy course of the evolution of man's consciousness through the progressive stages of the mineral, vegetable and animal kingdoms of life?

The obvious remedies for this situation are to use no remedies. For example, if one engages in a secluded life of mere physical renunciation, one is more likely to drive underground than eliminate the dirt of impressions from one's mind...

By becoming physically free of the bindings created by the impressions in your mind, you have not rooted them out of your mind. Although your *body* may be temporarily freed, as it is in the sound-sleep state, yet your *mind* remains bound by the impressions. Even when the body itself is dropped you do not become free, for your mind remains bound by the impressions which the mind has created.

Even as the mind cannot be freed of bindings by mere physical renunciation, so the heart cannot be purified by mere mechanical following of the external form and fads of religion. One must act on principles and not by rituals...

It is better not to worship if your heart is not in it. Any prayer made mechanically in a spirit of show or ceremony is all a farce. It results in greater bindings through one's pretence to purity. Similarly, a self-imposed fast, if not observed through a sense of obedience or through love of truth, may make a clock the object of your fast through watching to see when it is time to stop. Such actions tighten more than they loosen the bindings of impressions...

The best way to cleanse the heart and prepare for the stilling of the mind is to lead a normal, worldly life. Living in the midst of your day-to-day duties, responsibilities, likes and dislikes, becomes the very means for the purification of your heart...

For the purification of your heart, leave your thoughts alone but maintain a constant vigil over your actions... Let

> the thoughts of anger, lust and greed come and go freely without putting them into words and deeds. Then the related impressions in your mind begin to wear out and become less and less harmful. But when you put such thoughts into action – whether overtly or secretly – you develop new impressions which root even more firmly in your mind... Therefore, when you feel angry or have lustful thoughts, remember Baba at once. Let my name serve as a net around you. Remember me so often that your mind is at a loss to find other thoughts to feed on... If you cannot remember me constantly, then always repeat my name on going to sleep and on waking up.[3]

Early in 1956 Baba went into retirement at Satara, and on 15th February he announced that he would be in complete retirement for one year, except for a visit to the West which he had promised for July. As the time for this drew near, he sent out a message to his Western followers:

> A great so-called tragedy is facing me and my lovers. My long-expected humiliation is near at hand. This may happen tomorrow or any day of this year, or it may happen next year. The love, courage and faith of my lovers will be put to a severe test, not by me, but by Divine Law.[4]

In mid-July 1956, Baba was in London, staying at the Hotel Rubens near Victoria. There had been conflict among the British group,[5] and Baba devoted a morning to listening to the views of those involved. He obliged everyone to speak out openly, voicing their criticisms and complaints in front of one another. Finally he issued clear-cut instructions for future working; personally arranged for a transfer of funds to put the group back on its feet, and affirmed that he himself would be its President – an office which he never resigned and therefore, in the eyes of all its members, continues holding to this day.

Throughout his stay Baba showed that attention to detail and insistence on efficiency and punctuality with which his mandali were already familiar. He was at work each day by 5 a.m., and if he had ordered a meeting for 9 o'clock, he was in the room as the hour was striking. For the evening reception, held in one of the hotel's largest public rooms, a British devotee had arranged a spectacular setting. Against a background of purple hangings, on a settee placed in the centre of one wall, covered with satin and velvet cushions and flanked with massive flower displays, Baba looked truly regal, as some two hundred followers came up one by one to be greeted. It was a moving scene, and for most of those present it constituted their last visual memory of their Master, since he never again visited Britain.

From London Baba flew to New York where he stayed a week, followed by another at Myrtle Beach, and then went on to Australia. By mid-August he was back in India, in seclusion at Satara. In the last days of November he told those about him that the month or so preceding the end of his seclusion on 15th February 1957 would hold increased and concentrated suffering for himself, in which a number of his close ones would also share. They had not long to wait.

On Sunday, the 2nd December, Baba was returning to Satara from a day's visit to Poona. It was a dull, overcast day with little traffic and scarcely any foot passengers on the road. Eruch, skilled and careful, who had driven Baba many thousands of miles, was at the wheel with Baba beside him. In the back sat three of the mandali – Pendu, Vishnu (Vishnu N. Deorukhkar) and Dr Nilkanth N. Godse, known as 'Nilu'. Suddenly, as they were running easily and at moderate speed, the car went out of control and crashed against a low stone culvert, overturning and flinging most of its occupants out. This happened at about 5.15 p.m.[6] The road was good and there was nothing in sight, no other vehicle, no walkers, not even a stray goat or a squawking hen. There was neither puncture nor skidding, the speed was under 40 miles an hour and the car had previously been in good order. Eruch said later that the steering wheel "seemed to stop co-ordinating", the car swerved straight towards the culvert, and he remembered no more till he came to.

The accident was as serious as it was inexplicable. Baba's face and head were badly hurt and his tongue torn, in addition he sustained damage to his right hip, which later proved to be a fracture of the hip bone socket. Eruch suffered four broken ribs; Pendu's leg was seriously damaged, causing him afterwards to limp, and his mouth was injured in a way that would affect his speech for the remainder of his life; Vishnu was less seriously hurt; but Nilu was unconscious and appeared to be in a bad way.

Vishnu, on coming to, found himself alone in the back of the car. Climbing out, he went to the front and saw Baba in the front seat with blood on his clothes and face. After some moments he asked Baba if he was badly hurt. Baba nodded, pointing to his mouth and leg, but indicated to Vishnu to attend first to the three who had been flung out. Eruch meantime had managed, with a tremendous effort, to stand up and speak to Baba, supporting himself against the car. Three minutes after the crash a man going to Poona came along, lifted Baba and Vishnu into his own car and drove them back down the road to Satara. Not long after a truck arrived and carried the three others to the mandali's quarters. Eruch and Pendu were at once taken to hospital, but Nilu died in the truck without regaining consciousness.

Some days previous to the accident, Baba had smilingly told the mandali, "We may all die in a few days." Turning to Nilu, he said, "Don't worry about anything. Keep thinking of me constantly. I am the only One that exists, the only One that matters." During his period in hospital after the accident, Baba said of Nilu's death, "It is as he would have wanted it. He is blessed to be with me."

This period, winter 1956, was that of the Hungarian rising and its harsh suppression by the Russians. On the morning after the crash, Baba made one of his rare comments on public affairs, for though in normal circumstances he followed the day-to-day progress of events closely, he almost never spoke of them except in general terms. But now he said with gestures to those about him: "The Hungarians are suffering much in their present struggle. Many lie wounded and helpless on the roads, away from their loved ones and from care and relief from pain. At least, I am lying on a bed, with the care of good doctors, and the love of all my lovers, present and absent."

The injuries to Baba's face and mouth required stitching but did not take long to heal. What proved far more difficult to treat was the damage to his hip. After a week in Satara, when complications had set in and the pain was exceedingly severe, Baba accepted the doctor's pleas that he should be conveyed to Poona where better facilities existed. Here the plaster cast, which had been put around his pelvis and entire right leg, was removed, and his right leg put into traction, with all the acute suffering this can entail.

At a time when the pain was excruciating, Baba traced with his finger a little circle on the spot where the fracture had occurred and then made a wide circle in the air. "The suffering of the whole universe," he indicated, "is concentrated in this little spot. This is a tangible expression of the universal suffering I bear."[7]

Despite the pain, he expressed more than once to those about him: "I am happy. It is as I wanted it." He also said: "Nobody suffers in vain, for true freedom is spiritual freedom and suffering is a ladder towards it... Men unknowingly suffer for God, and God knowingly suffers for man."[8]

By the end of the first week of January 1957, Baba was sitting up in bed for a few minutes at a time and taking more solid food. At the request of his advisers, however, and in view of the slow progress he was making and the continued pain, a famous London orthopaedic surgeon was consulted, X-rays of the hip being flown over for him to examine. He had treated Baba previously and now said he would be willing to postpone all other work and fly out to India to perform a specialist operation, which he said was essential if Baba were ever to recover completely and be able to walk naturally. Baba sent his thanks but refused the operation, and it was accepted by those about him that he refused because his suffering formed an essential accompaniment to his inner work. "The accident has been a blessing for the universe," he said one evening when the pain was bad, "and a curse for Baba."

Towards the end of 1957 a blind chiropractor from New York, Dr Harry Kenmore, arrived and began to give Baba treatment, with which Baba said he was very pleased: "He has done his best with satisfactory results." Late in November Baba stated that the sahavas, for which his followers all over the world had been hoping, were to be held, first for the Easterners at Meherabad in February 1958, and for the Westerners at Myrtle Beach in May. To them Baba sent the following message:

> My suffering is daily becoming more intense, and my health is daily getting worse, but my physical body continues to bear the burden. Despite it I shall hold the *sahavas*. I expect from you a deep understanding of my self-imposed suffering, begotten of compassion and love for mankind. Also understand, therefore, that I shall not undergo medical examinations or treatments for my injured hip either in America or Australia. No doctor or treatment will be of any help before the pain I am undergoing has served its purpose.
>
> This *sahavas* will be unique in the sense that you will witness and share my present universal suffering by being near me as my fortunate companions – being with the Ancient One, who will be completely on the human level with you...
>
> I may give you more, much more, than you expect – or maybe nothing, and that nothing may prove to be everything. So I say, come with open hearts to receive much or nothing

> from your Divine Beloved. Come prepared to receive not so much of my words but of my Silence.[9]

For the Eastern sahavas, devotees were organised into two groups according to language, each group remaining for five days. In all more than 1,500 persons attended, each of whom was embraced by Baba on arrival and departure. One devotee from Hamirpur in Northern India, where there exists a long tradition of devotion to Baba, walked the entire distance of more than 1,000 miles, over mountains and rivers and through jungles, taking forty days.

The scene when the sahavas ended was something that could happen only in India. Meherabad is about six miles from the nearest railway station. But with the help of a high official, who was also a devotee, it was arranged that special trains should stop on the track at Meherabad for the departure of each group.

> There were streamers of little Baba-flags (of seven colours) round the engine, and a big one hoisted in front. Outside some of the compartments were pasted pictures of Baba, and there were also banners with the words
>
> Avatar Meher Baba
> Is the Soul of souls,
> The Beloved of the gods,
> The Life of His lovers
> And the Slave of His dear ones.
>
> (When the train was full, Baba's car was driven down so that he could wave goodbye.) Immediately there rose tremendous cheers of "BABA! BABA! Avatar Meher Baba ki Jai!!"[10] from every compartment, and when it was obvious they were all intending to leave the train to surge towards Baba's car, He waved a hand and gestured they should not come down... Baba acknowledged the salute of the engine driver and gestured that he should start the train. After a very

> long piercing whistle the 'Baba-train' moved forward, and as the long line of packed compartments filed past Beloved's car, the air thundered with reverberating cries of "Avatar Meher Baba ki Jai." Many were standing on the running boards, the rest leaning way out of the windows till we thought some would surely fall out; some hands folded reverently, hundreds of others waving ecstatically. Baba acknowledged their love with joined hands, or waved and gestured, "I am happy; take Me with you." When the train was out of sight Baba turned to us and said, "They take with them a spark of Me – and will spread My Love everywhere."[11]

Three months later the Western sahavas was held at Myrtle Beach in South Carolina. Two hundred and twenty-five men and women assembled from all over the US and Mexico, from France, Switzerland, Israel and Britain. The sahavas took a dramatic course. On the first full day Baba faced the assembled followers with a straight demand for acceptance of himself as Avatar and the obedience which must follow such acceptance.

"What I want is love and obedience... Discourses and messages are good, but are mere words... In the spiritual path there is no room for compromise. Raise your hands who cannot obey me." None raised a hand. "Now raise your hands all who will *try* to obey me!" Everyone raised his hand.[12]

In spiritual matters the compromise most acceptable to Western minds is to regard the Master as a saint or unusually holy man. Once planted in this convenient niche and suitably labelled, he can be left to go on being holy while the disciple feels no obligation either to obey his instructions or refute his claims. But Baba would have none of this.

> I am not a saint. I am the Ancient One; and I tell you, the time has come. When I drop my body, I shall remain in all who love me. I can never die. Love me, obey me, and you will find me.

After listing different types of obedience, leading up to "a fifth obedience which is very rare, absolute obedience, in which light becomes dark[13] and dark becomes light because the Master says so," Baba went on: "It is impossible to obey me one hundred per cent unless you have one hundred per cent love for me and accept me one hundred per cent as God incarnate. So it is for you who have raised your hands to do my will. The purpose of my coming to the West has been accomplished. Tomorrow we will start discourses..."

But tomorrow they did not start discourses, and on the day following when they met again it was to hear from Baba that he was thinking of cutting the sahavas short, cancelling a proposed visit to Australia and flying straight back to India. Faced with the consternation of the company who had made plans to remain for three weeks, Baba reminded them that only the day before yesterday they had all raised hands signifying obedience – and now his first instruction was to remain happy whether his stay among them was cut short or not. He told them not to think about their homes and worldly interests, but to concentrate on Baba, and he reminded them of the words of his favourite poet Hafiz: "To be with a Perfect Master for one moment is equal to a hundred years of sincere prayer with all one's heart and soul." Don Stevens then read a message to all from Baba.

> I am the Ocean of Love. Draw as much of this love as possible. Make the most of this opportunity. It rests with you to draw as much love as you can out of the Ocean. It does not rest with me to explain to you how you should love me. Does a husband or a wife explain to one another how to love? One thing is certain; I want to give you my love. It depends on each of you to receive it. The easy way to receive it is to forget your home, family and all worldly affairs, when you are here, and be receptive to my love. This is the first thing. The second thing is to have a good night's rest and feel fresh

> when you come here for my *sahavas* each day. I am God: If you remain drowsy in my presence, you will miss me and your drowsiness will oblige you to remain absent from my presence, in spite of your daily attendance.

Understanding the bias of modern people who want everything kept on the intellectual plane so that it can be apprehended, chewed over, discussed, Baba stressed that his sahavas was not some sort of seminar or study course:

> *Sahavas* is the intimacy of give and take between the lovers and the Beloved. There is no need to explain this give and take, for to create an atmosphere of explanations and discourses is to mar the dignity of love which is established only in the closest intimacy... Take fullest advantage of this opportunity in the living presence of the *Avatar*. Forget everything else but my *sahavas* and concentrate all your attention on me. I am the Ancient One.

Through the parable of a pet lion, Baba summed up the need for absolute surrender to God.

> My lovers may be likened to one who is fond of lions and admires them so much that he keeps a lion in his own home. But being afraid of the lion he puts him in a cage. The lion is always encaged; even while he feeds the lion, he feeds the pet animal from a distance and from outside the cage. Baba is treated like the lion by the lovers. There is love; there is admiration; there is an intense desire to see Baba comfortable and happy; and Baba is also frequently fed by love of the lovers. But all this is done, keeping Baba segregated from one's own self. What is wanted of the lovers is that they should open the 'cage' and, through intense love, throw themselves inside the cage to become food for the lion of love. The lover

should permit himself to be totally consumed through his own love for the Beloved.

What stands in the lover's way? The intellect, the sense of personal identity, fear to merge and to surrender. So the lover takes refuge in mentalisation, in discussion, but "In spite of all explanations and reading of books, words remain mere words. They do not take one any further than intellectual satisfaction. Only love for God works the miracle, because love is beyond mind and reason. Where then is the necessity to read?"

Despite his suggestion of an early departure, Baba, as often, had regard to the general wish and remained to the end of the month, making his stay one of fourteen instead of eighteen days, and going on afterwards to Australia for another three. And despite his rejection of discourses and explanations, he allowed discourses to be given and discussions to take place. Throughout all explanations and discussions, Baba stressed only one theme – obedience and love.

> Once you were a child; now you have grown up. During the period from childhood until now you have gone through moments of great joy and sorrow. Where has all that gone? The fact is neither joy nor sorrow was there; it is due to *maya* (illusion) that you think of and experience things which have no foundation. Within 20 or 30 years you will also forget the thoughts and events of today. So the best thing for you to do is just to love me. Love me honestly, work for me, I alone endure; all else is but a passing show! There should not be any trace of show in the work you do for me. You should have no expectations of reward for any work you do.

And when someone was introduced to Baba with all his qualifications listed as is the American custom, Baba replied: "I am unmindful of these qualifications. The only qualification I want you to have is love. I see whether one loves or not," and then added with that childlike directness that took away the pain of a rebuke, "You love me and I am pleased with you."

For Westerners man has traditionally been associated with intellect and action, woman with intuition and feeling. Baba had said that his work in the West would be done by women, and several times during the sahavas he emphasised the importance of woman's role, symbolised throughout his life by the special position he always gave to Mehera and the women mandali. Here too he made use of a parable.

> God is One. He is both father and mother in One. He is in everyone and in everything; but God is beyond this too. I will tell you about God in the Beyond state. In the Beyond state God is both God the father and God the mother simultaneously.
>
> Now we will discuss the worldly father and mother. Suppose a couple has seven sons. It is natural for the father to love those sons who are useful to him, who are healthy, intelligent, brilliant... Now the six sons of this worldly father are healthy, strong, intelligent and good in all respects; the seventh son is a disabled weakling, innocent, simple and guileless. The father has no love for this seventh son and loves only his six sons. But the mother loves her seventh son the most because he is weak, sick, disabled, simple and guileless.
>
> God is both the father and mother in One. The *Avatars* are Sons of the Father in the Beyond state. All past *Avataric* periods witnessed the presence of the *Avatar* as the healthy, bright, wise son of God. All this means that the *Avatar* always remained the Beloved Son of the Father. Note that the *Avatar* always takes a male form and mingles with mankind as man.
>
> Hitherto, God in the Beyond state did not have occasion to play the part of God the Mother. In this *Avataric* period, God the Father is very pleased with me at my being infinitely bright, wise, efficient and perfect in all respects (*Ustad*

> or 'shrewd') as my Father wants me to be, and I am the beloved Son of my Father. At the same time, in this form I am physically disabled. In America, in 1952, I was injured on the left[14] side of my physical frame from leg to face. In India, in 1956, I injured my right side from the head down to the leg. Besides being physically disabled, I am also infinitely simple and guileless. Thus, I am also the well-beloved Son of my God the Mother. So, in this incarnation, God has the occasion, as it were, to play the part of both Father and Mother.

Under the heading 'My Wish', a short discourse was read of which Baba said, "Listen carefully; it is very important for my lovers." It consisted of a brief list of instructions.

> The lover has to keep the wish of the Beloved. My wish for my lovers is as follows:
>
> 1. Do not shirk your responsibilities.
> 2. Attend faithfully to your worldly duties, but keep always at the back of your mind that all this is Baba's.
> 3. When you feel happy, think: 'Baba wants me to be happy.' When you suffer, think: 'Baba wants me to suffer.'[15]
> 4. Be resigned to every situation and think honestly and sincerely: 'Baba has placed me in this situation.'
> 5. With the understanding that Baba is in everyone, try to help and serve others.
> 6. I say with my Divine Authority to each and all that whosoever takes my name at the time of breathing his last comes to me; so do not forget to remember me in your last moments. Unless you start remembering me from now on, it will be difficult to remember me when your end approaches. You should start practising from now on. Even if you take my name only once every day, you will not forget to remember me in your dying moments.

A week later Baba left for Australia, where, under the direction of Francis Brabazon, the Australian poet who would for years be one of his mandali, a centre had been constructed. Baba remained with his Australian followers for three days, and then flew back to India.

This had been his last visit to the Western world, and this was the last time most of his Western followers would ever see him.

Meher Baba with Mehera and Mani. Location: Meherazad, 1944. Khandoba Hill can be seen in the background. Photographer: Naggu / © MSI Collection.

Notes

1. Don Stevens passed away in London in 2011. He brought out a number of Baba books and, following Baba's instruction, saw to the translation of Baba's words into major European languages. (Ed.)
2. *Listen, Humanity*, from pp. 16–20
3. *Listen, Humanity*, condensed from pp. 38–45

4. *The God-Man*, p. 287
5. It is now known as the Meher Baba Association.
6. Some sources have 4.45 p.m. as the time of the accident. (Ed.)
7. *Family Letters*, "Special Circular..." 17th December 1956.
8. That is, man suffers, to attain knowledge of God, his own true Self. And God incarnate suffers for the betterment of humanity.
9. *The God-Man*, p. 296
10. Literally, 'Hail' or 'Victory to Avatar Meher Baba!' A form of salutation.
11. *Family Letters*, condensed from Letter 18
12. This and the remainder of the chapter are condensed from *The God-Man*, pp. 297–320
13. Note: 'becomes dark'; not simply that the disciple accepts the Master's statement without dissent.
14. Analytically, the left is regarded as the female side, the right as masculine.
15. Tom and Dorothy wrote... When you suffer, don't worry; say, 'It is Baba's grace.' (Ed.)

The East-West Gathering, Pune, November 1962. © MSI Collection.

Chapter 14

The Long Seclusion

During the twelve months following the 1958 sahavas Baba withdrew more and more from outward contact. His recent visits to the West were the last, he said, that he would make, and he warned all his followers to expect no more discourses, interviews or gatherings. Even correspondence was not allowed except as a cable in an emergency. Baba spoke often of a coming crisis and the breaking of his silence which would ensue: "On my own I shall not break my silence. Universal crisis will make me do so."

At the beginning of March 1959, Baba went for one week to Bombay where he paid visits to a school and an industrial home for the blind. Though he said nothing to indicate this at the time, these were almost the last such visits he would make. For the next ten years his outward life would be lived in only two places less than a hundred miles apart – Meherazad, the cluster of buildings in a garden setting a few miles north of the small town of Ahmednagar which had been his principal 'home' since 1944, and Guruprasad, an ornamental bungalow on the outskirts of Poona up in the hills, to which Baba and the mandali moved every year for three months from April to June. Guruprasad belonged to a devoted follower, the Maharanee of Baroda, who kept the house with its acres of grounds and gardens available so that Baba could avoid the extreme heat of the plains in summer.

At first Baba used the visits to Guruprasad to allow breaks in his seclusion and to continue those special receptions for the poor, the outcast and the suffering which he had maintained for the past forty years. As knowledge of Baba spread slowly over the continent a tremendous pressure was building up among those who wished to see and touch him, or who hoped to derive benefit, spiritual or material, from being in his presence. In May and June 1960, Baba gave darshan to crowds estimated at more than 10,000 in one day, assembling from all parts of India. During June also there were two of those receptions for the poor to which he always brought a special intensity of love. The description which follows is taken from the *Family Letters* written by Baba's sister Mani (Manija Sheriar Irani). These letters, sent out every two or three months to Western followers, form the only connected record for the last ten years of Baba's life on earth, but many will have had glimpses of the following scene in films and videos of Baba's life.

At this Poona program, 160 poor people, both men and women, each received Rs.5 from Baba's hand after He had placed His head on the feet of each one… Baba sat in a chair before an old table with improvised steps that served as a 'platform'. Each one climbed on to this, and stood before Baba for Him to bow down, while his recipient was strictly instructed not to express thanks or reverence by word or gesture. To have seen Baba place His forehead on these unshod, dusty (and often gnarled and horny) pairs of feet, is not only a deeply moving emotion of the moment, but a never to be forgotten experience.

The Ahmednagar program[1] was for 150 very poor people, mostly lepers (many of them in a highly advanced state of malignancy), each receiving Rs.5 and a piece of cloth from Baba after He had washed their feet with loving care and touched their feet with His forehead. Eruch tells us this program took nearly two hours, and the exertion left Baba drenched in perspiration as well as from the water that had splashed on Him when washing the lepers' feet with His beautiful bare hands. While the *prasad* (gift) of money is an unfailingly welcome relief, in the case of the lepers it seemed overshadowed by their touching incredulity and happiness at Baba's expression of Love for them, these usually shunned and 'untouchable' children of God.[2]

From Meherazad, at the end of June, Baba sent out a message to his followers reinforcing the warnings already given:

> I want you to remain undisturbed and unshaken by the force of life's currents, for whatever the circumstances they too will be of my own creation.
>
> I want you to remain absorbed as much as possible in thinking of me during my seclusion of six months, when circumstances… will try to drift you away from me. This is the reason why I have repeatedly stressed, while at Guruprasad, that the time has come when I want you all to cling to my

> *daaman*[3] with both hands – in case the grip of one hand is lost, your other will serve in good stead.
>
> And lastly, I want you all to remember not to disturb me in any way during my seclusion, not even by writing to me to acknowledge this or to reaffirm your love for me.[4]

All his life, from the moment when he first became conscious of his Avatarhood, Baba had made a practice of retiring into seclusion. But now his seclusion appeared unusually intense even to those who had been with him from the earliest days. At the end of 1960 Eruch wrote in a letter, "Beloved Baba seems now to be interested in being totally disinterested! He appears to be absorbed in something very serious and, alone with His unique Silence, He has obviously silenced all activities immediately around Him. He does not want to hear anything and He does not want to see anything, nor take part in the usual conversation we hold while we sit near Him... The atmosphere around Meherazad is charged with a sort of 'stillness' – not inactivity (far from it!) but a sort of HUSH personified."

This deep seclusion was prolonged, with only an occasional brief interlude, until November 1962. At the start of that month he gave for four days his last darshan for lovers from all over the world. This was at Guruprasad to which Baba returned especially for this purpose. Westerners were present in the mornings, Easterners in the afternoons; just under 140 came from America, Europe, Australia, New Zealand, and about 3,000 from all over India, Iran and Pakistan, special platforms and canopies having been erected in the grounds to accommodate so many.

The period at which this gathering took place was one of extreme political crisis. China, having absorbed Tibet – regarded for centuries as the world's 'spiritual powerhouse' – had launched her armies against India, so that the country was then actually at war. On the far side of the world the two supreme powers of the time, the USA and the USSR, which had been squaring up to one another ever since the end of the Second World War, seemed about to come to final grips over the projected setting up in Cuba of Russian missile bases. This must have been in the minds of all those present as Baba's message of welcome was read out.

> My dear Children. Your coming from different places and across oceans has pleased me. And although no sacrifice to be near me is too great, I am touched by the sacrifice that some of you have made... It is a coming together of children of East and West in the house of their Father.
>
> All religions of the world proclaim that there is but one God, the Father of all in creation. I am that Father.
>
> I have come to remind all people that they should live on earth as the children of the one Father until my Grace awakens them to the realisation... that all divisions and conflicts and hatred are but a shadow-play of their own ignorance.
>
> Although all are my children they ignore the simplicity and beauty of this Truth by indulging in hatreds, conflicts and wars that divide them in enmity, instead of living as one family in their Father's house... It is time that they become aware of the presence of their Father in their midst and of their responsibility towards Him and themselves.[5]

In a series of profound messages Baba spoke of the nature of creation, giving a picture of the expanding universe such as no previous Avatar had ever outlined, and stressing the unique importance of our own planet in the divine scheme.

> In the Creation are millions of galaxies, the centre of which is the planet we know as our earth. In the galaxies are developed life forms, and in some planets evolution is completed and human beings exist. But only on earth do human beings reincarnate and pass through the involutionary process to God Realisation...

> Only on this earth can God be realised. It is not possible for men to contact the worlds that contain the kingdoms of evolution but are without spiritual development. On these other worlds there are beings that have more intelligence than exists in men. The earth is the centre of creation because men are made in God's image, and only human beings on earth are capable of advancement. (Baba ended with the dry comment) Through your learning the simplest things have been made very difficult.

CB Purdom, who had not seen Baba for more than four years, was struck by his changed appearance. "His expression was as bright, his eyes as keen as ever, and his alertness seemed not to have diminished, but he was withdrawn, and for much of the time looked far away, as though not belonging to the world. He constantly smiled and was ready to joke, and his humour had not deserted him, but there was a certain indifference that I had not noticed before. Above all there was an immense sadness that moved me strangely. When he walked one saw that he went heavily."

Two days later Baba gave those present a stern rebuke, which might also have been directed towards the world in general:

> I had to give you a message on Thursday because you expected one; and the theme of the message was on your being my children, because despite much talk about a Baba-family there is more a semblance than a reality of kinship among you who are the children of One Father.
>
> True children of One Father do not greet one another with smiles and embraces and at the same time harbour grudges and ill-feeling, but have an active concern in their hearts for the well-being of one another and make sacrifices for that well-being.
>
> If you make me your real Father, all differences and

contentions between you, and all personal problems in connection with your lives, will become dissolved in the Ocean of my Love...

Unless there is a brotherly feeling in your hearts, all the words that you speak or print in my name are hollow; all the miles that you travel in my cause are zero; all organizations for my work are but an appearance of activity; all buildings to contain me are empty places and all statues that you make to embody me are of someone else.

I have been patient and indulgent... because you have been very young children in my love, and children must have some sort of games to play. But now you are older and are beginning to realize that there is a greater work ahead of you than what you have been doing. And you have been searching your minds and hearts as to what this work might be.

It is not a different work... it is the same work done in a different way. And that way is the way of effacement, which means the more you work for me the less important you feel in yourself. You must always remember that I alone do my work... I allow you to work for me so that you have the opportunity to use your talent and capacities selflessly and so draw closer to me...

When you put my work before yourself the work will go right, though not necessarily smoothly. And when the work does not go right it means that you have put yourself between it and its accomplishment.

The way of my work is the way of effacement, which is the way of strength, not of weakness; and through it you become mature in my love...

Towards the close of the gathering a newspaperman asked Baba about the situation in the war with China, and what its outcome would be. "As I am the Ancient One and as I am in India," Baba answered, "in the final outcome India will be victorious." This was reported next day all over the country, omitting everything except the last four words.

Before the darshan ended Baba permitted the mandali to bow down before him one by one. It was the first time for twenty-two years that he had allowed this, and it seemed to signify an even deeper withdrawal in which the breaks would be fewer and briefer still. From time to time during his annual stay at Guruprasad there would be 'song feasts' in which famous Indian singers took part and visitors would be allowed to come, especially on Sunday afternoons. At times too the visitors would themselves put on plays and entertainments for Baba.

Two and a half years later in May 1965, there were six days of further darshan for Eastern followers, some of whom travelled great distances to be present – one group from Iran spending no fewer than eleven days on their laborious train journey. For the end of the same year a corresponding sahavas was projected for the Westerners, but before December came it was postponed, and continued to be put off year after year as Baba's seclusion was extended. This seclusion was the opposite of retirement. It was not a withdrawal from work but a withdrawal into work.

What the true nature of this work might be, even those whose lives were spent in Baba's company knew little. All they gleaned from a rare comment was, first, that it went on unceasingly. "You see Me doing all this," Baba had told them during an interlude at Guruprasad in June 1963, "but simultaneously My work continues. It is as breathing is to you – you talk, work, play, eat, sleep, etc. but you never stop breathing. It is the same with My work which continues without a stop whatever else I may appear to be doing."[6]

Secondly, they understood that it was directly related to the world situation at any given moment and carried out 'on the inner planes', invisibly and imperceptibly, as in the way that Baba worked to influence the minds of audiences absorbed in some spectacle or entertainment.

Thirdly, those around him could see for themselves that it involved intense suffering both bodily and mental. "After I return to Meherazad," he had said in the summer of 1963, "there will be an increase in pain and suffering... and chaos, the world over. It will be a reflection of the suffering I will undergo during the nine months..."

This statement had been made shortly before Baba began his last, seemingly unending – indeed literally unending though not quite unbroken – seclusion, which would continue for longer than five years. If for the world as a whole these years were ones of "suffering and chaos", including the horrors of the Vietnam War; the assassination of the American president, John F. Kennedy; and the Six-Day War in Israel – with the spate of hijackings, killings and further outbreaks of war which followed; for India Baba's words would prove especially prophetic. The nation had to face war and natural disasters of flood and famine on a gigantic scale; the death of two leaders, Nehru and Shastri; accompanied by almost continuous political unrest, reaching a new climax in the 1980s with the assassination of Indira Gandhi, the growth of the Sikh movement for secession, and the separatist movement in Ceylon.

At first Baba's physical pain centred round the hip joint which had been injured in the crash and which he steadfastly refused to have operated on. "The pain is bad, but the extent of my work being done is good." As the years went by, and with the help of the blind chiropractor, Dr Harry Kenmore, this was much eased, but now there came a new source of suffering, the physical cause of which may have been displacement resulting from the original hip injury. In a Family Letter of April 1965, Mani wrote:

> Besides the continuous pain in His hip-joint and His inability to walk freely, He has had since the last many months pain in the cervical spine, i.e. in the nape of the neck and extending

> down to the shoulders. Of late the pain has become intense... When, on one of his recurrent visits to Meherazad, Dr Ginde expressed his distress and surprise at the stubbornness of the pain, beloved Baba patted him lovingly on the arm and said, "Don't worry. It is all by my will. I alone know the cause of my pain, and it will go away after July. All the same I want you to go on doing your best to lessen it," (adding after a while) "and I will do my best to increase it!"... Baba has told the mandali more than once, "It is but the (yoke of) universal suffering round my neck" – and indeed the surgical collar that He wears seems to us painfully symbolical of this fact.

Five months later, announcing the cancellation of the Western sahavas planned for December, Baba said: "The world situation is very bad, and growing worse daily. The pressure of my universal work is affecting my health tremendously, and the pain in my neck is beyond limit."

Not all the record of these years is of suffering, however. There are glimpses of Baba, seated on a high stool because movement was painful, playing table tennis with the mandali, or out in the garden enjoying a game called 'Seven Tiles', in which the driver and gardeners took part as well. In this Indian version of skittles or bowls, seven pieces of stone or tile are balanced on top of each other, and the player tries to knock them all down with a ball. Baba also took great pleasure in the gardens, in watching the animals and birds both tame and wild. He enjoyed listening to music:

> Teatime at Meherazad (wrote Mani) is a happy hour for us women, when we sit together at the dining table with the Beloved; and mingling with snatches of conversation and the tinkle of teaspoons in cups, is the music from our transistor radio... This would find Baba drumming briskly on the table in rhythm with the music, the response from our brass tea-

kettle being a jerky little dance as it would bob up and down with the vibration of the table.

Children and childlike people afforded him relief. He responded instantly to the loving acceptance of children, who had no requests to make, were not interested in hearing discourses, but wanted only to press as close to him as they could. At Guruprasad in an assembly so crowded that there seemed no inch of floor space left, Baba singled out and silently beckoned to him a little girl hardly four years old. She made her way forward, bowed solemnly before him, and then smiled ecstatically as Baba drew her to him, embraced her and caressed her cheeks. She had come, it was later learned, from a place a long way from Poona. Her parents were not with her. Hearing that some neighbours were travelling to Poona to see Baba, she had urged and insisted with tears that her mother allow her to go with them and see him.

In another crowded gathering during the same stay, there was a mother having trouble with two boisterous children. No one supposed that Baba had even noticed her, occupied as he was with receiving a long line of visitors and being garlanded. But when the woman finally reached Baba, he asked:

"Do these kids trouble you?"

"Yes, Baba, indeed they do!" she answered feelingly.

"If only two children can make your life a hell," Baba asked her, "can you imagine my plight who has billions of children?"

One of the mandali whose company Baba specially enjoyed was Kaka Baria, a companion from the earliest days who had travelled several times with Baba to the West, and taken part in many 'mast hunts'. At Meherazad he acted as manager, and it was he who had originally given the place its name. Totally unselfconscious, Kaka would join in any entertainment and often provided one himself by his unique use of language. "Waddling beside Baba like a protective hen" he would keep up a running fire of observations and comments. Undaunted by a memory which faltered as he aged, Kaka would make up any words he found himself short of, and drop in alternative expressions which roughly resembled those he was trying to recall. Of him, Baba said: "While everybody adds to my burden, Kaka removes a fraction of it."

Just occasionally too the pain would lift, and in June 1967, Mani reported happily from Guruprasad:

> Each morning and afternoon we have seen the Beloved striding the length of the marble tiled verandah, to and from the mandali's hall. Added to our joy at seeing Him walk like this is seeing the pleasure it gives Him, when at the end of a stride He may ask with a delighted smile, "How do I walk?"

In general, however, the record of these years is one of unending work and increasing pain. Of the pain in his neck Dr Ram Ginde, the leading neurosurgeon from Bombay who was also a devoted follower, wrote to Dr Goher, a member of the mandali and Baba's personal physician: "Whatever I know from the knowledge of His cervical condition, I have tried to do in all sincerity. But I must admit... my utter failure in regard to relieving Beloved Baba's pain. I plead quite helpless in treating Him who is as powerful as, nay more powerful than, an ocean and as helpless as a kitten at one and the same time."

Not surprisingly, as they puzzled over this mysterious pain, those around Baba recalled that back in 1940, Chatti Baba – one of the greatest of masts, then living at Meherabad with Baba – had said that all suffering borne by Baba arose out of his compassion and love for humanity. The suffering yet to come upon the earth was so great that it would not be able to sustain the burden, and so Baba would take one end of the yoke upon his own shoulder.

In a message sent out on 1st March 1968, postponing the end of this seclusion once again until the 21st May, Baba wrote:

> None can have the least idea of the immensity of the work I am doing in this seclusion. The only hint I can give is that compared with the work I do in seclusion all the important work of the world put together is completely insignificant. Although for me the burden of the work is crushing, the result of my work will be intensely felt by all people in the world.

But Baba's seclusion did not end in May, any more than it had ended in March, or in February, or in November. He continued his work throughout his yearly visit to Guruprasad and on through the month of July after his return.

At last, on the evening of Tuesday, 30th July 1968, he declared:

> MY WORK IS DONE. IT IS COMPLETED ONE HUNDRED PER CENT TO MY SATISFACTION. THE RESULT OF THIS WORK WILL ALSO BE ONE HUNDRED PER CENT AND WILL MANIFEST FROM THE END OF SEPTEMBER.[7]

Meher Baba. Location: Guruprasad, Pune. Date: 2–6 May 1965.
Photographer: Meelan / © MSI Collection.

Notes

1. This took place one week later, after the return from Guruprasad to Meherazad.
2. *Family Letters,* Letter 35
3. *Daaman* is literally the hem of the garment. And if the right hand is thought of as masculine intellect and reason, which may be argued or ridiculed out of its convictions, the left can represent our feminine aspect of perception, intuition, faith.
4. *The God-Man,* p. 356
5. This and following quotes on '62 gathering: *The God-Man,* pp. 361–9
6. *Family Letters,* Letter 53. Remaining quotes in chapter from *Family Letters* (dated 1963–68).
7. *Family Letters,* Letter 78

L-r: Dr Ginde, Eruch, Mani & Dr Donkin. Location: by the Samadhi, Upper Meherabad, February 1969. © Meher Nazar Publications.

Chapter 15

The Last Sahavas

When Baba emerged from that last long-sustained seclusion, it was with his physical nature almost at breaking point. To a few specially summoned to Meherazad in October 1968, he said:

> No doubt you people and my lovers everywhere have been wondering why, when my period of intense Work in seclusion has finished, I have still not allowed my lovers to see me.
> The strain of that 18 months' Work was tremendous. I used to sit alone in my room for some hours each day while complete

> silence was imposed on the mandali... The strain was not in the work itself although I was working on all planes of consciousness, but in keeping my link with the gross plane. To keep this link I had continuously to hammer my right thigh with my fist... it will yet take some time for all traces of the strain to disappear.[1]

Baba went on to announce the news all were eagerly awaiting: a great gathering was to be held in Guruprasad for both Easterners and Westerners. It was to last for a fixed number of hours each day from the 10th April to the 10th June 1969. As always, the most careful preparations had been put in train with detailed instructions for all planning to attend – not forgetting a message of comfort for those wishing to come but unable to do so. Some of those hearing the announcement were apprehensive as to whether Baba's body could endure the strain of such an arduous programme, but he reassured them:

> It will be easy for me to give my lovers my darshan, so you are not to feel concerned about it. I will give darshan reclining and that will be no strain on my body. It will be different from all previous darshans and it will be the last in silence. Although I will be reclining I will be very strong. My physical condition now is because of my work, but by then my work will be complete and my exultation will be great.[2]

Mani's letter carrying to those overseas the news of the forthcoming sahavas ended with Baba's words:

> I have been saying: the Time is near, it is fast approaching, it is close at hand. Today I say: *the Time has come*. Remember this!

Though Baba had appeared to make light of anxiety over his

health, those about him felt growing apprehension especially from the beginning of December when he began to suffer muscular spasms. A blood check was called for, and the doctors simply could not believe what it showed. They called for a second, which confirmed the first, and Baba was given two blood transfusions. Dr Ginde, who was summoned from Bombay, later recalled: "I saw Beloved Baba again on December 19th, 1968, as by then His health had deteriorated further. Beloved Baba had become pale due to anaemia; there was swelling around His feet and ankles. He was unable to sit up. He was getting spasms of His limbs..."[3]

On the 22nd December, Mehera's birthday was celebrated as it had always been, and on the following day Baba took part in the wedding of his nephew Dara to Amrit, the daughter of Shatrughan Kumar. Dara was the son of Baba's younger brother Adi S. Irani, who had come over from England with his wife, Freny and their daughter Shireen.

From the 26th December the spasms increased, and Baba repeatedly told the mandali, "The time is very near." On 9th January 1969, when Freny, Adi's wife, came to see him before going back to England, Baba told her not to worry about his health, since, "All will be well by the end of this month."

Up till the 13th January,[4] Baba was still going over every morning and afternoon to the room occupied by the men mandali, as had long been his custom. But on 14th January, the doctors advised him not to leave his bed or his room, and so from that date the mandali would visit him three or four times daily.[5] From 28th January, the spasms became far worse. Eruch, who was present throughout this time, reports:

> The spasms lasted almost continuously for about sixteen hours... leaving Baba quite exhausted and restless. The sensation was like that of a very severe electric shock received by a person who accidentally touches a main, and it took four

> of the mandali to hold His body down in bed. Every jerk from a spasm almost broke Baba's back, and any movement on His part like raising His hands or fingers to tell us something, would result in a jerk that lifted the body from head to foot. Baba even found breathing difficult...
>
> On January 30th, Baba announced that He wanted five disciples to be always near Him, among whom Padri and Chhagan were specially mentioned.
>
> The mandali began their watch throughout the day and that night attempting with Baba's encouragement, to press hard on His body to eliminate the spasm if possible, or else to hold His body down if the spasms came, in order to avoid jerks to His spinal cord that were causing Him severe pain in the back and shoulders. While we were pressing His body, we would first feel ripples passing under our hands and when they got stronger, we knew He was going to have another massive spasm.[6]

As the day went on Baba told Dr Donkin, "This is my crucifixion"; and at 9.30 that night he said to Bhau Kalchuri, one of the mandali who had been doing night duty for him for many years, "I am not this body." At 3.45 a.m. the mandali were summoned, and groups of men and women remained in constant attendance throughout the rest of the night and the following morning. At one point in the morning Baba sent Aloba over to the mandali's room for a board on which were written up three couplets from his favourite poet Hafiz. They were ones he had quoted many times, and it was as if he wished to imprint them finally upon their memories.

> I am the slave of the Master who has released me from ignorance; whatever my Master does is of the highest benefit to all concerned.
>
> Befitting a fortunate slave, carry out every command of

> the Master without any question of 'why' and 'what'.
>
> About what you hear from the Master, never say it is wrong, because, my dear, the fault lies in your own incapacity to understand Him.

Baba enquired a number of times for Dr Ginde, who had been summoned from Bombay, making the gesture of tracing out a 'G'. The least movement could precipitate a spasm and each time he would wince at the pain; he had also developed severe pain in his back. To relieve the spasms Padri was giving Baba homoeopathic pills which had to be administered every ten minutes. Padri gave Baba the fourth dose at 12 noon, and Baba for the last time enquired whether Dr Ginde had yet come. Hearing he had not, Baba gestured, "It is getting late." At 12.15 p.m. Baba was seized with a particularly severe spasm.

> He was sitting on His surgical bed with His back and head raised. Baba flexed His arms and closed His mouth tightly. His respiration suddenly stopped. There was no relaxation after the spasm and Baba became motionless. Eruch, using his wits, tried to open Baba's mouth. He found that Baba's tongue had fallen back. Eruch put his mouth on Baba's mouth and began to breathe into his lungs forcibly. This mouth to mouth resuscitation was carried on for nearly thirty minutes. Francis and Bhau relieved him for a short while. Adi (Adi K. Irani) was immediately phoned to bring Dr Brieseman and an oxygen cylinder from the Mission (Evangeline Booth) Hospital at Ahmednagar. Pendu kept his hand on Baba's pulse. Dr Goher was busy giving several injections in an attempt to revive Baba.
>
> At about 12.40 p.m. Dr Ginde arrived followed by Adi and Dr Brieseman. They brought an oxygen cylinder with them. Eruch had collapsed on the floor out of sheer exhaustion. Dr Brieseman gave a cardiac massage. He then checked Baba's

> heart with a stethoscope and passed it on to Dr Donkin, who, after examining Baba, gave it to Dr Ginde. The three doctors discussed something which the mandali did not understand. Dr Ginde checked Baba's eye reflexes. The heart had stopped, the reflexes were gone and life was extinct![7]

And now it became clear why Baba had been so insistent on Dr Ginde's arrival. The women mandali were distracted; they could not believe Baba had laid down his body and thought he must be in a coma or a trance. Among the men "all minds seemed to have come to a standstill." Dr Ginde thereupon took charge. He told them they must not be emotional but practical, and himself wrote out Baba's death certificate. As they were discussing how to act, Eruch recalled Baba's having told him more than once, "Wherever my body drops, bring me and put me in the crypt at Meherabad."

Dr Ginde said that if Baba's body was to be taken to the crypt, the removal should be carried out within six hours, and on learning that the crypt floor was of stone, he said that the stone slabs would have to be taken up. Padri was charged with the task, went over to Meherabad and got to work. It was the noise of Padri's digging which first warned the villagers of Arangaon that something was amiss. Meantime Chhagan Master (Sitaram D. Deshmukh), another of the mandali, had been sent to Ahmednagar to have a wooden board prepared on which Baba's body could be laid, together with a cover for the coffin in which later it would be interred.

Baba's body was now lifted on to a stretcher and laid on his aluminium bed, and the men of the mandali came one by one to bow down to their Master for the last time in the place which had been his home and theirs for more than twenty years. Late in the afternoon an ambulance arrived to carry Baba's body to the Tomb at Meherabad, and as it left a cry was raised of: "Avatar Meher Baba Ki Jai." When the ambulance reached Meherabad and crept slowly up the hill, the Arangaon villagers, already alerted by the noise of digging, guessed what had happened, and the news spread rapidly.

Of Meherabad Hill Baba had once said:

> The major portion of my Universal work was done on this hill. I have selected this spot for my last resting place; when I drop the body, it shall rest here, in my Tomb. I have fasted here for six months. I used to lie down here in the crypt taking only water and coffee... After I drop my body the physical remains will rest here, and this hill will become an important place of pilgrimage for the world. After seventy years... a big township will grow around here.[8]

The sun was setting and the moon rising as Baba's body was lifted from the ambulance and placed in a cabin opposite the door of the Tomb. Then, after Padri had announced that the floor was dug and the Tomb all in order, the stretcher was carried from the cabin to the entrance and laid on the wooden board brought by Chhagan. Under one end Eruch had put three stone slabs from the floor, and now a pillow was placed beneath Baba's head. A scarf, which had already been tied round his head and chin, was rearranged. Baba lay now with his head to the north and his eyes closed, facing the steps by which his followers would descend into the crypt.

Some time before this, when Baba had asked the mandali whether it would be all right if he gave the forthcoming darshan lying down, they had supposed he was referring to his state of health which might prevent his sitting up for the whole period, and agreed. Thereupon Baba asked them to raise his head so that his lovers could see him from a distance. It was only now that they realised his meaning.

Almost immediately after Baba laid down his body, the men mandali had discussed the message to be sent out to the world.

Finally they agreed on the wording:

> AVATAR MEHER BABA DROPPED HIS PHYSICAL BODY AT TWELVE NOON 31 JANUARY AT MEHERAZAD TO LIVE ETERNALLY IN THE HEARTS OF ALL HIS LOVERS. BELOVED BABA'S BODY WILL BE INTERRED AT MEHERABAD ARANGAON ON 1 FEBRUARY AT 10 A M IN THE TOMB HE HAD ORDERED TO BE BUILT LONG AGO.[9]

All afternoon Adi K. Irani, Baba's secretary and lifelong companion, had been cabling this message to Baba centres and lovers in India and abroad. The All India Radio put the news out the same evening, repeating the announcement several times on the following day, sometimes with a brief sketch of Baba's life. Next day the BBC also announced his passing and overseas newspapers carried the news. Throughout the world the reaction of most Baba lovers was of disbelief; on being told the news, they supposed that either their informant or the newspaper must be mistaken. The small telegraph office in Ahmednagar was overwhelmed with cables calling for confirmation, denial or fuller information.

But from neighbouring districts numbers of followers who had heard the radio simply left everything and set off for Meherabad. Many came without waiting to get leave from work, not stopping to collect clothes or cash or food. They came as on a pilgrimage whose purpose justifies all sacrifice and the cutting through of all convention. By sunrise they were swarming in to Meherabad on foot or bicycle, in ox-carts or horse-drawn vehicles. Special buses had been laid on for the six miles between Ahmednagar and Meherabad. Other devotees who lived farther off and could not reach Meherabad by ten o'clock on the Saturday, the time announced for the interment, sent cables pleading that this be put off until they could arrive.

The time had originally been fixed on medical advice, that

since the body had not been embalmed it must be buried within twenty hours. However Mehera and Mani recalled Baba's conveying to them by signs on the last morning that "after seven days he would be one hundred per cent free." They interpreted this as meaning that interment should not take place for seven days, but that his body should be left uncovered, if possible, for the full period. It was in accordance with this decision that Baba's body had been laid in a reclining position, garlanded and covered with flowers regularly renewed, and surrounded by blocks of ice which were changed every few hours. Guarded continually, it was open to all from near and far who sought to pay their final tribute.

Dr Bharucha was one of those who had heard the news on the radio on the morning of 1st February. It took him five hours from his home in southern India to reach Bombay. From Bombay another train brought him and his friends on to Poona, where they caught a bus at 2.30 a.m. to reach Ahmednagar at 5 a.m. on 2nd February.

> From a distance the white walls of the Tomb could be seen. We did not wait to loosen our shoe laces but just knocked off our shoes and went in after kneeling at the threshold. What a sight awaited us! How can words express what we saw and felt at that time… Down in the crypt was Beloved Baba lying motionless, covered with a pink sheet and roses around His head and on His body. Only Baba's face down to His ears could be seen… His eyes were closed. His face looked a bit pale. His big forehead shone in the fluorescent light… He looked as if He were sleeping… For several minutes we could not get our eyes off Baba. We then heard Eruch saying from somewhere, "Go down the steps and touch His feet."

And now from early on the morning of Saturday, 1st February, the crowds were starting to arrive. They were drawn by the deep Indian conviction that, while it is always blessed to be near the Perfect Master, it is a duty when he lays down his body to express love and devotion by one's presence. Soon every foot of space was occupied by campers, many of whom had nothing to lie on nor to cover themselves with at night. The big hall at Lower Meherabad where Baba used to hold meetings and sahavas gatherings was crammed, and the verandahs surrounding it as well. On the railway which cuts Meherabad in two, drivers obliged their passengers by stopping trains in the open to allow them to scramble out. Others, whose trains could not stop, sounded their whistles in salute.

The mandali and their helpers were concerned to do everything they could for the devotees. A makeshift awning was put up in front of the Tomb to provide shade. No food was available nearer than Ahmednagar so that many, having brought nothing with them, lived on water. But on the next day, Sunday, Chhagan – who, with Padri, had spent the whole of Friday night watching in the Tomb – organised the cooking of quantities of rice and vegetables in Ahmednagar and its transport to Meherabad. Before long, too, a small canteen opened up.

There was no electricity in Meherabad, but devotees from Andhra set up a generator supplying power for some forty fluorescent lights. At sunset this would be turned on to light up the Tomb and the surrounding area, making Meherabad Hill conspicuous for miles around in the darkness. Catching sight of it, passengers in trains and buses would stand up and bow, and trains would sound their whistles. Some of the lights shone on a dais, at one end of which groups of singers from various centres kept up sacred songs and music almost until daylight. Some were reminded of Baba's humorous remark made years before on returning from a tour in Andhra: "My lovers sang outside my window all night while I rested."

All who came had only one concern – to have a last sight of Baba and to take his darshan. They came bringing flowers and garlands which were collected from them at the door. A continuous flow of people moved up to the entrance, bowed or knelt down, left their flowers, and moved on. Others came inside and bowed. Others again went on down the five steps to touch Baba's feet for the last time. Once inside they were unwilling to leave and had to be asked to make room for other waiting devotees. Some picked up fallen flowers or petals which they would cherish all their lives, or carry back as a blessing for families left behind. Two volunteers were continually present in the Tomb, one to keep off flies and mosquitoes with a fan, while the other collected flowers at the door or swabbed the floor with a wet cloth to keep down dust.

For a full week the Tomb remained open, apart from a short period during two nights. Three times each day the doors were closed for a brief spell while Eruch with a couple of helpers changed the blocks of ice surrounding Baba. For every task there was a rush of volunteers eager to find some way of expressing the love which filled their hearts and could often be seen pouring down their cheeks.

Each day began with prayers in which all took part, and with a report from Dr Goher as to whether the body had yet to be interred. On the eighth day, Friday, 7th February, it was generally known that the sahavas would end and interment take place soon after midday. Newspapers had also announced that this was the final day, and the crowds pouring in had swelled accordingly. It was the week of the full moon, and those in Meherabad had been astir since 3 a.m.; by 4.30 all had assembled at the entrance.

As it happened, the 7th February was Baba's birthday by the Zoroastrian calendar (25th February by ours), and it had been announced that at 5 a.m., his actual birth moment, all should salute Baba. The mandali had always saluted him on his birthday during his lifetime, with the cry of "Avatar Meher Baba Ki Jai" three times repeated, and so precisely at 5 a.m. the shouts rang out from the crowd. From 7 a.m., no one was allowed inside the Tomb except the two attendants who were fanning Baba's body, but so many begged a share of this last task that they were allowed only two minutes of service each.

During that morning as the thousands of devotees, those who had spent the night there and others newly assembled, stood silently round the Tomb, their hearts were full of memories of Baba and their minds of his treasured sayings:

> Things that are real are always given and received in silence.
>
> I am the One so many seek and so few find. No amount of intellect can fathom Me. No amount of austerity can attain Me. Only when one loves Me and loses one's self in Me, am I found.
>
> When I drop My body, I will remain in all who love Me. I can never die. Love Me, obey Me, and you will find Me.

There were some Westerners present too, a handful who, on hearing the news, had also left everything and come here. They perhaps remembered other of his sayings:

> God is not to be found in the skies or in the caves of the Himalayas. God is in the heart of each one. Once your heart is clean, God will shine out of it.
>
> However far man may fling himself into outer space… man will not change – wherever he goes he will remain what he is. It is when man travels within himself that he experiences a metamorphosis of himself. It is this journeying that matters, for the infinite treasure – God – is within man, and not to be found anywhere outside himself.

At a quarter past midday a threefold cry of "Avatar Meher Baba Ki Jai" rang out once more. The doors of the Tomb were closed. Mehera and the women mandali entered for the last time as the crowd stood by in total silence. When they withdrew, the men mandali gathered and placed the coffin cover over their beloved Master. The lid was heaped with flowers, and earth placed over it. Finally the crypt itself was levelled up with earth. By five o'clock the work was done and the Tomb swept and cleaned. Most of the lovers had left by now, and as the sun began to sink the last small groups were making their way home. They carried their sorrow with them, but they carried something else as well. For in the words of Dr Bharucha, "Once an inner contact is established with Baba, the Divine Shepherd folds His sheep with His love, wherever He is, wherever they are, irrespective of time or space."

Those who had lived close to Baba for many years, the men and women mandali, suffered an intensity of deprivation which made them feel, and possibly sometimes wish, that life itself were ending. Two of them did die very shortly, Kaka Baria within a month and Dr Donkin a few months later. All, living or dying, would echo the words of Mani: "To have what one wants is to have everything. To us, being with Baba was everything – and we had it."

Those throughout the world who had made contact with Baba in one way or another turned to their memories with heartfelt gratitude. Those who had made the journey experienced the joy of knowing that all their effort was worthwhile since they had been able to pay tribute to their Master at his last sahavas.

And those who had failed to make the journey could think over his tender, humorous reminder:

> I am in each heart, but I am sleeping there. It is my old, old habit. In order to awaken me you should always call out to me, saying "Baba, Baba, Baba!" Then I, who am sleeping in your heart, will not find any pleasure in remaining asleep. Let alone sleep, I shall not find time even to doze! I shall then slowly be awakened in your heart by your constant

calls. Once I am awake in your heart, you too will awake and remain awake forever. Therefore, repeat my name constantly and awaken me in your heart so that you become awake for all time.

Meher Baba inside his tomb-shrine. Location: Meherabad Hill, India, 1954. Photographer: Panday / © Meher Nazar Publications.

Notes

1. *Family Letters*, Letter 79
2. *Love Alone Prevails*, p. 675
3. This and much else in this chapter is taken from *Meher Baba's Last Sahavas*.
4. Some sources have 12th January. (Ed.)
5. Cf. *The Ancient One*, p. 143
6. *The Ancient One*, pp. 144–5
7. *The Ancient One*, pp. 144–5
8. *Last Sahavas*, p. 19
9. *Family Letters*, Letter 81

Part II: The Message of Meher Baba

Introduction

As with every Avatar, Meher Baba has given mankind the example of his life, and though repeatedly stressing that his mission is not to teach but to awaken, he has also left a body of teaching which opens up a new and dynamic chapter in religious thought. With parts of this teaching readers have already become acquainted, through the expositions Baba gave to his followers throughout his life. But such expositions and declarations were made on particular occasions to meet some special situation, either among his followers or in the world at large.

What we shall try to do in this second section of our book is to give the reader a connected impression of Baba's teaching as a whole, and of the way that teaching relates to, and at times runs counter to, current orthodox religious beliefs. Baba's exposition of the nature of the universe is contained largely in his book *God Speaks*; that about human life and its purpose is to be found mainly in his *Discourses*, originally published in India in five volumes between 1939 and 1943, but recently reedited and republished in a single volume.[1]

Anyone who ventures on a study of these books must be prepared for his or her attitude to life to be challenged and indeed transformed. Long-held opinions and assumptions, backed by centuries of religious orthodoxy, will be shown to be partial or misleading. A new picture opens up of our purpose on earth; the slow course of our spiritual development across aeons of time; and of a sublime destiny which gives purpose and meaning to all our earthly sufferings and struggles.

On 10th July 1958, the anniversary of the day on which he began his unending silence, Baba made an explicit statement on his role as Avatar,[2] or Messenger of God, to the present-day world.

> I have come not to teach but to awaken. Understand therefore that I lay down no precepts…
>
> Because man has been deaf to the principles and precepts laid down by God in the past, in this present Avataric form I observe Silence. You have asked for and been given enough words – it is now time to live them…
>
> You have not to give up your religion, but to give up clinging to the outer husk of mere ritual and ceremonies.
>
> (And, in a powerful indictment of the present age, Baba demanded) How many Christians follow Christ's teaching to 'turn the other cheek', or 'to love thy neighbour as thyself'? How many Muslims follow Muhammad's precept to 'hold God above everything else'? How many Hindus 'bear the torch of righteousness at all cost'? How many Buddhists live 'the life of pure compassion'? How many Zoroastrians 'think truly, speak truly, act truly'? God's truth cannot be ignored; and thus by mankind's ignorance and weakness a tremendous adverse reaction is produced – and the world finds itself in a cauldron of suffering through wars, hate, conflicting ideologies, and nature's rebellion in the form of floods, famines, earthquakes and other disasters.[3]

Long before this time, in his first direct public message to the

West delivered in 1932, Baba stressed that he had not come to establish any new religion, but to arouse people to the truth embodied in all the great religions:

> I am not come to establish any cult, society or organisation – nor to establish a new religion. The Religion I shall give teaches the knowledge of the One behind the many. The Book I shall make people read is the book of the heart, which holds the key to the mystery of life.[4]

What is the truth which underlies all the great religions? And what does Baba mean by 'the knowledge of the One behind the many'?

Historically, mankind has always placed God at a distance. Primitive peoples, awed by the wonder of creation and the power of natural forces, looked upon the skies as God's abode, worshipping him in the sun which gives light and heat. But as knowledge of the physical world expanded, the sun – though remaining a powerful symbol of God-given illumination – was no longer itself the object of worship; and, though God was thought of as having his existence 'in the heavens' or 'beyond the skies', this was a poetic, not literal, expression of belief.

In the Western world, as elsewhere, early religions imagined a multiplicity of gods and goddesses, presiding over particular places, activities or spheres of interest. The first monotheistic religion to establish itself is generally accepted to have been Judaism at a date of around 1300 BCE.[5] The worship of a single divine being constituted a huge advance on previous ideas of worship, and it is on Judaism as the first truly monotheistic religion that Jewry bases its claim to be 'God's chosen people'.

With the coming of Christianity, the ties between God and mankind were drawn closer still into what may be regarded as a 'spiritual family relationship'. The essence of the Christian faith is the belief that Jesus was in a literal sense the Son of God, who lived on earth, suffered and was crucified, in order by his sacrifice to win God's forgiveness for his erring children. Thus, through the mediation of Christ, God takes on a more intimate and personal role as the loving Father of mankind.

But what Baba tells us is nothing less than that man and woman are, in their own true nature, divine – "spiritual in essence, eternal in nature, and of infinite resources". During the long process of evolution, however, men and women have inevitably lost sight of their true nature and, assuming the material world to be reality, have identified with their physical nature throughout all evolutionary transformations. And so now, having at last attained human form, they continue to regard the physical body as their true self, and believe that when this dies, they die too. In reality, though, death is not a passing *out of* life and a final separation from the physical world; it is a passing *over* into a temporary state of existence in which every man or woman has the opportunity to learn the lessons of his/her recent incarnation, before, after a varying span of time, reincarnating in a new body in which the process of development and self-realisation can be resumed.

Likening the body to a coat which is put on, worn out, and later replaced by another, Baba explains that we have all passed over and returned innumerable times. Only when the individual soul attains at last to a realisation of its own divine nature does it become free from the round of births and deaths. In all this, Baba's teaching links with the Buddhist belief that the attainment of Nirvana puts an end to the repetitious round, or 'Wheel', of births and deaths; also with the Vedantic belief that the ultimate goal of life is, through innumerable incarnations, to become one with God. Where Baba goes far beyond a general acceptance of reincarnation, however, is that he does not regard spirit as at war with matter, but declares *all matter to be an unconscious form of spirit*. Insisting that religion and science are not antagonistic but complementary, his cosmic view sees evolution as forming part of a single age-long progress from total unconsciousness to the fully conscious acceptance of one's own divine nature – a state to which the term 'God-realisation' is applied.

In one of the most powerful and moving passages in the whole of the *Discourses*, Baba has set out this new vision of the universe.

> Consciously or unconsciously, every living creature seeks one thing. In the lower forms of life and in less advanced human beings, the quest is unconscious; in advanced human beings it is conscious. The object of the quest is called by many names – happiness, peace, freedom, truth, love, perfection, Self-realisation,[6] God-realisation, union with God. Essentially, it is a search for all of these, but in a special way. Everyone has moments of happiness, glimpses of truth, fleeting experiences of union with God; what they want is to make them permanent. They want to establish an abiding reality in the midst of constant change.
>
> This is a natural desire, based fundamentally on a memory – dim or clear as the evolution of the individual soul may be low or high – of its essential unity with God. *For every living thing is a partial manifestation of God, conditioned only by its lack of knowledge of its own true nature.* The whole of evolution, in fact, is an evolution from unconscious divinity to conscious divinity, in which God Himself, essentially eternal and unchangeable, assumes an infinite variety of forms, enjoys an infinite variety of experiences, and transcends an infinite variety of self-imposed limitations. Evolution from the standpoint of the Creator is a divine sport, in which the Unconditioned tests the infinitude of His absolute knowledge, power and bliss in the midst of all conditions. But evolution from the standpoint of the creature, with its limited knowledge, limited power, limited capacity for enjoying bliss, is an epic of alternating rest and struggle, joy and sorrow, love and hate – until in the

> perfected person, God balances the pairs of opposites, and duality is transcended.
>
> Then creature and Creator recognise themselves as one; changelessness is established in the midst of change; eternity is experienced in the midst of time. God knows Himself as God, unchangeable in essence, infinite in manifestation, ever experiencing the supreme bliss of Self-realisation in continually fresh awareness of Himself by Himself. This Realisation must and does take place only in the midst of life; for it is only in the midst of life that limitation can be experienced and transcended, and that subsequent freedom from limitation can be enjoyed.[7]

The above passage, so profound and so contrary to accepted patterns of belief, may demand many rereadings for its full implications to be taken in. All the great religions of the world accept that mankind is dependent upon God; but what Baba is here telling us is that God is also dependent upon mankind. Mankind depends on God for the experience of true spirituality; God depends on mankind for the achievement of full consciousness of his own divinity, for it was only by becoming man that God attained to full consciousness of his divine nature.

In the light of Baba's words, the relationship between God and the individual assumes new and deeper meaning. A demand for ultimate perfection made by God on the individual is replaced by an unending cooperation in achievement for the benefit of all creation.

From this two questions inevitably arise:

1) If man and woman are indeed 'spiritual in essence and eternal in nature', how have they come to identify with the physical body, accepting the material world as reality and regarding their spiritual nature either as illusion, or as something shadowy and difficult to apprehend?

2) If the body is no more than a coat to be discarded after

a brief earthly use, what is it which survives through the long series of incarnations, carrying over the lessons learned from one life to the next?

In the following sections we shall seek Baba's answers to these two all-important questions as given to us in his *Discourses*.

Notes

1. This refers to the 7th edition in 1987. (Ed.)
2. The deeper meaning of the title *Avatar* will emerge in a later chapter.
3. *The God-Man*, pp. 343–6
4. *The God-Man*, p. 101
5. In Egypt under Pharaoh Amenhotep IV, at a slightly earlier date (1353–1336 BCE), a form of monotheistic religion had been introduced. But this was abolished under his successor, (Tutankhamun) who restored the previous multiplicity of gods.
6. Baba uses 'Self' with a capital letter for the spiritual self, the soul, which is an individual's true Self. He uses 'self' for the everyday self which is identified with the ego.
7. *Discourses*, pp. 266–7

Meher Baba. Location: Ganeshkhind, Pune. April, June, or August 1957. Photographer: Meelan / © Meher Nazar Publications.

Section 1

Ego: The Great Misleader

Back in 1932, when Meher Baba paid his second visit to England, he gave an interview to a well-known journalist, James Douglas, in the course of which Douglas asked Baba: "What is your secret?"

Baba replied: "The elimination of the ego."

What does this mysterious sentence mean? What *is* the ego? What purpose does it serve? Why does it have to be eliminated?

In his *Discourses* Baba devotes much space to answering these questions, and in a three-part discussion on "The Nature of the Ego and Its Termination", he begins by explaining why the ego had to come into existence.

> Human consciousness would be nothing more than a repository for the accumulated imprints of varied experiences,

> if it did not also contain the principle of ego-centred integration, which expresses itself in the attempt to organise and understand experience. The process of understanding experience implies the capacity to hold bits of experiences together as parts of a unity and the capacity to evaluate them by their being brought into mutual relationship... (Hence) mental energy would be caught up endlessly in the multitudinous mazes of dual experience, and would all be wasted and dissipated, if there were no *provisional nucleus*.
>
> The ego takes stock of all acquired experience, gives a certain amount of stability to conscious processes, and also secures a working equilibrium, which makes for a planned and organised life.
>
> It would be a mistake, therefore, to imagine that the arising of the ego is without any purpose. Though it arises only to vanish in the end, it temporarily fulfils a need that could not have been ignored in the long journey of the soul. The ego is not meant to be a permanent handicap, since it can be transcended and outgrown through spiritual endeavour. But the phase of ego formation must nevertheless be looked upon as a necessary evil, which has to come into existence for the time being.[1]

To show the essential part played by the ego, Baba gives the example of the dog in which, as in all animals, the ego is still undeveloped. We are all familiar with the way in which a dog, when something angers or frightens it, starts to bark. But after barking for a while, the dog suddenly forgets what made it angry, scratches itself and wanders off.

So the question arises – if the ego serves a useful purpose in one's development, why does it have to be got rid of? To this Baba's answer is explicit. Because the ego is a limiting factor, and it is only by breaking the ego-shell that a human being can progress beyond the stage in which each individual looks upon his/her self as the centre of a personal universe, just as the chicken can only grow when it breaks out of the egg.

Baba sums up our need to 'terminate' and outgrow the ego, in the following manner.

> Since the ego takes shelter in the false idea of being the body, it is a source of much illusion which vitiates experience. It is of the essence of the ego that it should feel separate from the rest of life by contrasting itself with other forms of life. Thus… the ego creates an artificial division between external and internal life in the very attempt to feel and secure its own existence. This division in the totality of life cannot but have its reverberations in the inner individual life over which the ego presides as a guiding genius. While always striving to establish unity and integration in experience, the ego can never realise this objective. Though it establishes a certain kind of balance, this is only provisional and temporary; its incompleteness being evident from the internal conflict which is never absent so long as experience is faced from the ego point of view.
>
> From moment to moment the mind of man is passing through a series of conflicts, harassed by conflicting desires and tendencies… The ego attempts to solve its inner conflicts through false valuation and wrong choices. It is characteristic of the ego that it takes all that is unimportant as important, and all that is important as unimportant. Thus, although power, fame, wealth, ability, and other worldly attainments and accomplishments are really unimportant, the ego takes delight in these possessions and clings to them as 'mine'. On the other hand, true spirituality is all-important for the soul, but the ego looks upon it as unimportant… The ego thus represents a deep and fundamental principle of ignorance, which is exhibited in always preferring the unimportant to the important.

The ego's basic motivational drive is the satisfaction of desires; its symbol an ever-open mouth whose hunger can never be appeased. The more it gets, the more it wants, whether of power, fame, riches, pleasure, love. Its constant cry is 'I want! Give me!' It is the prime 'taker', and, should it ever 'give', does so because it expects personal advantage to result.

When, despite all its worldly acquisitions, the ego still feels empty and incomplete, its answer is always to fortify itself through still more acquisitions instead of cultivating detachment from them. It is thus the ego which supplies the driving force for the increasingly acquisitive, competitive and violent world in which we live.

It is impossible for the ego, whose fundamental belief is its own uniqueness and isolation, to accept that all life is one; that we are linked, through spirit, not only with each other but with creation as a whole; that the misery and degradation of some must inevitably affect the quality of life for all. On the contrary, the ego tends to look on the sufferings and humiliations of others *as evidence of its own superiority*. And, so far from seeing life as a unity, regards existence as a struggle in which it is essential to 'come out on top' and, acting on this belief, makes life far more of a struggle than it need or ought to be.

Since the ego's driving force is self-interest, it is evident that, so long as human beings are governed by their egos, no form of political organisation, no plan for social betterment, no church or religious institution, however lofty its ideals, will ever achieve its aims. Instead of transforming the quality of life, it will itself undergo transformation, or rather *decomposition*, since the egos of those taking part will before long start using it as a vehicle for their own profit or aggrandisement.[2]

We can see all this in the world of politics and business, but it is also possible – if one makes the effort to detach oneself and listen intently to one's own pattern of thought – actually to hear one's own ego speaking. In most of us indeed it keeps up a continuous monologue based on the idea of 'I' and 'mine' and centring round the themes 'I want', 'I mean to have'. As a rule the tone of this monologue is aggressive, for most egos are touchy and quick to take offence: 'I'll soon put a stop to that'... 'They'd better mind their step'... 'He can't go on treating me like this'. At other times or in other persons, its tone is feeble and self-pitying: 'I've really had about as much as I can take'... 'I don't know why things like this always happen to *me*'... 'I just don't see how I can go on coping'. Or else, faced with disappointment and frustration, the ego takes off into boastful fantasies and daydreams. In these it asserts its superiority and is acclaimed by humiliated rivals, so consoling itself by a withdrawal from reality for its own inner emptiness.[3]

Every thought, emotion, action which springs from the idea of exclusive, separate existence is a manifestation of the ego. All such reflections as 'I am someone of such and such a type, someone different and special', and that *my* home, *my* car, *my* clothes are different from those of other people; all emotions tending to exclude or reject others – hatred, resentment, fear, greed, jealousy, contempt – fortify and feed the ego. Under its domination we all do actions of which we afterwards say: "I just don't understand how it happened!" or "I don't know what came over me," as though the action concerned were not our own but the result of some outside force taking control.

Meantime, through the sense of separation which these negative emotions stir up and maintain, and through the words and acts which are the consequence of that sense of separation, there has occurred a narrowing-down of the range and scope of life, so that in excluding others it is we ourselves who experience exclusion, and the man or woman who tries to 'concentrate entirely on my own life' ends up having little or no life to concentrate upon. Thus the consequence of being subject to the ego is to make each man or woman a prisoner of his or her own selfishness, like the prince in the fairy story who was locked up inside a tree.

But direct self-assertion is far from being the only method employed by the ego to ensure its survival. We all at times come up against experiences which are too much for us. Face-to-face with the disaster we have brought upon ourselves or on those dearest to us, we may resolve to curb our ego-centredness; to reform our nature; to think and work for others. Good resolutions, however, though an essential first step, do not necessarily deal a death blow to the ego, or even curtail its activities to any great extent. For, as Baba explains:

> If the ego faces curtailment in one direction, it seeks compensating expansion in another. If it is overpowered by a flood of spiritual notions and actions, it tends to fasten upon this very force which was originally brought into play for the ousting of the ego. If a person attempts to cultivate humility in order to relieve himself of the monstrous weight of the ego… the ego can, with surprising alacrity, transfer itself to this attribute of humility.[4] It feeds itself through repeated assertions such as 'I am spiritual'… Thus arises what might be called a *spiritual* ego, or an ego that feels its separateness through the attainment of things considered to be good and highly spiritual. But from the truly spiritual point of view, this type of ego is as binding as the primary and crude ego which makes no such pretensions.[5]

Preachers and politicians, who adopt policies which in themselves are just and generous, may all too soon find themselves more concerned about their reputation as idealists than about the ideals they advocate, and, to complete the picture, not only feelings of superiority or inferiority, but even *the notion of equality*, advocated by idealists in good faith, can be seized upon by the ego. So long as a man or woman is under the ego's domination, support for equality merely –

> marks a point of transition between the two attitudes (of superiority and inferiority) rather than permanent freedom from the distinction between the 'I' and the 'you'... Such negative assertion of the ego in the form of equality is utterly different from the sense of unity characteristic of the life of spiritual freedom. Although the sense of equality is made the basis of many social and political ideals, the real conditions of a rich co-operative life are fulfilled only when the bare idea of equality is replaced *by the realisation of the unity of all life.*

Faced with the ego's capacity to wind itself into and take over even generous impulses and efforts to serve our fellow beings, what are we to do? How can we detach ourselves from our egos, and kill the hydra-headed monster once and for all? The first essential, Baba tells us, must be a search for right values.

> If the mind is to be freed from conflict it must always make the right choice and unfailingly prefer the truly important to the unimportant... only through the pursuit of true and permanent values is it possible to attain a poise that is not detrimental to the dynamic and creative flow of mental life... The problem of the conflict of desires thus turns out to be the problem of conflicting values, and the solution of mental conflict demands of us a deep search for the true meaning of life. It is only through wisdom that the mind can be freed from conflict.
>
> (And Baba goes on:) Having once known what the right choice is, the next step is to stick to it firmly... The life of true values can become spontaneous only when the mind has developed the unbroken habit of choosing the right values. Three-quarters of our life is made up of ordinary activities; and though conflict over ordinary matters may not cause much mental agony, it still leaves in the mind the sense of uneasiness that something is wrong. The conflicts that turn

> upon ordinary matters are rarely even brought to the surface of consciousness. Instead they cast a shadow on one's general feeling about life as if from behind a screen. Such conflicts have to be brought to the surface and frankly faced before they can be adequately solved... On such occasions an attempt should be made to analyse one's mental state through deep introspection.[6]

Valuable as such analysis can be in bringing hidden conflicts to light, however, these can only be *resolved* when a man or woman has developed 'a burning longing for some comprehensive ideal.' And, though modern psychology has supplied us with a practical technique for unearthing the sources of conflict within ourselves, the value of which Baba recognises, it has its own limitations, since

> ... it has yet to discover methods of awakening inspiration or supplying the mind with something which makes life worth living. This indeed is the creative task facing the saviours of humanity.
>
> The establishment of a true ideal is the beginning of right valuation. Right valuation in turn is the undoing of the constructions of the ego, which thrives on false valuation... In the ripeness of evolution comes the momentous discovery that life cannot be understood and lived fully as long as it is made to move around the pivot of the ego. Man is then driven by the logic of his own experience to find the true centre of experience and to reorganise his life in the Truth... The false nucleus provided by the ego must disappear if there is to be a true integration and fulfilment of life.

How is this "true centre of experience" to be built up, and the "false nucleus" of the ego dethroned? Baba's answer is logical and simple. Since the ego is an affirmation of separateness "the only experience that makes for its slimming down is the experience of love... The ego is the affirmation of being separate from others, while love is the affirmation of being one with others. Hence the ego can be dissolved only through true love."

The manner in which such dissolution may be effected will be examined in the next section. Meantime it can be said that Baba's three Discourses on "The Nature of the Ego and Its Termination", together with the related Discourse on "Selfishness", constitute an exposition so profound, so penetrating in analysis, so closely-knit in argument, so illuminating in the possibilities unfolded for a new approach to life, that if one were to devote ten years to studying them and seeking to be guided by them, one would be repaid many times over in the expansion of consciousness and the enrichment of life.

Notes

1. This and next extract abbreviated from: *Discourses*, pp. 160–3
2. The perversion of political ideals through selfishness is the underlying theme of George Orwell's famous satire *Animal Farm*.
3. James Thurber's story, *The Secret Life of Walter Mitty*, is such an ego fantasy. And much of the 'stream of consciousness' writing, which was started by the last chapter in James Joyce's *Ulysses*, consists of the musings of different egos. The phrase an 'ego trip' conveys a general truth in popular terms.
4. Readers may recall, in Charles Dickens' *David Copperfield*, the repeated claim of Uriah Heep to be "so very 'umble."
5. This and next extract abbreviated from: *Discourses*, pp. 170–3
6. This and following quotes abbreviated from: *Discourses*, pp. 163–5

Meher Baba. Location: Ganeshkhind, Pune, 1957. Photographer: Meelan / © Meher Nazar Publications.

Section 2

Love: The Creative Force

We naturally tend to think of love solely in human terms. But love, in one form or another, Baba tells us, is built into the whole pattern of creation.

> Life and love are inseparable from each other. Where there is life, there is love. Even the most rudimentary consciousness is always trying to burst out of its limitations and experience some kind of unity with other forms. Though each form is separate from other forms, in reality they are all forms of the same unity of life. The latent sense of this inner reality makes itself felt even in the world of illusion (i.e. the material world) through the attraction one form has for another.
>
> The law of gravitation, which planets and stars are

subject to, is in its own way a dim reflection of the love that pervades the universe. Even the forces of repulsion are in fact expressions of love, since things are repelled from one another because they are more powerfully attracted to something else. Repulsion is a negative consequence of positive attraction. The forces of cohesion and affinity, which prevail in the very constitution of matter, are positive expressions of love. A striking example at this level is the attraction the magnet exercises for iron. All these forms of love are of the lowest type since they are conditioned by the rudimentary consciousness in which they appear.

In the animal world, love becomes more explicit in the form of *conscious* impulses directed towards different objects in the surroundings. Such love is instinctive and takes the form of gratifying different desires through the appropriation of suitable objects. When a tiger seeks to devour a deer, it is in a very real sense 'in love' with the deer. Sexual attraction is another form of love at this level. All expressions of love at this stage have one thing in common, they all seek to satisfy some bodily impulse or desire through the object of love.

Human love is much higher than these lower forms because human beings have fully developed consciousness. Though human love is continuous with the subhuman forms out of which it developed, it differs in one respect, since its operations have to be carried on side by side with a new factor, which is reason. Sometimes human love manifests itself as a force divorced from reason and running parallel to it, sometimes as a force that comes into conflict with reason. Finally, it expresses itself as a constituent of the harmonised whole in which love and reason have been balanced and fused into integral unity... When this is achieved, both love and reason are so completely transformed as to precipitate the emergence of a new level of consciousness which, compared to normal human consciousness, can best be described as *superconsciousness.*

Human love (Baba goes on to say) is encircled by a number of obstructive factors, such as infatuation, lust, greed, anger and jealousy. In one sense, even these obstructive factors are either lower forms of love or the inevitable side results of these lower forms of love. In infatuation a person is enamoured of a sensual object; in lust he develops a craving for sensations in relation to it; and in greed he desires to possess it. Of these three lower forms of love, greed has a tendency to extend from the original object to the means of obtaining it. Thus a person becomes greedy for money, power or fame, which can be instruments for possessing the different objects that are craved. Anger and jealousy come into existence when these lower forms of love are threatened or thwarted.

These lower forms of love obstruct the release of pure love. The stream of love can never become clear and steady until it is separated from these limiting and perverting forms of lower love. The lower forms are the enemy of the higher... Therefore love has to be carefully distinguished from the obstructive factors of infatuation, lust, greed and anger. In infatuation, the person is a passive victim of the spell of conceived attraction for the object. In love there is an active appreciation of the intrinsic worth of the object of love.[1]

In the four Discourses which Baba devotes to love in its various aspects, he directs particular attention to differentiating between love and lust, which we all at one time or another tend to confuse.

In lust there is reliance upon a sensual object and consequent spiritual subordination of oneself to it, whereas love puts one into direct and co-ordinate relation with the reality behind the form. Therefore lust is experienced as being heavy, and love as being light. In lust there is a narrowing down of life, and in love there is an expansion of being. To have loved someone is

> like adding another life to your own. Your life is, as it were, multiplied, and you virtually live in two centres. If you love the whole world, you live vicariously in the whole world; but in lust there is an ebbing down of life and a sense of hopeless dependence upon a form regarded as another. Thus in lust there is accentuation of separateness and suffering, while in love there is the feeling of unity and joy. Lust is a craving of the senses; love is the expression of the spirit. In lust there is excitement, but in love there is tranquillity.

Baba's words on lust are amplified in what he has to say about sex, which he describes as, "One of the most important problems with which we are confronted, one of the 'givens' in human nature which, like everything else in life, comes to be considered through the opposites created by the limited mind," and he records our situation faced by these opposites with profound sympathy and understanding.

> Just as the mind tries to fit life into a scheme of alternatives – such as joy or pain, good or bad, solitude or company, attraction or repulsion – so in relation to sex it tends to think of indulgence and repression as alternatives from which there is no escape.
>
> It seems as if the mind must accept one or the other; yet it cannot wholeheartedly accept either. When it tries repression, it is dissatisfied and thinks longingly of indulgence. When it tries indulgence, it becomes conscious of its bondage to the senses, and seeks freedom by reverting to mechanical repression... However, in spite of repeated disappointment in indulgence as well as in repression, the mind usually does not renounce the root cause of unhappiness – which is *craving*... Only when aspirants become fully awake to the inevitable bondage and suffering caused by craving, do they begin voluntarily to disburden themselves of craving through

> intelligent understanding. Once the mind is free from craving, it can no longer be moved by the false promises of either indulgence or mechanical repression... Mind turns to the mechanical repression of craving because of disappointment, but it turns to spontaneous renunciation of craving because of disillusionment or awakening.[2]

Disappointment, as we can usually see in the case of others, if not always in our own, is an emotional state rooted in self-pity. It implies that we have been 'let down' in our justified expectations, but that these may well succeed if we try again, or in a new direction, which is exactly what we all tend to do in our sex lives.

Disillusion, however, is based on reason, and what it tells us is that we have been pursuing illusion and that, so long as we choose to delude ourselves, we cannot possibly find what we are seeking. It is not therefore related to self-pity but to *self-reproof*. Disillusion leads to an awakening, awakening to the need to face reality, which brings us eventually to the recognition that, since it is craving which was the source of self-deception, it is craving which must be got rid of.

The situation of someone planted between the alternatives of indulgence and repression – and hazily beginning to perceive they will find peace in neither – has been eloquently expressed from what might seem an unlikely source. Lord Byron wrote from Italy to his friend John Hobhouse: "I feel and I feel it bitterly that a man should not consume his life at the side and on the bosom of a woman... that even the recompense – and it is much – is not enough... but I have neither the strength of mind to break the chain nor the insensibility which would deaden its weight. I cannot tell what will become of me."

Many have felt as Byron felt and vacillated between two extremes, not knowing "what will become of" them. When we look at life from a broader standpoint, we find the same picture of vacillation. The age into which we have lately moved is called 'the permissive age', but it might equally well be called an age of indulgence. There have in the course of history been many periods of indulgence or permissiveness, just as there have been many periods of repression. The one, as Baba shows, is both the cause and consequence of the other. The pendulum swings across the centuries just as it swings in the smaller timescale of our own lives. The present period of indulgence follows upon a period of repression, the Victorian Age, in which the normal sexual restraints and taboos were reinforced by many which were abnormal and excessive. Older people alive today[3] were brought up in this repressive atmosphere and suffered from its restrictiveness. As a result the belief has spread that problems over sex only arise because the 'natural self' has been inhibited. If this natural self were allowed full freedom from an early age – the argument runs – there would be no inhibition and no suffering. However, it is assumed, a completely free enjoyment of sexuality would lead sooner or later to love and happy marriage, without the need for special effort on our part, that is, simply 'in the course of nature'.

What Baba now tells us, though, is the very opposite of this agreeable fantasy. Promiscuity, he says, does not lead to freedom but to bondage, and bondage to lust, which is more potent than any drug.

> In promiscuity the temptation to explore the possibilities of mere sexual contact is formidable. If the mind tries to understand sex through increasing the scope of sex, the delusions to which it becomes a prey are as endless as the scope of sex itself. Only by the maximum restriction of the scope of mere sex can the aspirant arrive at any real understanding of the values attainable through the gradual transformation of sex into love... Again, in promiscuity the suggestions of lust are necessarily the first to present themselves to the mind,

> and the individual is doomed to react within the limitations of this initial perversion and thus close the door to deeper experiences.
>
> Truth cannot be grasped by skipping over the surface of life and multiplying superficial contacts. It requires a preparedness of mind which can centre its capacities upon selected experiences. This process of discrimination between lower and higher, and the transcendence of the lower in favour of the higher, is made possible through wholehearted concentration and a true interest in life. Such concentration and interest is impossible when the mind becomes a slave to the habit of wandering between many possible objects of similar experience.[4]

Baba's theme of the enslaving power of sensuality pursued for its own sake cannot fail to awaken echoes in many hearts. The sensual life, inevitably one of promiscuity in greater or less degree, is based on a double delusion: first, that happiness can be found through the multiplication of desires and their satisfaction; and secondly, that it is possible to remain in control of desires to which one continually gives way, though common sense tells us this is impossible. The same theme, familiar throughout art and literature, is to be found most potently in myth, that great repository of the world's unconscious knowledge. Medusa, the Gorgon, whose head, beautiful but horrible, turned everyone who looked on her to stone, was represented with the serpents of desire around her face instead of hair, and with serpents also at her girdle.

In more recent times the story known to everyone is that of Don Juan, whose name has passed into everyday language. There are many versions of his story but, in most, Don Juan, after a life devoted to seduction, betrays a girl of noble family, and then kills the father who is seeking to avenge her. Sometime later, seeing a stone effigy of the dead father on his tomb, he flippantly invites it to dinner. The effigy, representing Don Juan's humanity now turned to stone, does indeed come to dinner, and this visit proves to be the harbinger of Juan's death. In both myths the implication is the same. Lust pursued for its own sake inevitably leads to callousness towards others and their claims; in time, therefore, it separates a man or woman from their own humanity. The capacity to experience love is lost in the pursuit of physical sensation, and the victimiser, become their own victim, is turned inwardly to stone. Robert Burns[5] (1759–96), who had experienced both the depths of sensual passion and the heights of human feeling, has expressed this memorably in his "Epistle to Davie":

> I waive the quantum o' the sin,
> The hazard of concealing;
> But och; it hardens a' within,
> And petrifies the feeling!

From a consideration of promiscuity and its effects, Baba turns to a comparison with married life. Here, too, sex is involved but, he explains

> Sex in marriage is entirely different from sex outside marriage. In marriage the impressions of lust are much lighter and can more easily be removed... In married life two souls become linked in so many ways, that they are called upon to tackle the whole complex problem of personality, rather than a simple problem created by some isolated desire... Promiscuous sex attempts to separate the problem of sex from other needs of the developing personality, and to solve it in isolation from them. Although this kind of solution might seem easy, it turns out to be utterly superficial, and has the further disadvantage of side-tracking the aspirant from attempting the real solution... In married life there is ample

> room for varied experience, with the result that the different tendencies latent in the mind begin to organise around the crystallised scheme of married life...
>
> Married life develops so many points of contact between two souls that severance of all connection would mean deranging the whole tenor of life. Since this difficulty of breaking away from one another encourages inner readjustment, marriage affords an opportunity for the souls to establish a lasting understanding which can cope with the most complex and delicate situations.[6]

It is sometimes argued that marriage is 'out-of-date' and has no place in the modern world. Free and independent spirits, it is suggested, should live freely and independently, pairing and parting without obligation. Divorce should require nothing more than the consent of both parties that their association has now ended; financial and other details can be worked out by lawyers acting for both sides. Apart from the question of children, whose need for stability and parental love is ignored under such a system, there is the fact stressed by Baba that a serious relationship has no opportunity to develop if the tie can be broken with a word or at a whim. Some cases of grievous hardship are indeed produced by marriage laws, but the institution itself represents far more than a mere legality; it stands for nothing less than the longing and aspiration of men and women to reach together a deeper understanding and experience of life than either could attain alone.

> The spiritual value of married life (Baba goes on to explain) is directly related to the nature of the factors determining its daily course. If based on shallow considerations, it can deteriorate into a partnership in selfishness aimed against the rest of the world. If inspired by lofty idealism, it can rise to a fellowship which not only calls forth increasing sacrifices for

each other, but actually becomes a medium through which the two souls can offer their united love and service to the whole family of humanity. When married life is thus brought into line with the Divine Plan for the evolution of the individuals, it becomes a blessing for the children who are its fruit and who absorb a spiritual atmosphere from the very beginning.

In turn the married life of the parents is enriched by the presence of the children. Children give parents an opportunity for expressing and developing spontaneous love in which sacrifice becomes easy and delightful, and the part played by children is of tremendous importance for the spiritual advancement of the parents themselves. It therefore follows that when children make their appearance they ought to be welcomed wholeheartedly.

For the man or woman truly in search of inner freedom, the alternative to married life is celibacy, and Baba tells us,

> It should be borne in mind that the life of freedom is nearer to the life of restraint than to the life of indulgence. Hence for the aspirant, if restraint comes easily, celibacy is preferable to married life. Such restraint, however, is difficult for most persons and sometimes impossible, so for them married life is more helpful. Just as celibacy requires and calls forth many virtues, so married life in turn nourishes the growth of many spiritual qualities of the utmost importance. The value of celibacy lies in the habit of restraint and the sense of detachment and independence it gives. The value of marriage lies in lessons of mutual adjustment and the sense of unity with the other…
>
> For the celibate as well as for the married person the path of inner life is the same. When drawn by the Truth aspirants long for nothing else, and as Truth increasingly comes within their ken, they gradually disburden themselves of craving.

> Whether in celibacy or marriage, they are no longer swayed by the deceptive promises of indulgence or mechanical repression, and so practise internal and spontaneous renunciation of craving until freed from the deceptive opposites.

Having shown, in his Discourse on marriage, the heights to which human love can attain, Baba goes on to show that such perfected human love can lead on to something greater still, to which he gives the name 'pure love', and this in turn to 'divine love' in which a person finally becomes one with God.

> Pure love is the bloom of spiritual perfection. Human love is so tethered by limiting conditions that the spontaneous appearance of pure love from within becomes impossible. So when pure love arises in the aspirant, it is always a gift. Pure love arises in the heart of the aspirant in response to the descent of grace from a Perfect Master. When pure love is first received as a gift of the Master, it becomes lodged in the consciousness of the aspirant like a seed in favourable soil; and in the course of time the seed develops into a plant and then into a full-grown tree.[7]

Lest it be assumed that we have to go looking for this 'Master' in order to have grace descend upon us, Baba has made clear that our task is not to wander around in search of such a being, but to prepare ourselves inwardly to receive his grace. "As soon as the disciple is ready the grace of the Master descends, for the Master, who is the ocean of divine love, is always on the lookout for the soul in whom his grace will fructify." And in the passage just concluded, Baba's use of the phrase "pure love from within" shows he is referring to the Eternal Master Within, namely God, with whom Baba is One, and with whom we, as he is constantly telling us, are, in our True Selves, also One. Hence his reiterated

"You and I are not We but One."

He continues...

> The descent of the grace of the Master is conditioned, however, by the preliminary spiritual preparation of the aspirant. This preparation for grace is not complete until the aspirant has built into his spiritual make-up some divine attributes. For example, when a person avoids backbiting and thinks more of the good points in others than of their bad ones, can practise supreme tolerance, and desires the good of others even at cost to himself, he is ready to receive the grace of the Master... The kind of love awakened by the grace of the Master is a rare privilege. The mother who is willing to sacrifice all and to die for her child, and the martyr who is prepared to give up his life for his country, are indeed supremely noble; but they have not necessarily tasted this pure love born through the grace of the Master. Even the great yogis who, sitting in caves and on mountain tops, are completely absorbed in deep *samadhi* (meditative trance), do not necessarily have this precious love.
>
> Pure love awakened through the grace of the Master is more valuable than any other stimulus. It not only combines in itself the merits of all the disciplines, but excels them all in its efficacy to lead the aspirant to his goal. When this love is born, all his thoughts turn away from the self and come to be exclusively centred on the divine Beloved. Through the intensity of this ever growing love, he eventually breaks through the shackles of the self and becomes united with the Beloved. This is the consummation of love. When love has thus found its fruition, it has become *divine*...
>
> Divine love arises after the disappearance of the individual mind and is thus free from the trammels of the individual nature. In human love the duality of the lover and the Beloved persists, but in divine love the lover and the Beloved become

> one. At this stage the aspirant has stepped out of the domain of duality, and becomes one with God; for Divine Love *is* God. When lover and Beloved are one, that is the end and the beginning.

And in a wonderfully lyrical passage, full of encouragement and reassurance, Baba tells us –

> It is for love that the whole universe sprang into existence, and it is for the sake of love that it is kept going. God descends into the realm of Illusion because the apparent duality of Beloved and lover is eventually contributory to His conscious enjoyment of His own divinity. The development of love is conditioned and sustained by the tension of duality. God has to suffer apparent differentiation into a multiplicity of souls in order to carry on the game of love...
>
> Love is the reflection of God's unity in the world of duality. It constitutes the entire significance of creation. If love were excluded from life, all the souls in the world would assume complete externality to each other; and the only possible relations and contacts in such a loveless world would be superficial and mechanical. It is because of love that the contacts and relations between individual souls become significant. It is love which gives meaning and value to all the happenings in the world of duality, but it is at the same time a standing challenge to duality. As love gathers strength, it generates creative restlessness and becomes the main driving power of that spiritual dynamic which ultimately succeeds in restoring to consciousness the original unity of Being.

Notes

1. This and next extract: *Discourses*, abbreviated from pp. 110–3
2. *Discourses*, abbr. pp. 99–101

3. In 1980s. (Ed.)
4. *Discourses*, abbr. pp. 102–3
5. The celebrated Scottish poet and lyricist. (Ed.)
6. This and next extracts: *Discourses*, abbr. pp. 101–6
7. This and remaining extracts: *Discourses*, abbr. pp. 113–6

Meher Baba in Seclusion in the Cage Room. Location: Upper Meherabad. Date: 30 July 1931. Photographer: Padri (Faredoon Driver) / © MSI Collection.

Section 3

Reincarnation & The States of 'Hell' and 'Heaven'

In the introduction to the second part of this book, two questions were posed. The first – as to how man and woman, being "spiritual in essence and eternal in nature", came to identify themselves with their physical body – has now been answered; and the path they must follow to find liberation has been indicated by Baba as the path of love.

But there remains the second question: since the body is no more than a coat to be discarded after earthly use, what is it which survives the long series of incarnations, enabling us to carry over the lessons of one life to the next – thus making progress possible across scores of lives and through an infinite range and variety of experiences?

In the first of a series of seven Discourses devoted to "Reincarnation and Karma"[1] Baba explains:

> Immortality of the individualised soul is made possible by the fact that the individualised soul is *not* the same as the physical body. The individualised soul continues to exist with all its sanskaras (impressions) in the inner worlds through its subtle[2] and mental bodies, even after it has discarded its gross body at the time of death. Hence, life through the medium of the gross body is only a section of the life of the individualised soul; the other sections of its life have their expression in other spheres.
>
> Nature is much greater than can be perceived through the ordinary senses of the physical body… The finer aspects of nature are not perceptible to the ordinary individual, but are nevertheless continuous with the gross aspect which is perceptible to him. The finer and hidden part of nature has two important divisions, namely the subtle and the mental, corresponding to the subtle and mental bodies of man… When the soul has incarnated in a physical body, it expresses its life in the gross world. When it drops the outer sheath (the physical body), it continues to have its expression of life either in the subtle world through the subtle body, or in the mental world through the mental body…
>
> In normal cases, death occurs when the sanskaras (impressions) released for expression in that reincarnation are all worked out. When the soul drops its physical body, it is completely severed from all connections with the gross world, though the ego and the mind are retained with all the impressions accumulated during the earthly career. Unlike the exceptional cases of spirits which are still obsessed with the gross world,[3] ordinary souls try to reconcile themselves to the severance, and conform to the limitations of changed

conditions. They are now in a state of subjectivity, in which a new process begins of mentally reviewing the experiences of the earthly career by reviving the sanskaras (impressions) connected with those experiences. Thus death inaugurates a period of comparative rest consisting in a temporary withdrawal from the gross sphere of action. It is the beginning of an interval between the last incarnation and the next.[4]

To sum up: when the individual soul has discarded its gross body, it no longer has any consciousness of the gross world, but it retains the impressions from the past life within its mental body. During the interval between death and its next reincarnation, the soul's consciousness is entirely concentrated upon these impressions. It is not aware of the subtle environment, which should not be thought of as having any kind of 'geographical' existence. Baba goes on:

> In life after death the experiences of pain and pleasure become much more intense than they were in earthly life. These subjective states of intensified suffering and joy are what we know as 'hell' and 'heaven'. *Hell and heaven are states of mind; they should not be looked upon as being places…*
>
> In the earthly career, desires – as well as the pleasures and suffering they bring – are experienced through the medium of the gross body… Therefore the processes of consciousness have to pass through an additional veil which lessens their force, liveliness and intensity – just as rays of light are dimmed when they pass through a thick glass – but when the body has been given up, they undergo a relative increase in intensity.
>
> In the heaven state the fulfilment of desires is not, as in the gross sphere, dependent upon having the object of desire. Fulfilment comes merely through thinking of that object. For example, if a person wishes to hear exquisite music, he

experiences this pleasure merely by thinking about it, and the pleasure he derives from the thought of exquisite music is much greater than the pleasure derived in his earthly career from the actual hearing of sounds...

In fact, even in the earthly sphere, some individuals develop this capacity for making their pleasure independent of the possession of a gross object. Beethoven was completely deaf; yet through the exercise of imagination alone, he was able to enjoy his own compositions intensely. In a sense, even on earth he might figuratively be said to have been 'in the heaven state'. In the same way, a person who meditates on the Beloved with love derives happiness merely through the thought of the Beloved, without requiring His physical presence... So too, the finer desires – idealistic aspirations, aesthetic and scientific interests, goodwill towards friends and neighbours (with the resultant personal love and fellow feeling) – contribute to the life of enlightenment and happiness prevalent in the heaven state.

Certain other desires, by contrast, have a direct relation to the possession and assimilation of gross objects through the gross body. In these 'coarse' desires – such as lust, gluttony, or the craving for alcohol or drugs – there is not only a preponderance of sensations derived from contact with the object, but also of those sensations which constitute the response of the body itself. Such coarser desires contribute to the hell state... Any imaginative idea or thought of the gross objects serves only to accentuate the urge to reach out for them, and, since those gross objects are no longer available, suffering is intensified.

Hell and heaven are *both* states of bondage, however, and subject to the limitations of the opposites of pleasure and pain. Both are states whose duration is determined by the nature, amount and intensity of the accumulated impressions, so that, from this point of view, heaven and hell are shadows cast by one's earthly life. Though time in the subtle world is not the same as time in the gross world, the important fact is that both the hell and heaven states are far from lasting. After having served their purpose in the life of the individualised soul, they both come to an end.

Heaven and hell would, however, serve no especially useful purpose if they were to consist merely of mental revival of the earthly past. That would mean bare repetition of what has already occurred. On earth, the consciousness of most persons is predominantly objective and forward-looking under the pressure of unspent sanskaras (impressions). But in the after-death states, consciousness is predominantly subjective and retrospective. All its earthly experiences are now available for reflection in a form more vivid than is possible through memory during earthly life. The shots have all been taken on the mind's cinematic film, and they can now be studied through magnified projection on the screen of subjective consciousness.

The lessons learned by the soul through such stocktaking and reflection are confirmed in the mental body by the power of their magnified suffering or happiness. The truths absorbed by the mind in the life after death become in the next incarnation a part of its inborn wisdom.[5]

It will be apparent from the above that 'heaven' and 'hell' are not alternatives, but complementary states. Every soul will experience some degree of 'hell' and some degree also of 'heaven', the proportion of each depending on his or her actions in the preceding life. Readers may find themselves contrasting the logic and justice of 'hell' and 'heaven' as described by Meher Baba, with the picture presented by mediaeval Christianity, which has lingered on into our own time. That a soul should be damned eternally for the misdeeds, however grievous, of a single lifetime inevitably strikes us as unjust in view of the utterly different backgrounds from which individuals come, the handicaps from which they suffer or the advantages they enjoy, and the very different opportunities available to them.

Equally, the idea that a soul can progress so rapidly in a single lifetime as to be capable of eternal bliss through proximity to the Divine Being baffles a present-day comprehension. If eternal bliss is to come within reach of human beings, it can surely only be as the result of arduous spiritual effort sustained over many lives. And the concept of a Judgement Day, following which one half of mankind will ascend to eternal happiness, while the remainder sink into lasting torment, is an insult to the Divine Being – a scenario which not even the glories of the Sistine Chapel can render anything but repellent.

As against the contradictions and injustices of such a destiny, that unfolded by Baba in his Discourses on "Reincarnation and Karma" reveals a sublime blending of justice and compassion. *The whole of mankind is seen as progressing towards a goal which all will ultimately attain, though at varying rates and over different measures of time.* For one and all the goal is the state known as 'God-realisation', that is the becoming conscious and the full acceptance of one's own True Self, which is "spiritual in essence, eternal in nature". We are all children of God, though few indeed are aware as yet of our sublime destiny.

A divine streak is woven into us all, and it is this divine streak which is real and lasting; and the material world which is illusory. Our pilgrimage is not outward across space but inwards towards the divine Reality. Hell and heaven – so far from being ultimate destinies to which mankind will be consigned, sheep in one direction, goats in another – are temporary states between one life and the next, and both are beneficial to the soul. In the 'hell' state we recognise our follies and misdeeds more painfully, and therefore more clearly, than we were able to do on earth; and in the 'heaven' state we derive comfort and confidence from whatever good we were able to accomplish and whatever service we may have rendered to others. Thus we can form resolutions to be put into effect on our return to earth.

It would seem to follow that, in so far as we are able to face our own inadequacies and wrongdoings in this life, and modify the greed and selfishness of our egos, we may hope to reduce the length and intensity of the 'hell' state, through having learned some part of the necessary lessons in advance.

In the third part of his long Discourse on "Reincarnation and Karma", subtitled "The Existence and Memory of Past Lives", Baba goes on to explain why the memory of our previous incarnations is closed off from us in this one.

> Those who have immediate access to the supersensible truths concerning the life of the soul and its reincarnation know, through their unclouded perception, that so-called birth is only an incarnation of the individualised soul in the gross sphere. The unbroken continuity of the life of the reincarnating soul is punctuated by birth and death, both of which are comparable to gateways in the stream of life as it advances from one type of existence to another. Both are equally necessary in the greater life of the soul, and the interval between death and birth is as necessary as the interval between birth and death.
>
> Just as those who consider death to be the termination of individual existence, those who consider the birth of the body to be its beginning are also confronted with a conflict between their false assumptions and the claims of rationalised intuition. From the standpoint of individual justice, the uneven distribution of good and bad in relation to material happiness or prosperity seems seriously to impugn the rationality and justification of the entire scheme of the universe. To see the virtuous at times suffering deeply and the vicious possessing the amenities of pleasure, creates insurmountable difficulties for anyone who looks upon life as being intended to fulfil an

eternal and divine purpose...

But in spite of all appearances to the contrary, the human mind has in it an inborn tendency to try to restore a deep and unshakeable faith in the intrinsic sanity and value of life. Except where artificial resistances are created, it finds acceptable those explanations that are in conformity with this deeper law of the spirit.

Those who have direct access to the truth of reincarnation are even fewer than those who have direct access to the truth of the immortality of the individual soul. The memories of all past lives are stored and preserved in the mental body, but they are not accessible to normal consciousness because a veil is drawn over them. When the soul changes its physical body, it acquires a new brain. Under ordinary circumstances, only the memories of the present life can appear in consciousness, because the new brain acts as a hindrance to the release of memories gathered in past lives through the medium of other brains.

In rare cases, some memories of past lives do leak into the present life in the form of dreams. A person may see in his dreams people he has never seen in his present life. However, the memory of past lives does not come back to a person, except in abnormal and rare cases, unless he/she is sufficiently advanced from the spiritual point of view.

At first sight it might seem that absence of memory of previous lives is a total loss, but this is far from being the case. Spiritual evolution consists in guiding life in the light of the highest values perceived through intuition, and not in allowing it to be determined by the past. *The task of Emancipation consists in securing freedom from the past rather than in being governed by it.*

Life would be infinitely more complicated if one who is not spiritually advanced were burdened with the conscious memory of numberless past lives. He would be dazed and unsettled by the diversity of settings in which persons would appear to him in the light of his memory. Those whom he once looked upon as belonging to him might be seen in this present life belonging to someone else. Possessiveness of all types must be purged from the mind before the aspirant is spiritually prepared to withstand the disturbing influence of memories from past lives.

When an individual is spiritually prepared, he is completely desireless and full of impersonal love. All entanglements of the personal ego have disappeared from his mind. He can look upon his old friends and enemies with equanimity. He is so lifted out of his limitations that he is the same to relations and non-relations from his past and present lives. He is free from the idea of any pressing claims and counterclaims on his part against others, or of others against himself, because he has realised the deeper truth of the unity of all life and the illusoriness of mundane happenings.[6]

From this explanation as to why memory of previous incarnations is withheld from us, Baba goes on to explain the specific conditions which govern each new incarnation.

Notes

1. *Karma* is generally translated as 'fate', meaning those circumstances in a person's life which are preconditioned by his or her previous lives.
2. Baba uses the term *subtle body* to describe the vehicle (or nucleus) of our desires and vital forces which carries forward from one life to another. The *mental body* is the seat of the mind. Unlike the brain, which dies with the body, the mind also continues from one life to another, carrying forward the mental impressions.
3. Baba has explained that in certain cases of untimely death, particularly suicide, in which a soul's sanskaras have *not*

been fully worked out, the discarnate soul continues to crave gross satisfactions which are no longer available to it, and suffers accordingly.

4. *Discourses*, pp. 304–6. The above is condensed from a Discourse on "The Significance of Death" which particularly requires to be read and studied in full.
5. *Discourses*, condensed from pp. 307–12
6. *Discourses*, abbr. pp. 313–6

Meher Baba. Location: Meherabad, November 1930. © Meher Nazar Publications.

Section 4

Karma: The 'Inexorable Must'

At the sahavas (gathering) which he gave for his devotees at the Meher Spiritual Center, Myrtle Beach, on the South Carolina coast in May 1958, the following statement from Baba was read out:

> Everything and everyone in the universe is constrained to move along a path prescribed by its past. There is an inexorable 'must' that reigns over all things large or small.

The freedom man appears to enjoy is itself subject to inner compulsions: and the environmental pressure, which limits the scope of reactions or moulds the reacting self, is itself subject to the inexorable 'must', which is operative in the past, present and future.

Man has his name, his sex, his personality, his colour, his nationality, his characteristics, his pain and pleasure and all that he may possess because he *must* have all these.

This overpowering compulsion is exercised by the force of innumerable impressions gathered in the past. The rule of this inexorable 'must' governs and reshapes the so-called destiny of man in every incarnation as long as the 'self' of man remains conscious of impressions. The principle of 'must' which overrides human plans is based on divine law which both adjusts and gets adjusted by evolutionary impressions. It is only the divine will that can supersede the divine law.

The so many deaths during the one whole life, beginning from the evolution of consciousness to the end of the involution of consciousness, are like so many sleeps during one lifetime.

One who lives for himself is truly dead, and one who dies for God is truly alive.[1]

From this statement it might appear that – since the circumstances of every individual life, as well as our reactions to every situation in which we find ourselves, are all governed by past impressions – there can be no such thing as free will, with little possibility of changing our nature or modifying our future. That this is not the whole truth of the matter, however, is made plain in Part VI of Baba's long Discourse on "Reincarnation and Karma", in which his theme is "The Operation of Karma Through Successive Lives".

In the successive incarnations of an individual soul, there is not only a thread of continuity and identity, but there is also an uninterrupted reign of the law of cause and effect through the persistence and operation of karma. The successive incarnations with all their particulars are unfailingly determined by rational law, *so that it becomes possible for the individual soul to mould its future through wise and intelligent action.* The actions of past lives determine the conditions and circumstances of the present life, and the actions of the present life have their share in determining the conditions and circumstances of future lives. Successive incarnations of the individual soul yield their full significance only in the light of the operation of the law of karma.

A person's intermittent incarnations in the gross world are only apparently disconnected. Karma persists as a connecting link and determining factor through the mental body, which remains a permanent and constant factor throughout all the lives of an individual soul. The law of karma and its manner of operation cannot be fully understood as long as the gross body and the gross world are considered to be the only facts of existence. Karmic determination is made possible by the existence of the subtle and mental bodies and worlds.

The plane on which one can possess physical consciousness is the gross world. The planes on which one can possess consciousness of desires are in the subtle world, and the planes on which the soul can have mental consciousness are in the mental world. The source of desire is to be found in the mind, which is on the mental planes. Here the seed of desire is attached to the mind and exists there in a latent form – just as the tree is latent in the seed. The mind retains all impressions and dispositions in a latent form, and the limited 'I', or ego, is composed of these sanskaras (impressions). *It is this ego-mind which constitutes the kernel of the existence of a reincarnating individual.*

The ego-mind, based in the mental body, takes lower

bodies according to the impressions, or sanskaras, stored in it. These impressions determine whether an individual will die young or old; will experience health or illness, or both; will be beautiful or ugly; will suffer from physical handicaps, such as blindness, or will enjoy general efficiency of the body; will have sharp or dull intellect; will be pure or impure of heart, fickle or steadfast in will; will be immersed in the pursuit of material gain or will seek the inner light of the spirit.

The ego-mind, in its turn, becomes modified through the deposited impressions of karma, which include not only physical action, but thought and feeling. And the circumstances of each incarnation are adjusted to the composition and needs of the ego-mind. Thus, if a person has developed certain capacities or tendencies in one incarnation, he takes them on into succeeding incarnations; and activities left incomplete in one can be completed in following incarnations... Those also who have been closely associated with each other, whether through good or bad dealings, tend to make recurring contacts. Thus the game of duality is carried on long enough to gather so much experience of the opposites that the soul, out of the fullness of its experience, eventually becomes ripe for dropping the ego-mind and turning inward to know itself as the Oversoul.

If there has been a give and take between certain persons which forges karmic and sanskaric links between them, creating claims and counterclaims, they have to come together and carry on fresh dealings in order to meet these claims and counterclaims. That which a person gives with a selfish motive binds him in the same way as that which he takes with a sense of separateness. The transaction of give and take need not be purely on a material plane in the form of goods or money, or in the performing of physical tasks. It can consist in the exchange of views or feelings...

The quick and unfailing responsiveness of souls is expressed in the law that hate begets hate, lust begets lust, and love begets love. This law operates not only during a single lifetime but across several lives. An individual feels impelled to hate or fear an enemy from past lives, although the present life may have given him no apparent reason for this attitude. In the same way he or she, is impelled, for no apparent reason, to love and help a friend from previous lives… The rhythm in which two souls start their relationship tends to perpetuate itself, unless the souls, through fresh intelligent karma, change the rhythm and raise it to a higher level of quality…

Karmic determination is popularly designated as 'fate'. Fate, however, is not some foreign and oppressive principle. *Fate is man's own creation pursuing him from past lives; and just as it has been shaped by past karma, so it can also be modified, remoulded and even undone through karma in the present life.* Karma on earth plays an important part in shaping and reshaping the impressions in the ego-mind, and giving it a momentum which decides a person's further destiny. It is in the arena of earthly existence that creative and effective karma can be expressed, through the medium of the gross body. Proper understanding and use of the law of karma enables man to become master of his own destiny through intelligent and wise action. *Each person has become what he is through his own accumulated actions. And it is through his own further actions that he can mould himself according to the pattern of his heart, or finally emancipate himself from that karmic determination, which has governed him throughout the long sequence of lives and deaths.*

Broadly speaking, karma is of two kinds: that which binds and that which helps towards Emancipation and Self-realisation. Good as well as bad karma binds as long as it feeds the ego-mind through wrong understanding. But karma becomes a power for Emancipation when it springs

> from right understanding and wears out the ego-mind. Right understanding in this respect is best imparted by the Perfect Masters, who know the soul in its true nature and destiny, along with the complications created by karmic laws.
>
> The karma that truly counts comes into existence after a person has developed a sense of distinction between good and bad. During the first seven years of childhood, the impressions released for expression are very faint, do not leave strong or effective impressions on the ego-mind, nor play an important part in shaping the child's future. True and effective karma, which moulds the ego-mind and its future, begins after the individual has developed a sense of responsibility. This sense of responsibility depends on a sense of the distinction between good and bad, which as a rule dawns fully only after one has passed the first years of childhood.[2]

The concept of free will is thus seen to be one which involves the right use of time. None of us can produce great and lasting changes in our character or situation merely by wishing for such changes to occur. If a man or woman resolves to become a great saint or a great artist, he or she is embarking on a course which can only yield its full results over a sufficient span of lives. The same will be true to a lesser degree of someone who sets their heart on becoming a great athlete or mountaineer. All talent, all spiritual development, demands the appropriate amount of time to prove effective, and even where such talent appears to blossom suddenly partway through a lifetime, it will be because of efforts previously made but slow to take effect. "Which of you," Christ asked, "by taking thought can add one cubit unto his stature?"[3] But, with a firm enough determination and a sufficient span of time, anything and everything becomes possible.

From the physical world we may take the parallel of a large and powerful vessel. If the captain decides to turn around and move in the opposite direction, he cannot achieve this instantly;

his purpose can only be carried out over the appropriate time and distance, and the larger the vessel, the more of both will be required. In the long term, therefore, free will is limitless; but in the short term it is governed by the 'inexorable must' of our character, our circumstances, and all the limitations we have imposed on ourselves through the impressions accumulated over our past lives.

> In the world of values (Baba concludes) the law of karma can be compared to the law of cause and effect which governs the physical world. If there were no law of cause and effect in the physical world there would be chaos; and people would not know what to expect. Similarly, if there were no law of karma in the world of values, people would not know whether to expect good or bad consequences from a given action. In the physical world there is a law of conservation of energy, whereby no energy is ever lost. So too in the world of values, once karma comes into existence, it persists until either it bears its own fruit or is undone through counteracting karma. Good actions inevitably tend to good results, and bad actions lead to bad results.
>
> *Karmic determination is therefore not some blind external power, but the condition of true responsibility*. It means that an individual will reap as he sows. What a person gathers by way of experience is invariably connected with what he does. If he has done an evil turn to someone, he must accept the penalty and welcome the evil rebounding on himself. If he has done someone a good turn, he must receive the reward in due course, and enjoy the good rebounding on himself. What he has done for another he has done also for himself, although it may take time for him to realise that this is exactly so. The law of karma is an expression of justice and a reflection of the unity of life in the world of duality.[4]

In the passages above Baba has answered some of the deepest and most perplexing questions which have haunted the minds of men and women from the start of human consciousness. How can any order based on justice be said to exist in the universe, when men and women are born into such different and contrasting situations? Why should some die almost as soon as they are born and others live on into a ripe old age – indeed, in some cases, live on longer than they wish to live? How does genius come into existence? What makes it possible for a child to be born who becomes in a few years a Mozart, a Leonardo da Vinci, a Plato, an Einstein – or perhaps a Nelson or Napoleon?

From Baba's explanation it is now seen that *all* achievement is the result of sustained effort over a span of lives. It might be thought that, once a man or woman has experienced the satisfaction of great achievement, he or she would be born again and again in order to repeat the success and continue harvesting its benefits. But apart from the fact that success never brings all the achiever hoped for – since there is an element of frustration and disappointment in all human existence – *there lies within every soul the urge to complete an experience by also experiencing its opposite.*

In a Discourse entitled "The Beginning and the End of Creation", which is placed almost at the start of his long volume *Discourses,* Baba has explained this seeming paradox.

> The sanskaras deposited by specific actions and experiences render the mind susceptible to similar actions and experiences. After a certain point is reached, however, this tendency is checked and counteracted by a natural reaction consisting of a complete changeover to its direct opposite, making room for the operation of opposite or contrary sanskaras.
>
> Often the two opposites form part of the same chain of imagination. For example, a person might first experience that he is a famous writer – with wealth, fame, family and all the

> agreeable things of life – but later in the same life, undergo the experience of losing everything he has. Sometimes it seems that a chain of imagination does not contain both opposites in the same lifetime. For instance, a man might experience throughout his life that he is a powerful king always victorious in battles. In this case he will have to balance such experiences by experiencing defeats in the next life before his chain of imagination is complete. *The purely psychological compulsion of the sanskaras is thus subject to the deeper need of the soul to know its Self.*
>
> Or suppose that a person has killed someone in this life. This deposits in his mental body the sanskaras of killing. If consciousness were solely determined by the initial tendency, he would go on killing others ad infinitum... There would be no escape from this recurring determinism, were it not that the logic of experience provides a necessary check. The killer comes to realise before long the incompleteness of his one-sided experience, and unconsciously seeks to restore the balance by going over to its opposite. Thus the individual who has experienced killing will develop the psychological need and susceptibility for getting killed. In killing another person, he has appreciated only one part of the total situation. From this arises an inner compulsion to complete that experience by attracting to oneself the opposite of what one has gone through.[5]

From this it can be seen that the murderer or other criminal who congratulates himself on having 'got away with it', because the crime has not been detected and punished during his lifetime, has in fact only postponed the penalty he is certain to bring down upon himself in a future incarnation.

Every form of experience impels the individual soul to seek and experience its opposite in the course of time. And the same innate compulsion which drives the individual soul to experience success and failure, riches and poverty, health and sickness, love and hatred, also involves it in experiencing both male and female incarnations. Why this should be so Baba explains as follows:

> In qualities of the heart women are usually superior to men, and in qualities of the head and will men are usually superior to women. The interesting point is that the same soul excels in the qualities of heart or head, according to whether it incarnates in a female or male form. The alternate development of specific spiritual qualities goes on through the alternation between male and female forms until development is all-sided...
>
> Before the soul is set free from all sanskaras, it will have assumed numerous forms both male and female, since if the soul were to incarnate only in one or other, its experience would remain one-sided and incomplete. When the soul takes a female body, the male tendencies are, in general, suppressed into the unconscious part of the mind where they are held in abeyance and only the female tendencies released for expression. Similarly when the soul takes a male body, the female tendencies are in abeyance, and the male tendencies are released for expression.
>
> Identification with the body involves identification with the sex of the body... Since the other part of the mind is repressed and latent in the unconscious, there arises in the conscious part a sense of incompleteness, with a tendency to restore completeness through attachment to persons of the opposite sex... *From this point of view sexual attraction might be said to be a result of the effort the mind makes to unite with its own unconscious part.*
>
> Sex is a manifestation of the ignorant attempt the conscious mind makes to compensate for the fragmentation entailed in identification with the sex of its body... But once the soul seeks to overcome sexual duality through

detachment from the opposite sex, it is paving the way for understanding the experience associated with the opposite sex from *within*. A man then tries to understand a woman, not through his own maleness, but through an imaginative reaching out towards what the woman feels herself to be in her own personal experience. In the same way, a woman then tries to understand a man, not through her eyes as a female, but through the imaginative reaching out towards what a man feels himself to be, in his own personal experience. Thus detachment from the bodily form of the opposite sex facilitates a true comprehension of the experience associated with the opposite sex because it removes the barrier created by sex-obsessed imagination... When inner understanding of the relevant experiences is complete, aspirants no longer experience themselves as male or female, but as being *beyond the distinction of sex*.

To be free from attachment to the opposite sex is to be free from domination by the sex of that body into which the soul has incarnated, thereby annihilating most of those sanskaras which compel the soul to identify itself with the body. The transcending of sexual duality does not in itself overcome all duality, but it goes a long way towards facilitating the ultimate transcendence of duality in all its forms. Complete solution comes only when the wider problem of all duality is solved through divine love, in which there is neither 'I' nor 'you', neither man nor woman.

The purpose of male and female incarnations is the same as the purpose of evolution itself, which is to enable the soul to arrive at its own undivided and indivisible existence.[6]

We can sum up the complex meaning of this section in Baba's words already quoted: "Thus the game of duality is carried on long enough to gather so much experience of the opposite that the soul, out of the fullness of its experience, eventually becomes ripe for dropping the ego-mind and turning inward to know itself as the Oversoul."

Notes

1. *The God-Man*, pp. 321–2
2. *Discourses*, from pp. 327–331
3. St Matthew, 6:27
4. *Discourses*, pp. 332–3
5. *Discourses*, from pp. 26–8
6. *Discourses*, condensed from pp. 323–6

Meher Baba. Location: Bindra House, Pune, 21 September 1952. © Meher Nazar Publications.

Section 5

The Search For Happiness

Since we are all driven by the inexorable 'must' to follow a particular path through life, the question arises as to how, under such compulsion, a man or woman can find happiness and avoid despair and misery. Are we not all, like old-time serfs, drawing the heavy wagon of our destiny, with no more than momentary alleviations and only the most distant assurance of ultimate release? What can we do to better our lot in the meantime? How far is happiness attainable on earth, and if it is, how can we attain it?

In two short Discourses entitled "The Conditions of Happiness", which are placed almost last among the seventy Discourses, Baba gives answers to these problems.

> Every creature in the world (Baba tells us) is seeking happiness, and man is no exception. Man appears to set his heart on many kinds of things, but ultimately all that he desires or undertakes is for the sake of happiness. If he seeks power, it is because he expects to derive happiness from its use. If he strives for money, it is because he thinks it will secure the means for his happiness. If he seeks knowledge, health or beauty, if he applies himself to science, art or literature, it is because he feels his happiness depends on them. If he struggles for success or fame, it is because he hopes to find happiness in their attainment... Happiness is the ultimate motive power, driving him in all he does...
>
> Man does not seek suffering, but it comes to him as an inevitable consequence of the manner in which he seeks happiness. He seeks happiness through the fulfilment of his desires, but the tree of desire bears fruits of two kinds; one sweet, which is pleasure, one bitter, which is suffering. It cannot be made to yield just one kind of fruit. Man pursues pleasure furiously and clings to it fondly. He tries desperately to avoid the impending suffering, and smarts under it with resentment. But his fury and fondness avail little, for his pleasure is doomed to fade and disappear. Equally his desperation and resentment are of no avail, since in the very moment when his desires are fulfilled, any happiness they yield has already started to fade and vanish. *Worldly desires can never, because of their transitory nature, lead to abiding happiness.*[1]

At some point in time, usually after many lives and much experience, the truth inevitably begins to dawn on a person that if the satisfaction of worldly desires has never brought, and can never bring, lasting happiness, he/she must follow a different path. Then their mind may turn towards detachment from material satisfactions and the search for a way of life that will afford true peace of mind. But unless this is rooted in something deeper than disappointment or the failure of some ambition, it will not be long before a recurring flood of attractions and desires sweeps away their resolution.

Sometimes it may happen that the death of a beloved friend or relative – bringing the reminder that before long we too must die and leave behind everything we have acquired or achieved – gives us a shock which compels us to realise the hollowness of the life we have been living. Under such impulse, a man or woman may embark on a determined search for a more sincere and meaningful manner of life, renouncing all worldly ambitions and allurements, and for a while such effort may be sustained. But if it is no more than a reaction to painful experience, it will not be long before memory of that experience fades, and the old life is resumed.[2] The only detachment that endures, Baba tells us, is one based on true understanding.

> *The detachment that really lasts is due to the understanding of suffering and its cause.* It is securely based upon the unshakeable knowledge that all things of this world are momentary and passing. As long as there is attachment to worldly objects of pleasure, a man perpetually invites upon himself the suffering of not having them – or the suffering of losing them after having got them. Complete detachment is one of the essential conditions of true and lasting happiness.
>
> Desirelessness (Baba goes on to explain) makes an individual firm as a rock. Then he is moved neither by pleasure nor by sorrow; he is not upset by the onslaughts of opposites. One who is affected by what is agreeable, is bound to suffer from what is disagreeable. If a person is encouraged in his endeavours by an omen considered to be auspicious, he is bound to be discouraged by one considered to be inauspicious. So too, if a person is pleased at receiving

> praise, he is bound to be miserable at receiving blame. The steadiness and equanimity to remain unaffected by any opposites is possible only through complete detachment.

And here Baba adds some words on the nature of different kinds of suffering, words which – since we all without exception experience a full range of suffering during our lifetimes – are to be borne in mind during such dark periods.

> Humanity is subject to much suffering, physical and mental. Of these two, mental suffering is the more acute. Those with limited vision think that suffering can only be physical. Their idea of suffering is some kind of illness or torture of the body, but mental suffering is worse than physical suffering. Indeed physical suffering sometimes comes as a blessing by weaning one's attention away from mental suffering. Even yogis who can endure great physical suffering find it difficult to keep free from mental suffering, which is rooted in the frustration of desires.
>
> If a person does not want anything, he is not unhappy under the most adverse circumstances. The state of complete desirelessness is not unattainable since it is latent in everyone. And when through complete detachment one arrives at the state of wanting nothing, one taps the unfailing inner source of eternal happiness – which is not based upon the objects of this world, but is sustained by Self-knowledge and Self-realisation.

What Baba means by Self-realisation, the true goal of all creation, is explained in the second of his Discourses on "The Conditions of Happiness", which is entitled "Contentment, Love, and God-realization". But first he tells us that the process of purging the mind of its many desires cannot be anything but painful while it lasts.

The suffering involved in purging the mind of its many desires exists – even when the soul may be ready to renounce them – because this decision of the soul runs counter to the determination of the ego-mind to survive and control through pursuing its habitual desires. Renunciation of desires curtails the very life of the ego-mind. Therefore, it is a process invariably accompanied by acute suffering. But such suffering is wholesome because it liberates the soul from bondage, bringing with it the sense of greater freedom which comes when desires gradually disappear from the mind. If an infected swelling on the body is opened and allowed to drain, it gives much pain but also great relief. *Similarly, the suffering from renunciation of desires is accompanied by the compensating relief of a progressive initiation into the limitless life of freedom and happiness.*

Man has complicated his life by the growth of artificial and unnecessary desires, but is reluctant to abandon them unless the lesson that desires are born of ignorance is impressed upon his mind through acute mental suffering. The suffering which purges the soul of desires is as necessary as medicine to a sick person.

It remains true, however, that ninety-nine per cent of human suffering is not necessary (and could well be avoided). Through obstinate ignorance people inflict suffering upon themselves and their fellow beings, and then ask, "Why should we suffer?" Suffering is often symbolised by scenes of war: devastated houses, broken and bleeding limbs, the agonies of torture and death. But war does not involve *special* suffering; people are suffering all the time. They suffer because they are not satisfied – they want more and more. War is an outcome of this universal disease of dissatisfaction, rather than an embodiment of representative suffering. It is through their own greed, vanity and cruelty that people bring untold suffering upon themselves and others.

Everyone is seeking his or her personal happiness even at the cost of the happiness of others, and it is this which gives rise to cruelty and to unending wars. But as long as a person thinks only of his own happiness, he will never find it. Someone who is deeply selfish can, in the pursuit of his individual happiness, become utterly callous and cruel to others. But this recoils upon himself since it poisons the very spring of his own life. Loveless life is most unlovely; only a life of love is a life worth living.

The elimination of desires, however, though freeing one from self-created suffering and carrying one a long way along the road, cannot of itself take one to the final goal of positive happiness.

True happiness begins when one learns the art of right adjustment to other persons, and right adjustment involves self-forgetfulness and love. Hence arises the spiritual importance of transforming a life of the limited self into a life of love.

Pure love is rare because it is extremely difficult to purge consciousness of the deep-rooted ignorance which expresses itself through the idea of 'I' and 'mine'. For example, even when a man says he *loves* his beloved, he often only means that he possessively *wants* the beloved to be with him.

Pure love cannot be forced upon someone, nor can it be snatched away from another by force. It has to manifest itself within with unfettered spontaneity. *What can be achieved through bold decision is the removal of those factors which prevent the manifestation of pure love.* The achievement of selflessness may thus be said to be both difficult and easy. It is difficult for those who have not decided to step out of the limited self, and it is easy for those who have so decided. In the absence of firm determination, attachments connected with the limited self are too strong to be broken through. But if a

> person resolves to set aside selfishness at any cost, he finds easy entry into the domain of pure love. The limited self is like a coat worn by the soul. Through the exercise of will one can take off one's coat, and through firm resolution a man can decide to shed the limited self and be rid of it once and for all. By the exercise of bold, unyielding decision, the task that would otherwise be difficult proves to be easy. Only the intense longing for pure love – a longing such as that with which a hungry person longs for food – can give rise to such a decision.

And Baba concludes the two Discourses on "The Conditions of Happiness" with a promise, the promise that when the aspirant has made the sustained effort to rid him/herself of desires, and to put the happiness of others before their own, then help will always be forthcoming for the next stage of their journey.

> Once the aspirant has developed such an intense longing for pure love, he or she has become prepared for the intervention of a Perfect Master. Only the Master can awaken pure love through the divine love he imparts. There is no other way. Love is the most significant thing in life. It cannot be awakened except by coming into contact with the Incarnation of love. Theoretical brooding on love will result in weaving a theory about love, but the heart will remain as empty as before.
>
> When true love is awakened in the aspirant, it leads him/her to the realisation of God and opens up the unlimited field of never-fading happiness. The happiness of God-realisation is the goal of all creation, worth all the physical and mental suffering in the universe. Then all suffering is as if it had never been.
>
> The happiness of God-realisation is self-sustained, eternally fresh, unfading, boundless and indescribable. It is for this happiness that the world has sprung into existence.

Notes

1. All extracts in this section are condensed from *Discourses*, pp. 388–98
2. There is a special name for such detachment, which can be translated as 'cremation or burial ground detachment', because it usually arises at funerals and fades with a change of scene.

Meher Baba seated on his gaadi outside his tomb-shrine, circa 1928. © Meher Nazar Publications.

Section 6

God-Realisation: The Avatar's Role

What will have emerged from the preceding sections is, we believe, a picture of human life based on principles of absolute justice. As a man sows, so shall he reap – though not necessarily in his present lifespan. Karmic debts and dues are carried on from one life to the next, until the account is squared and obligations extinguished. Each one of us has undergone, and in almost every case will continue to undergo, a long sequence of lives, in both male and female forms. A vast range of experiences must be met with, each eventually to be completed by its opposite. A variety of talents – physical, mental, artistic and spiritual – will be developed; triumphs achieved and overturned; setbacks and handicaps of all kinds accepted and endured.

The goal of life for each one of us is the same. It is the eventual transcending of *all* human experience, painful or pleasurable, in the supreme and lasting bliss of God-realisation – which is the realisation and acceptance in full consciousness of our own spiritual nature. It is this realisation which gives meaning to our long sequence of lives. However remote and unattainable it may appear to us in the midst of our worldly preoccupations, ambitions and distractions, this is the bliss to which every human being will ultimately attain.

What then, in all this pattern of struggle and effort, is the role of the Avatar?

In the earlier part of this book[1] we quoted extracts from Meher Baba's statement made at Dehra Dun on 7th September 1953, reputed anniversary of the birth of Zoroaster, on his position as the latest in the line of Avatars. The role of the Avatar or God-Man, he explained, is to awaken in all the knowledge of our own true nature. By arousing love and a passion for service in our heart, the Avatar helps us to draw closer and closer to the divine within us, and so, over countless centuries, to become 'God-realised' – oneness with God being the sole purpose of life.

In the following year, on 30th September 1954, Baba's "Final Declaration" was read out, to a gathering of his followers from all over the world. It contained the following statement:

> I have not come to establish anything new – I have come to put life into the old... When my universal religion of love is on the verge of fading into insignificance, I come to breathe life into it and to do away with the farce of dogmas that defile it in the name of religions and stifle it with ceremonies and rituals...
>
> I have come to sow the seed of love in your hearts so that, in spite of all superficial diversity which your life in illusion

> must experience and endure, the feeling of oneness, through love, is brought about amongst all the nations, creeds, sects and castes of the world.[2]

Meher Baba's teaching on the nature of the Avatar and the special service he renders to humanity is set out fully in his Discourse entitled "The Avatar".[3] In this Baba answers such questions as why the Avatar appears at a particular moment in history; how he operates to awaken mankind to a knowledge of his true nature; and what it is in us which responds to the message the Avatar brings.

> Avataric periods are like the spring tide of creation. They bring a new release of power, a new awakening of consciousness, a new experience of life – not merely for a few, but for all. Qualities of energy and awareness, which had been used and enjoyed by only a few advanced souls, are made available for all humanity. Life, as a whole, is stepped up to a higher level of consciousness, geared to a new rate of energy. *The transition from sensation to reason was one such step;*[4] *the transition from reason to intuition will be another.*
>
> This new influx of the creative impulse manifests through the medium of a divine personality, an incarnation of God in a special sense – the *Avatar*. The Avatar was the first individual soul to emerge from the evolutionary and involutionary process as a Sadguru, and He is the only Avatar who has ever manifested or will ever manifest. Through Him God first completed the journey from unconscious divinity to conscious divinity, first unconsciously became man in order consciously to become God. Through Him periodically, God consciously becomes man for the liberation of mankind.
>
> The Avatar appears in different forms, under different names, at different times, in different parts of the world. As His appearance always coincides with the spiritual

regeneration of man, the period immediately preceding His manifestation is always one in which humanity suffers from the pangs of the approaching rebirth. Man seems more than ever enslaved by desire, more than ever driven by greed, held by fear, swept by anger. The strong dominate the weak; the rich oppress the poor; large masses of people are exploited for the benefit of the few who are in power. The individual, who finds no peace or rest, seeks to forget himself in excitement. Immorality increases, crime flourishes, religion is ridiculed. Corruption spreads throughout the social order. Class and national hatreds are aroused and fostered. Wars break out. Humanity grows desperate. There seems to be no possibility of stemming the tide of destruction.

At this moment the Avatar appears. Being the total manifestation of God in human form, He is like a gauge against which man can measure what he is and what he may become. He trues the standard of human values by interpreting them in terms of divinely human life.

He is interested in everything, but not concerned about anything. The slightest mishap may command His sympathy; the greatest tragedy will not upset Him. He is beyond the alternations of pain and pleasure, desire and satisfaction, rest and struggle, life and death. To Him they are equally illusions that He has transcended, but by which others are bound, and from which He has come to free them. He uses every circumstance as a means to lead others towards Realisation.

He knows that individuals do not cease to exist when they die and therefore is not concerned over death. He knows that destruction must precede construction, that out of suffering is born peace and bliss, that out of struggle comes liberation from the bonds of action. He is only concerned about concern.

In those who contact Him, He awakens a love that consumes all selfish desires in the flame of the one desire to serve Him. Those who consecrate their lives to Him gradually

> become identified with Him in consciousness. Little by little their humanity is absorbed into His divinity, and they become free…
>
> The Avatar awakens contemporary humanity to a realisation of its true spiritual nature, gives Liberation to those who are ready, and quickens the life of the spirit in His time. For posterity is left the stimulating power of His divinely human example – of the nobility of a life supremely lived, of a love unmixed with desire, of a power unused except for others, of a peace untroubled by ambition, of a knowledge undimmed by illusion. He has demonstrated the possibility of a divine life for all humanity, of a heavenly life on earth. Those who have the necessary courage and integrity can follow when they will.[5]

In the two Discourses on "The State of the Man-God"[6] and "The Work of the Man-God", following that on "The Avatar" from which the above majestic passages are quoted, Baba stresses still more forcefully what the attainment of God-realisation means to the aspirant, and also the heavy price that must be paid for such attainment.

> God-realisation is the very goal of all creation. All earthly pleasure, however great, is but a fleeting shadow of the eternal bliss of God-realisation. All worldly knowledge, however comprehensive, is but a distorted reflection of the absolute Truth of God-realisation. All human might, however imposing, is but a fragment of the infinite power of God-realisation. All that is noble and beautiful, all that is great and inspiring in the universe, is but an infinitesimal fraction of the unfading and unspeakable glory of God-realisation.
>
> But the eternal bliss, infinite power, unfading glory and absolute Truth of God-realisation are not to be had for nothing. The individual soul has to go through all the travail,

pain and struggle of evolution, reincarnation and involution before it can inherit this treasure, which lies hidden at the heart of creation. *The price it has to pay for coming into possession of this treasure is its own existence as a separate ego.* The limited individuality must disappear entirely if there is to be entrance into the unlimited state of Godhood.

In the ordinary man or woman, the limited individuality which is identified with a finite name and form, predominates and casts a veil of ignorance over the God within. If this ignorance is to disappear, the individual has to surrender his own limited existence. When he goes from the scene without leaving a vestige of his limited life, what remains is God. *The surrenderance of limited existence is the surrender of the rooted delusion of having a separate existence.* It is not the surrender of anything real: it is the surrenderance of the false and the inheritance of the Truth...

When the Sadguru (Man-God or Perfect Master)[7] descends into the world of forms from the impersonal aspect of God, he assumes universal mind; and he knows, feels, and works through this universal mind. No longer for him is the limited life of finite mind; no longer for him are the pains and pleasures of duality; no longer for him are the emptiness and vanity of separative ego. He is consciously one with all life. Through his universal mind[8] he not only experiences the happiness of all minds but also their suffering. Since most minds have a great preponderance of suffering over happiness due to ignorance, the suffering that comes to the Man-God because of the condition of others, is infinitely greater than the happiness.

The suffering of the Man-God is great; but the infinite bliss of the God state, which he constantly and effortlessly enjoys, supports him in all the suffering that comes to him, leaving him unmoved and unaffected by it.[9]

If this is the state of the Sadguru, the Perfect Master who, having attained God-realisation, comes back into the world in service to mankind as 'Man-God', what is the condition of the Avatar, or 'God-Man', during his life on earth? Are his sufferings 'real', as they would appear to an ordinary mortal? Or does his divinity protect him against suffering, so that he merely seems to be undergoing pain and torment? On this point Baba is explicit:

> When God *becomes* man, He as the God-Man literally suffers as man. Jesus Christ, as the Avatar, *did* suffer on the Cross. However, with the continuous Knowledge that His conscious Godhood gave Him, He knew at the same time that everything in the world of duality is illusion; and He was sustained by the Knowledge of His God state.
>
> The God-Man experiences all souls as His own. Although He knows Himself to be identical with God and is thus eternally free, He also knows Himself to be one with the other souls in bondage and is thus bound. Though He is conscious of the eternal bliss of His God state, He also experiences infinite suffering, owing to the bondage of others whom He knows to be His own forms. This is the meaning of Christ's Crucifixion…
>
> The God-Man is inseparably united with God forever and dwells in a state of non-duality in the very midst of duality. He not only knows Himself to be one with all, but also knows Himself to be the only One. He consciously descends from the state of being God to the state of experiencing God in everything. Therefore His actions in the world of duality not only do not bind Him but reflect the pristine glory of the sole Reality, which is God, and contribute towards freeing others from their state of bondage.

Earlier we referred to Meher Baba's statement that the Avatar comes to earth once in every 700 to 1,400 years "in different forms, under different names, in different parts of the world." And Baba has stated more than once that his next return as Avatar will take place seven hundred years from now, and into a world very different from the present one. In a message full of hope and promise for suffering humanity Baba has declared:

> When I come again after seven hundred years the evolution of consciousness will have reached such an apex that materialistic tendencies will be automatically transmuted into spiritual longing, and the feeling of equality in spiritual brotherhood will prevail. This means that opulence and poverty, literacy and illiteracy, jealousy and hatred – which are in evidence today in their full measure – will be dissolved through the feeling of the oneness of all men. Prosperity and happiness will then be at their zenith. (And, he repeated) My next advent, after I drop this body, will be after seven hundred years, and that will mark the end and the beginning of a cycle of cycles.[10]

Finally, Baba, as Avatar of this age, has stressed the importance of our own planet earth, not merely to ourselves who live upon it, but in the whole vast scheme of creation.

> Only on this earth can God be realised. It is not possible for men to contact the worlds that contain the kingdoms of evolution but are without spiritual development. On these other worlds there are beings that have more intelligence than exists in men. The earth is the centre of creation because men are made in God's image, and only human beings on earth are capable of advancement.[11]

In the preceding sections, we, the writers of this book, have attempted to convey some impression of Meher Baba's teaching and his message to mankind. We are conscious of the inadequacy of our efforts; but these will have served their purpose if they lead readers to apply themselves directly to the *Discourses* of Meher Baba, and to his all-important but perhaps difficult book, *God Speaks*.

In the following and final section we record the manner in which our own book, and its predecessor, *Much Silence,* came to have been written, and the experiences which led us to attempt so exacting a task.

Notes

1. Cf. above Chapter 12
2. *The God-Man,* pp. 273–4
3. Every advent of the Avatar (the God-Man, the Messiah, the Buddha, the Christ, the Rasool) is the direct descent of God on earth in human form – as the Eternal Living Perfect Master. The five Sadgurus (Perfect Masters) of the age precipitate this advent once in a cyclic period of 700 to 1,400 years. For a full explanation cf. *God Speaks* by Meher Baba. And see Chapter 2 above for the five Perfect Masters concerned with Meher Baba's advent.
4. Pioneers in this transition were the Greeks in the five centuries preceding the birth of Christ. Its centre was Athens, and its leading exponent Socrates, known to us chiefly through the writings of Plato.
5. *Discourses,* condensed from pp. 268–270
6. When man becomes God-realised but still retains consciousness of the world, he is called a Man-God, Perfect Master or Sadguru. But when God takes human form He is known as the God-Man, or Avatar.
7. Note that Baba is here speaking of the Man-God (Sadguru) not of the God-Man (Avatar).
8. It was this universal mind to which Jesus referred in his statement to the multitude: "Are not five sparrows sold for two farthings, and not one of them is forgotten before God?

But even the very hairs of your head are all numbered. Fear not therefore: ye are of more value than many sparrows." St Luke, 7:6–7

9. This and next quote: *Discourses*, from pp. 277–281
10. *The God-Man*, pp. 274–5
11. *The God-Man*, p. 366

Meher Baba at Meherazad, January 1948. Photographer: Charmian Duce Knowles. Image used with kind permission of Sufism Reoriented.

Section 7

Intuition: The Inner Voice

Dorothy writes:

In the early 1940s, I – with my husband, the late Hugh Kingsmill and four children – was living in a flat in Holland Park, London. Trying to bring up children under wartime conditions proved extremely stressful, and it was not long before I was having to spend much of my time lying in a darkened room, suffering the miseries of acute migraine headaches, unable to keep down what little food I ate.

I saw a number of doctors, none of whose treatment proved successful, until at last one of them suggested I should try psychoanalysis. The analyst, middle-aged and a staunch

Freudian, was confident of being able to help me; and, true to his word, within six months the vomiting stopped and the migraines lessened; by the end of the year, indeed, they had actually ended.

By now I had become absorbed in my analysis. My dreams were copious, and the analyst appeared to find them as interesting as I did myself; I was, however, beginning to differ from him at times as to how a particular dream should be interpreted. The summer was approaching, and the analyst decided he needed a holiday; before leaving, he instructed me to continue to write down my dreams, which I was happy to do. For about a week, however, I did not dream at all, and I found this disturbing. Had I, I asked myself, been dreaming so much because the dreams were trying to tell me something, or because the analyst demanded them in order to understand me?

When I did begin to dream again, the dreams took a strange form. Being tired, I had retired to bed early and fell asleep at once. In the course of the night, however, I woke – or dreamed I woke up – to find a presence, enveloped in a golden-pink glow of light, sitting by my bed. It had wavy hair down to the shoulders and was wearing a white robe, so that at first I thought it was a woman, before quickly realising that it was a man. The eyes held mine with a deep, penetrating gaze, which made me feel I already knew him, but without remembering how, or when, or where.

His glowing face wore a serene expression, and I felt myself enveloped in an intense love. Neither of us spoke, and I have no idea how long the experience lasted, but when I woke up next morning I felt I had seen a Divine Being, and been given spiritual guidance and instruction. Rushing to my husband's room, I poured out to him what had happened. While agreeing that I had had an extraordinary experience, the look of concern in his eyes, and the way he patted my head while assuring me that all was going to be well, warned me to control my intense elation.

After lunch I felt free to go to my room and write down my experience and the new insights it had given me; later, over a cup of tea with my husband, I started to read out what I had written. Part way through, however, he interrupted me, looking very serious, and said: "I can see the spiritual side of your nature has been stimulated, but I feel strongly that you'd be unwise to give such material to your analyst. I know little about psychoanalysis, but I *do* know that it's based on a materialist outlook. You've responded very well to the treatment so far, and are much better in health. I should indeed be distressed if you were upset again… Think about this seriously – you've a couple of weeks before the analyst gets back."

I did as he asked. I thought long and seriously, and in doing so began to understand why I had often disagreed with my analyst's interpretation of my dreams. Putting on my coat when my last session ended, I had asked somewhat petulantly: "Why do you always interpret flowers as orgasms? I love flowers. If I were a rich woman I'd surround myself with flowers – I'm not interested in orgasms."

"Exactly! That's what's wrong with you," the analyst answered sharply. "Your feet aren't on the ground. You float in the clouds with the *'Gita* under one arm and the *Upanishads* under the other, and a Bible hanging round your neck on a chain!"

I had laughed, but my query had been dismissed with a wave of the hand and a reminder to record my dreams for his return in three weeks' time. Thinking all this over, I began to feel alarmed. Was it true that I was "up in the clouds" and my feet "not on the ground"? Angrily I thought: "How does he suppose I run a large flat, and do all the shopping and cooking for six people?"

Soon, however, the anger turned against myself… You are not understanding, giving enough thought and consideration, to what you are being told. While I pondered, the tender, loving face of the Divine Being floated before me; I started to tremble, and at last burst into tears, saying to myself, "You *are* in a mess..."

Lying in bed that night, awake and restless, I decided that, despite my husband's warning, it was essential I should give the analyst on his return an account of my Divine Visitor. He would not like this, but since it seemed I was not fully understanding and absorbing what was being shown me, I must make every effort to be more aware. I went to sleep at once, to wake up in the morning refreshed and unable to recall my dreams; I would, I decided, give myself a short respite from recording any more.

The analyst had benefited from his holiday, and, after a few minutes' chat, asked for my material... While he read, I settled myself on the couch. His back was now towards me, and he could only have read a couple of pages or so when he flung them all down on his desk, swivelled his chair round, his whole being suffused with anger, then, collecting himself with an effort, said icily: "Let us begin!"

Alarmed, I was unable to speak, but at last managed to stutter: "It's all there... in the... er... writing." But it came out as sounds rather than words, and after a long silence, I was told: "I shall read your material at my leisure. What I want now is your spoken account."

For what seemed an eternity I was silent, then at last stammered, "I want to go home. *Please* may I go home? ... I shall be all right tomorrow."

Once in the street, I burst into tears and decided to walk home in order to calm down. "If he's as angry as that," I thought, "when he's only read a couple of pages, what's he going to be like when he's read the lot?"

Later, having gone to bed, I found myself muttering, "Divine Being, whoever you may be, help me, please! I'm confused and don't know what to do." I went to sleep at last, but awoke feeling I had received no answer to my cry for help and must get through the day as best I could.

Having arrived early instead of late, which was my usual bad habit, I was kept waiting quarter of an hour before being called into the consulting room. My "Good morning" was unanswered, and before I could reach the couch, a chair was pushed towards me and a cold voice said: "Kindly sit down."

Seating himself directly in front of me and leaning forward, the analyst said: "I want you to give your whole attention to what I am going to say. You read too much. You fantasise too much. You also consider yourself a religious person – you are *not*! Your so-called religion is no more than compensation for an unhappy childhood. Now you've invented a yes-man for yourself, and all this *rubbish*..." – he waved a hand towards his desk – "has simply come out of your head. I refuse to go on with your analysis until you stop this nonsense."

Rising to my feet, I snapped: "You're saying I invented all this? That it all came out of my own head?"

"Yes. I do. Fantasies of a conceited and self-willed woman."

Flushing with anger, I retorted: "If that material came out of my own head, if I invented it myself, then I've no need to come to you."

"Insolent – as well as self-willed and conceited," was his retort as, rising to his feet, he pronounced: "There will be no session this morning, and no more sessions until you stop this time-wasting nonsense. Is that understood?"

Without answering, I snatched my coat and rushed out of the room. As a rule I travelled by bus, my 58 minute session ending in time for me to get home and prepare lunch, but today I was glad to walk all the way. My head was throbbing and I felt unwell. The moment I got home I rushed to the bathroom and was sick – "Migraine!" I muttered to myself.

My husband was sympathetic and refrained from saying, "I told you so!" Somehow I managed to cook a meal, but could eat nothing and was glad to be tucked up in bed where I soon fell asleep. Around three o'clock Hugh tiptoed into the room to ask how I was feeling.

"Stunned," I answered. "But the sleep has done me good. Are you going out?"

"To Kensington Library – to pick up some books. Can I choose one for you?"

"Yes," I said, "but *nothing* serious. A sloppy novel, perhaps."

I was sitting up in bed drinking a cup of tea when Hugh got back, looking pleased with himself, and handed me a book, saying: "I've got the very thing you'll enjoy."

Glancing at its title, I read *The Perfect Master* by CB Purdom. "But I particularly asked for nothing serious!" I objected, and threw the book angrily down on the floor. Books to Hugh were sacred, and he picked it up carefully and laid it on my bed. It had fallen open at a portrait and, as I leaned forward, I gave a gasp.

"What is it now?" Hugh asked anxiously, holding his head.

With an effort I managed to say calmly: "It's Him... my Divine Being... the Silent Messenger who instructed me without words."

Hugh held his hand out for the book, studied the portrait carefully, and handed it back: "It certainly answers your description."

At this I lost control and began laughing and crying, saying over and over again: "It's Him! He hasn't forgotten me... He will help me... He *is* helping me."

Hugh sat down on the edge of the bed and took my hand: "Darling – I'm very happy for you. But this is a most extraordinary happening... Take it slowly. I'll read the book as soon as you've finished it – and we'll decide what to do then."

Putting the children to bed took some time; meanwhile Hugh was skimming through Purdom's book, and, when I rejoined him, drew my attention to a small notice at the back. A Mr William Backett, it said, giving an address in Ealing, would be pleased to provide further information to anyone interested.

"Action can begin tomorrow morning," Hugh observed and, knowing that I wanted to start reading it at once, handed me the book.

By five o'clock next morning I had managed a run-through read to the end and then, excited and exhausted, fell asleep till eight. Hugh had given himself the task of getting in touch with Mr Backett, and I spent the morning clearing up household chores. Meanwhile Hugh had invited Mr Backett to tea, and by five we were all sitting together in the study.

"There's nothing to be alarmed about," Mr Backett assured me, having heard my story. "You must have met Meher Baba in some previous life, and He's doing you the honour of contacting you again."

"Yes, of course," said Hugh with a politeness which told me how bewildered he felt. By the time Will Backett left, however, we had both learned a great deal. He himself had met Meher Baba on Baba's first visit to London in September 1931. He also knew Charles Purdom, and told us that he and Purdom, along with a Miss de Leon, were running a small Baba group in London which met regularly. I was invited to join this, and given an address for Miss de Leon who, we were told, had spent some time in India at Meher Baba's ashram. Having phoned next morning, I was invited to tea with her the same day.

An elegant and handsome woman, she talked about Baba with the same love and reverence Will Backett had shown; she urged me to join their group, and, as I was leaving, gave me five slender volumes – the *Discourses* of Meher Baba.

Over supper that evening I told Hugh that, having now found Meher Baba, I neither wanted nor needed further analytical treatment.

"I understand your not wanting to return," Hugh answered thoughtfully. "But I'm not sure about the 'not needing'. We must remember he *did* cure your migraines..."

"Nor," I interrupted, "can I forget his damnable rudeness."

Hugh patted my hand. "Yes, darling. It *was* overcharged – to say the least of it."

"Well then, can I ring him up in the morning and tell him I'm not coming back?"

"If you feel so strongly about it, then you must."

Having gone to bed determined not to return to analysis, I was perplexed to wake with the certainty that, whether I liked it or not, I must. I could recall no dreams; no visit from Baba; yet I knew it was He who was advising me to return, and telling me to achieve this through an apology to the analyst. Horrified at the idea, I rushed to Hugh's room for his advice. He listened patiently as I poured out my anger and confusion; then when the flow stopped, asked, "Isn't it possible – since you neither saw Baba nor heard Him speak – that it is your own common sense telling you that an apology and a return to analysis is advisable?"

"I don't think I've got that kind of sense," I said doubtfully, "and I've been much too angry to use it if I'd had it."

"Well, then, isn't it possible, in view of Baba's divine status, that he's helping you to get over being angry?"

Unable for the moment to take in this new point of view, I evaded answering. "I must see to the children and get breakfast – we'll talk later."

By the time breakfast ended – whether through my own common sense, which I had doubted, or through Meher Baba's wisdom and desire to help me, of which I was certain – I phoned the analyst and apologised humbly for having caused him pain. To my surprise he answered: "But it was I who had to cause *you* pain – in order to do what you're coming to me for – to help you. The migraine and sickness no longer trouble you. But they were only the effect of your problem – which is what we have now got to tackle. Come and see me tomorrow at your usual time. I'm grateful for your apology."

Over supper that evening Hugh told me how glad he was I was resuming analysis and that all had gone so smoothly. He had been reading Purdom's book and was impressed by both author and subject. Of Meher Baba he said: "It's clear he is not just a Master, but a perfected one. Purdom shows this clearly, and it's to his credit that he recognises it – helped considerably, of course, by his knowledge and interest in different aspects of theology. Despite my own lack of such knowledge, however, I intuit that Purdom has not fully grasped the true greatness of Baba."

"Oh!" I exclaimed excitedly, "What *is* that greatness?"

"Meher Baba lives in and works from a realm which lies far beyond theology in all its aspects and denominations. I don't claim to understand this – but I do know that such a realm exists. So I am especially happy He's contacted you, and that you're ready to place yourself in His hands. How He manages to speak to you without words, I haven't a clue – but He does, so let us be grateful!"

I went to bed that night feeling calm and happy. I recalled the words of the 14th century saint and mystic, Mother Julian of Norwich,

"All shall be well, all shall be well… All things shall be well."

The analysis was teaching me a lot – to be more aware and realistic, more grown-up. I was the mother of four children and had heavy responsibilities; I must act accordingly. And now, having been given the opportunity to put myself in the hands of a Perfect Master, I would do my best to obey Him in all things.

On my way to the analyst next morning I felt no guilt over my resolve to edit the material I gave him from now on. It was a kindness not to burden him with what he could not see, did not want to see, and could not and did not understand. When my session ended, I asked nervously: "Can I have the… er… rubbish material back, please?"

Briskly came the reply: "Certainly not. Analyst's perks!"

Despite the limitations under which it now proceeded, my analysis went on reasonably smoothly. Hugh bought me my own copy of *The Perfect Master*, and I was now a member of the

London group, so meeting Charles Purdom, who was naturally gratified by my enthusiastic appreciation of his book. Writer, editor, one of the planners of Welwyn Garden City, he was short and thickset, with a brusque, authoritative manner, but kind-hearted when one got to know him.

He was also, as the book made clear, a man of great erudition with a wide knowledge of comparative religion, and our friendship was much strengthened when we found that we both attached unique importance to the figure of Jesus, believing his advent as Saviour to have been the turning point in religious history. I was therefore all the more impressed when Purdom urged me to take Meher Baba's *Discourses* very seriously indeed: "They are sublime. You should read and re-read them constantly."

Since it was some months since Delia de Leon had given me the five volume set of Baba's *Discourses*, I was now well into them; and the more I read, the more I was overcome, not only by their profundity but by the poetic beauty in which Baba's teaching was expressed. I had become aware, however, of repetitions and at times a certain shapelessness, as though the spoken messages had not been edited for print. As I read, I frequently interrupted Hugh in whatever he was doing to read out some particularly impressive passage, so that before long he had taken to reading the volumes as I finished, and we could talk them over together. Hugh summed his impressions up to me as: "Baba's own language is majestic – sublime thought, beautifully expressed. But he seems to have dictated at different times to different persons – hence the repetitions... What the *Discourses* really need, I feel, is to be re-edited for Western readers."

"But wouldn't that be a very difficult and lengthy job?" I asked.

"It certainly would. But it could be of enormous benefit to a lot of people."

Two or three days later Hugh observed that he would be

happy to do the editing if Baba agreed. I was enthusiastic over the offer; but instead of writing himself, Hugh left it to me to put his proposal forward as best I could. I did so, but received no answer to my letter. As the weeks went by I became more and more distressed. Had I given offence? Shown myself presumptuous? Concern over this, however, became swallowed up before long by the stressful wartime conditions under which we all were living; and, to add to the many stresses, Hugh was showing signs of being a very sick man.

Eventually, in 1948, Charles Purdom told me he had received a request from Meher Baba "to edit and condense the five volume *Discourses* into one volume, in order to make them more acceptable for publication in the West."

By now we had moved down into the country, to a cottage in Partridge Green which we rented from an old friend, the novelist Antonia White. It was through Antonia that we came to know Tom Hopkinson. At that time editor of *Picture Post*, he came down to see us occasionally, and shortly before his death Hugh asked Tom to become one of his trustees.

Hugh died on May 15th, 1949, and a memorial service was later organised for him in London by two of his closest friends, Malcolm Muggeridge and Hesketh Pearson. I was both surprised and happy to see my analyst present, and touched that – though the analysis had now long been over – he offered to give me any help that was in his power.

It took Purdom some time to complete his exacting task, so that his edition of the *Discourses* did not appear until 1955, published by Gollancz, under a title chosen by Baba himself – *God to Man and Man to God*.

By now Tom and I were married, and we had both also met Meher Baba in London during 1952, when Baba was paying one of his visits to the West. When Purdom's book came out, Tom was working on the now defunct *News Chronicle* and, though not yet a committed Baba-lover, succeeded in getting a review of it on to the leader page. In it he wrote: "… The Discourses in this book were given by Baba to his followers over many years. They have been available hitherto only in a privately printed five volume edition. What Mr Purdom has done is to shorten them considerably… In so doing he has made available to the general reader a series of essays whose distinguishing quality is that they deal with the most profound subjects in the simplest language. They have, as it were, immense depth but without weight. They enter directly to the heart…"

It was nearly twenty years after this, in 1974 – by which time Tom had become as devoted a Baba-lover as myself – that our own book *Much Silence* was published, also by Gollancz. The title, taken from an African proverb, "Much silence makes a mighty noise", was a reference to Baba's vow of silence taken on July 10th, 1925.

In the opening pages of this book we explained why, when a new edition was called for, we decided not simply to reprint, but to rewrite, *Much Silence.* To complete the task has taken us some seven years, and in the course of those years – and particularly during 1989 – the whole of the political and social world has been transformed.

Barriers which divided 'East' from 'West' have dissolved or been swept aside. Tyrannies unchallenged for decades have been overthrown in a few weeks. Whole nations, as if guided by some common impulse, have demanded, and secured, their freedom. The process is not yet finished, and its consequences only begin to be assessed. But as a first step, the piling-up of armaments – which had seemed set to continue and increase indefinitely – has been curtailed. Armies, navies and air forces are being cut back. Nuclear weapons have been reduced in number, and some of the technology which provided them diverted into other, more beneficial channels.

Behind this political and material transformation lies a profound inner change, emotional, even spiritual, in nature.

Not yet throughout the world, but simultaneously in different continents and countries, there is a growing sense that all mankind is one; that nations, like members of a family, should help each other, and that there can be no lasting peace so long as some peoples and countries enjoy abundance, while others still lack the basic necessities of life.

Secondly, an awareness has sprung up and is growing, of the need actively to protect our common heritage – the earth and seas, with all the creatures that inhabit them, and even the atmosphere itself – against pollution and destruction. What had been the dream of a few advanced thinkers down the centuries – that the earth is a garden and mankind its gardener – is finding its way into the pattern of accepted beliefs. And this sense of responsibility towards our environment, the recognition that each generation should strive to pass on to its successor a world that is more fertile and productive – not one that is ravaged, depleted, even dangerous – is growing faster among ordinary men and women than among our rulers and political leaders.

Moreover, these changes in our ideas and in political and social fields, have been accompanied and supported by a range of practical and material developments, serving to unite the peoples of the world in ways which seemed inconceivable only half a century ago.[1] The spread of English to become virtually a universal language is one such development. The worldwide network of air communication is another. Television, with the use of satellites, making it possible to see what is happening in even remote corners of the world, is a third. And meantime, the mix-up of races and peoples which began centuries ago in the United States, has spread throughout Europe, Africa and much of Latin America and Asia. Populations are no longer local and indigenous, but various in colour, in origin, background and religion.

In the course of the twentieth century, the world pot has been stirred as it was never stirred before, and such stirring seems set not to diminish, but increase.

At such a time of crisis it was inevitable that, as the great Catholic writer Teilhard de Chardin[2] foretold, there would be a new spiritual manifestation, to assist and to explain the world transformation that is taking place. The writers of this book have no doubt that this spiritual manifestation, the Prophet and the Explainer of our age, took the form of Meher Baba, the Silent Messenger. And we both, now well on into our eighties, feel ourselves doubly fortunate to have looked upon the Silent Messenger in his bodily form, and to have lived long enough to see the changes he foretold beginning to take shape.

We ended *Much Silence* with a quotation from Baba's Discourse entitled "The New Humanity" and today, after fifteen years' further reading and study of his works – and much personal endeavour – we can find no nobler expression of God's promise and mankind's situation than the same extract in an extended form.

> As in all great critical episodes of human history, humanity is now going through the agonising travail of spiritual rebirth. Great forces of destruction seem to be dominant at the moment, but creative forces which will redeem humanity are also being released through several channels. Although the working of these forces of light is chiefly silent, eventually they are bound to bring about transformations which will make the further spiritual advance of humanity safe and steady. It is all part of the divine plan, which is to give to the hungry and weary world a fresh dispensation of the eternal and only Truth.
>
> The urgent problem facing humanity is to devise ways and means of eliminating competition, conflict and rivalry in all the various spheres of life. Military wars are the most obvious source of chaos and destruction. However, wars in themselves do not constitute the central problem for humanity, but are

> the symptoms of something graver at their root. The cause of the chaos that precipitates itself in wars is that most persons are in the grip of egoism and selfish considerations, and express their egoism and self-interest individually as well as collectively. This is the life of illusory values in which man is caught. To face the Truth is to realise that life is one, in and through its manifold manifestations. To have this understanding is to forget the limiting self in the realisation of the unity of life. With the dawn of true understanding, the problem of wars would immediately disappear…
>
> Even wars require co-operation, but the scope of this is artificially restricted by identification with a limited group or ideal. Wars indeed are often carried on by a form of love, though it is a love that has not been properly understood… If there is to be a resurrection of humanity, the heart of man will have to be unlocked so that a new love is born into it – a love that is entirely free from individual or collective greed…
>
> When it is recognised that there are no claims greater than the claims of the universal Divine Life – which without exception includes everyone and everything – love will not only establish peace, harmony and happiness in social, national and international spheres, but will shine in its own purity and beauty… Divine love will not only bring imperishable sweetness and infinite bliss into personal life, but will make possible an era of New Humanity which will learn the art of co-operative and harmonious life, free itself from the tyranny of dead forms, and release the creative life of spiritual wisdom. It will shed all illusions and become established in the Truth. It will enjoy peace and abiding happiness. It will be initiated into the life of Eternity.[3]

The perfection we all long for and seek, in whatsoever form we are envisaging it, Baba tells us, does not belong to God as God, nor does it belong to man as man; but we get Perfection when man becomes God or when God becomes man... This is what happens when man gives up the illusion of being finite and attains Godhood by realising his divinity. God's Perfection is revealed only when He manifests Himself as man. Thus we have Perfection when the finite transcends its limits and realises its infinity, or when the Infinite gives up its supposed aloofness and becomes man. In both cases, the finite and the Infinite do not stand outside each other. When there is a happy and conscious blending of the finite and the Infinite, we have Perfection.[4]

So to suffering humanity I say: *Have hope.* I come to help you win the one victory of all victories – to win your True Self. I bring the greatest treasure it is possible for man to receive – a treasure that includes all other treasures, that will endure forever, that increases when shared with others.

Be ready to receive it.

Notes

1. Tom wrote this in 1989. (Ed.)
2. Teilhard de Chardin (1881–1955) (Ed.)
3. *Discourses,* condensed from pp. 3–9
4. *Discourses,* from pp. 81–2

Appendix: Map of Meherabad

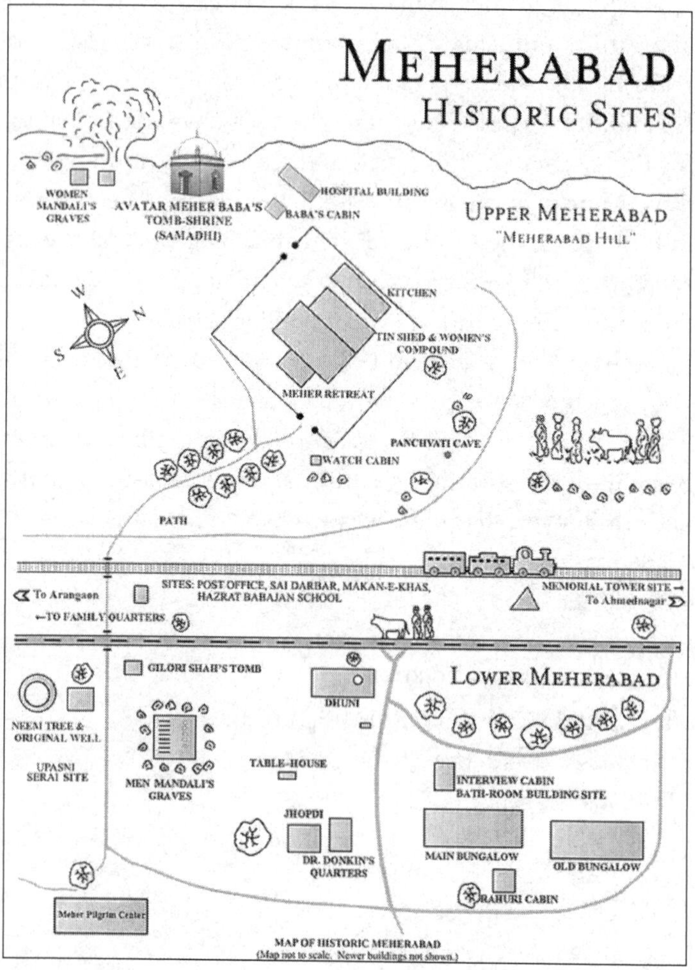

Map of Meherabad. © Avatar Meher Baba Perpetual Public Charitable Trust 2011.

Meher Ashram school was mainly based in Meher Retreat where pupils occupied the two lower level rooms. The "big hall" (Chapter 15) is in the Main Bungalow. Meherazad, Baba's main residence from the 1940s, is located beyond Ahmednagar, some 20km north of Meherabad.

Acknowledgements

The authors wish to thank Hilary Stabler, the (then) Secretary of the Meher Baba Association, for long and devoted work in producing the text of this book via a word-processor.

T. and D. H. 1989

Profound thanks are extended to Amanda Hopkinson for her kind permission on behalf of the estate of Tom and Dorothy Hopkinson, to publish *The Silent Messenger*; to the UK Meher Baba Association for supporting the project; to Shelagh Rowling and Sarah McNeill for their work with Tom and Dorothy's manuscript; to Maria Radoje and Richard Cork for initiating and shepherding it through to the publishing stage, and to all who have shared in the publication process in so very many ways.

Special thanks are also due to Martin and Christine Cook for their tireless work preserving and preparing Meher Baba's photographic legacy, to David Fenster of Meher Nazaar Publications and Pat Summer of the Mani Sheriar Irani (MSI) collection.

To create this book the authors relied considerably on what had already been written, and drew a great deal from many sources. Special obligations are owed to the following works, and sincere thanks to the copyright holders for permission to make quotations. To the Avatar Meher Baba Perpetual Public Charitable Trust, Ahmednagar, India for *Donkin's Diaries*; *Tales from the New Life with Meher Baba*; *Eighty-Two Family Letters...*; *The Beloved: The Life and Work of Meher Baba*; *Glimpses of the God-Man, Meher Baba, Vol. II*; *Listen, Humanity*; *The Wayfarers: Meher Baba with the God-Intoxicated*; *Love Alone Prevails: A story of life with Meher Baba*; *Glimpses of the God-Man, Meher Baba*; *Discourses*; and *Map of Meherabad*. To Sheriar Press for *The Perfect Master*. To Meher Era Publications, for *Twenty Years with Meher Baba*; *Meher Baba on Love*; and *Meher Baba on War*. To Meher Spiritual Center,

Myrtle Beach, for *The God-Man*. To Avatar's Abode Trust for *The Silent Word: Being Some Chapters of the Life and Time of Avatar Meher Baba*, by Francis Brabazon, Copyright © 2006 Avatar's Abode Trust, PO Box 186, Woombye 4559, Queensland, Australia. To Mrs Dilmeher Bharucha-Bhola for *Meher Baba's Last Sahavas*. To Meher Baba Center, Los Angeles for *Avatar*.

The Ancient One, A Disciple's Memoirs of Meher Baba; and *Glow International* magazine have been quoted with permission from Naosherwan Anzar, Beloved Archives, 2016. *Ramjoo's Diaries, 1922–1929* has been quoted with the kind permission of Sufism Reoriented. *The Awakener Magazine* has been quoted with permission.

Other sources due acknowledgement, being integral to both *Much Silence* and *The Silent Messenger*, include MSS notes "I remember…" by Delia de Leon; and early issues of *Divya Vani* (Divine Voice) magazine which proved invaluable to the authors for checking and amplifying the record.

Bibliography

The published sources used for *The Silent Messenger* are given below. Anyone wishing to know more about Meher Baba may find this list a useful starting place. To this end, the most recent publication details are noted. Any earlier editions used by Tom and Dorothy occur in brackets.

An increasing number of books and messages can also be read and accessed online via the Avatar Meher Baba Trust website library: www.ambppct.org.

The Ancient One, A Disciple's Memoirs of Meher Baba, narrated by Eruch Jessawala. Ed. Naosherwan Anzar. New Jersey: Beloved Books, 1985.

Avatar by Jean Adriel. (CA: JF Rowny, 1947) Berkeley, CA: John F. Kennedy University Press, 1971. A personal narrative going up to the year 1943.

The Beloved: The Life and Work of Meher Baba by Naosherwan Anzar. Myrtle Beach, SC: Sheriar Press, 1974, 5th reprint in 2003. E-version at: www.belovedarchives.org – A pictorial biography.

Discourses by Meher Baba. 7th edition (SC: Sheriar Press, 1987) Myrtle Beach, SC: Sheriar Foundation, 1995. Originally published in India in five volumes between 1939 and 1943. The 7th edition has one volume. Reprinted earlier editions are also available. *Discourses* provides the backbone of Part II "The Message of Meher Baba". The best possible companion for anyone seeking spiritual direction.

Donkin's Diaries: Travels in India with Meher Baba 1939–1945 by William Donkin. Compiled by Sarah McNeill. Myrtle Beach, SC: Sheriar Foundation, 2011.

Eighty-Two Family Letters: To the Western Family of Lovers and Followers of Meher Baba written by Mani (Manija S. Irani).

(NY: Society for Avatar Meher Baba, 1969) Myrtle Beach, SC: Sheriar Press, 1976. These letters, sent out by Baba's sister Mani to followers all over the world, provide the only continuous record for Baba's last years.

Glimpses of the God-Man, Meher Baba, Vol I by Bal Natu. Walnut Creek, CA: Sufism Reoriented, 1977. A richly detailed account of Meher Baba in the years 1943–48.

Glimpses of the God-Man, Meher Baba, Vol II by Bal Natu. Bombay: Meher House Publications, 1979. A detailed account of Meher Baba in the years 1949–January 1952.

The God-Man by CB Purdom. (London: Allen & Unwin, 1964) Myrtle Beach, SC: Sheriar Press, 1971. An expansion of *The Perfect Master*, carrying the story on up to 1962. Draws on diaries of close disciples for the account.

God Speaks: The Theme of Creation and Its Purpose by Meher Baba. (NY: Dodd, Mead, 1973) Walnut Creek, CA: Sufism Reoriented, 1973. 4th printing in 2010.

Listen, Humanity by Meher Baba. Narrated and edited by DE Stevens. (NY: Harper & Row, 1971) New York: The Crossroad Publishing Co., 1998. Part I is Don Stevens' account of a gathering of Baba followers in India in November 1955. Part II gives extracts from Baba's teaching, with information by Baba himself, particularly about his early life.

Love Alone Prevails: A story of life with Meher Baba by Kitty Davy. (SC: Sheriar Press, 1981) Myrtle Beach, SC: Sheriar Foundation, 2001. From Kitty's meeting Baba in 1931 to reflections half a century later.

Meher Baba on Love, compiled by KK Ramakrishnan. Pune, India: Meher Era Publications, 1972. Compilation of Baba's messages on love.

Meher Baba on War, compiled by KK Ramakrishnan. Pune, India: Meher Era Publications, 1972. Baba's messages on war and related subjects.

Meher Baba's Last Sahavas by Dr HP Bharucha Navsari. India:

self-published, 1969. This 50 page pamphlet is a first-hand record of the week of Baba's lying-in-state.

The Perfect Master: The Early Life of Meher Baba by CB Purdom. (London: Williams & Norgate, 1937) Myrtle Beach, SC: Sheriar Press, 1975. The story of Baba's life and work up to 1936.

Ramjoo's Diaries, 1922–1929: A Personal Account of Meher Baba's Early Work by Ramjoo Abdulla. Ed. Ira G. Deitrick. Walnut Creek, CA: Sufism Reoriented, 1979. This book is an invaluable source of information on the Meher Ashram and the later history of its students.

The Silent Word: Being Some Chapters of the Life and Time of Avatar Meher Baba by Francis Brabazon. Australia: Meher Baba Foundation, 1978. Baba's life story to the closing of the Prem Ashram in January 1929. *The Silent Word* is a work of prose flowing with the lyricism found in Brabazon's poetry.

Tales from the New Life with Meher Baba, narrated by Eruch, Mehera, Mani & Meheru. Berkeley, CA: The Beguine Library, 1976. A transcription of taped accounts with the mandali recalling extraordinary memories of living The New Life.

Twenty Years with Meher Baba by Dr Abdul Ghani Munsif. Pune, India: Meher Era Publications, 1975. Originally a series of articles covering the period 1920–40 by Dr Ghani.

The Wayfarers: Meher Baba with the God-Intoxicated by William Donkin. Foreword by Meher Baba. (CA: Sufism Reoriented, 1969) Myrtle Beach, SC: Sheriar Foundation, 2000. The extraordinary record of Baba's work with the 'masts' or God-mad.

Magazines referred to in The Silent Messenger:

The Glow, now known as *Glow International.*
See www.belovedarchives.org.

The Awakener Magazine. Available online www.theawakenermagazine.org.

MANTRA
BOOKS

EASTERN RELIGION & PHILOSOPHY

We publish books on Eastern religions and philosophies. Books that aim to inform and explore the various traditions that began in the East and have migrated West.

If you have enjoyed this book, why not tell other readers by posting a review on your preferred book site.

Recent bestsellers from MANTRA BOOKS are:

The Way Things Are

A Living Approach to Buddhism

Lama Ole Nydahl

An introduction to the teachings of the Buddha, and how to make use of these teachings in everyday life.

Paperback: 978-1-84694-042-2 ebook: 978-1-78099-845-9

Back to the Truth

5000 Years of Advaita

Dennis Waite

A demystifying guide to Advaita for both those new to, and those familiar with this ancient, non-dualist philosophy from India.

Paperback: 978-1-90504-761-1 ebook: 978-184694-624-0

In the Light of Meditation

Mike George

A comprehensive introduction to the practice of meditation and the spiritual principles behind it. A 10 lesson meditation programme with CD and internet support.

Paperback: 978-1-90381-661-5

The Less Dust the More Trust

Participating in The Shamatha Project, meditation and science

Adeline van Waning, MD PhD

The inside-story of a woman participating in frontline meditation research, exploring the interfaces of mind-practice, science and psychology.

Paperback: 978-1-78099-948-7 ebook: 978-1-78279-657-2

I Know How To Live, I Know How To Die
The Teachings of Dadi Janki
A warm, radical, and life-affirming view of who we are, where we come from, and what time is calling us to do
Neville Hodgkinson
Life and death are explored in the context of frontier science and deep soul awareness.
Paperback: 978-1-78535-013-9 ebook: 978-1-78535-014-6

Living Jainism
An Ethical Science
Aidan Rankin, Kanti V. Mardia
A radical new perspective on science rooted in intuitive awareness and deductive reasoning.
Paperback: 978-1-78099-912-8 ebook: 978-1-78099-911-1

A Path of Joy
Popping into Freedom
Paramananda Ishaya
A simple and joyful path to spiritual enlightenment.
Paperback: 978-1-78279-323-6 ebook: 978-1-78279-322-9

Ordinary Women, Extraordinary Wisdom
The Feminine Face of Awakening
Rita Marie Robinson
A collection of intimate conversations with female spiritual teachers who live like ordinary women, but are engaged with their true natures.
Paperback: 978-1-84694-068-2 ebook: 978-1-78099-908-1